C0001960??

A Difference of Op
My Political Journ

'Jim's insights span one of the most important and transformative periods of Scotland's history and he is right to say that idealism and passion are not enough alone to change the world. I hope others of my generation will look to his vast experience and timely lessons explored here and take on the mantle of socialism for the coming decades'

Cat Boyd, co-founder, Radical Independence Campaign

'Jim Sillars hails from Burns country and is the living embodiment of the bard's "man of independent mind". Required reading for anyone who wants to understand the strange death of Labour in Scotland and the demise of Alex Salmond'

Michael Forsyth, Secretary of State for Scotland 1995–97

'From the Attlee landslide in 1945 to Harold Wilson's devolution woes, from SNP MP on the inside to outside strategic critic, his take on independence remains original and unique. This memoir straddles some momentous events which are told with real insight from a man with a ringside seat'

Bernard Ponsonby, Special Correspondent, STV

'Jim Sillars is the grit in the oyster of complacency – there is a challenging thought on almost every page for every thinking person'

Nigel Griffiths, Deputy Leader
of the House of Commons 2005–07 and
MP for Edinburgh South 1987–2010

A DIFFERENCE OF OPINION

MY POLITICAL JOURNEY

JIM SILLARS

BIRLINN

First published in 2021 by
Birlinn Limited
West Newington House
10 Newington Road
Edinburgh
EH9 1QS

www.birlinn.co.uk

ISBN: 978 1 78027 683 0

British Library Cataloguing-in-Publication Data
A catalogue record for this book is available from the British Library

Designed and typeset Initial Typesetting Services, Edinburgh

Printed and bound by Clays Ltd, Elcograf, S.p.A.

*To my late brother Robert
and my sister Jean*

Contents

Acknowledgements

That I have survived the slings and arrows that fill the political air I have lived in for sixty years to reach my present age I owe to the care and support given to me by my son, Matt Sillars, my daughter, Julie Martin, and my stepdaughters, Petra Reid and Zoe MacDonald. All four experienced turbulence in their lives through my involvement and that of Margo MacDonald in the storms of politics. I owe all of them a debt of gratitude.

That I am able to understand the world of today, which now seems a historical time away from the one I was born into in 1937, is, in good part, due to my ten grandchildren – Stephen, Roseanne, Matthew, Lena, Rebecca, Josephine, Beth, Peter, John and Adam. Our close relationships, our discussions and arguments have contributed to the continuing evolution of my take on the world, as reflected in the later parts of this book. The births of the first two took Margo and me into a world outside of politics and the others who followed made that 'just family' part of our lives even more enjoyable.

Alex Neil MSP and Professor Joe Farrell have gone through the mill with me on a number of occasions and I have been fortunate to have had their company on my political journey. No one has ever had better friends. To them must be added Iain Lawson and Gil Paterson MSP whose support in the campaigns I have been part of, as recorded in these pages, was immense.

There is too a younger generation who have ensured that I was not put out to grass too early and have kept me – and my mind – active. They are Peter Kearney, Calum Miller, Jim Eadie, Tom Walker and Colin Fox.

My thanks are due to Carole McCallum, archivist at Glasgow Caledonian University, for the access she gave me to the records of the STUC at the time I was an official there. The National Library of Scotland staff were, as ever, exceptionally helpful.

I also wish to record sincere, not just formal, thanks to Hugh Andrew and Tom Johnstone of Birlinn and the staff of the company. Their courtesy and friendliness have been greatly appreciated.

I must record a special thanks to my copy-editor Patricia Marshall and Birlinn's managing editor, Andrew Simmons. It has been a salutary and beneficial lesson for this writer to have my drafts pass through their hands. Their criticisms, suggestions and frankness have, I hope, made this book more interesting and informative for the reader than would otherwise have been the case.

Foreword

This book comes due to pressure on me from Professor Joe Farrell. He argued that there are events in my political life, lessons learned from them, some of the thinking I have done and expressed, that will not only be of interest to those involved or simply interested in politics but useful to the younger generation now taking its rightful place in the forefront of public life. I have been reluctant to comply with Joe's urgings, not from any false sense of modesty. In elected office or out of it, I have been influential in politics especially on the Left. The reluctance comes because I have always been able to keep my private life private. I intend keeping it that way. This is not an autobiography. I bring in personal matters only where circumstances or people have been important in shaping or influencing me politically. During an interview with a journalist who thought he was entitled to probe when I was an MP, I told him that, although the public paid me, they didn't own me. It is a principle I recommend to today's politicians.

I did not have a good formal education – this was partly my own fault and partly due to the system and attitudes in place in my school days. I have sought to make up for that by self-educating through reading, with an emphasis on history, geography, political biographies, memoirs, philosophy, economics and articles by numerous thinkers and opinion formers across a wide spectrum. I have not restricted myself only to socialist literature, although that has had a great influence on me. I think I am one of the last few survivors of a working-class political culture that produced its own leaders.

I have also learned a great deal from working in other countries and with people of other cultures. My two years studying law at Edinburgh University, when I was no longer an MP, was the best educational experience of my life and, while I did not complete the course, it gave my mind a cutting edge and stimulated my interest in spheres of knowledge into which I would not otherwise have ventured.

A Difference of Opinion

If 'democracy' is to be genuine, it must have not just diversity but a multiplicity of ideas that generate dispute and fire up debate. Explicit to that is the recognition that the 'other side' has legitimacy and that understanding where that legitimacy comes from can only be obtained from reading, talking to and discussing with those on that 'other side'. People who engage in politics and seek to shape public policy should make themselves study the other point of view and so recognise that no ideology or single set of opinions can make the claim to absolute truth and certainty.

Bertrand Russell has had the greatest influence on me. From reading him, I have developed a personal guide – to treat every 'ism', including my own socialism, with scepticism. I first made public reference to this principle in a debate at Glasgow University in 1976. It was immediately denounced by a young student as cynicism. It is not. It is a bar to dogma – a fault of all ideologues. And, if the young treat every 'ism' with scepticism, as essential to the rigorous interrogation of ideas and policies that can make or mar the lives of people, they will be better equipped to address the issues they will face.

Here, I come to another reason for my reluctance to write and publish – will the young really learn anything from my experience and, more particularly, the opinions I express in this book on contemporary matters, which do not fit into the present orthodoxies, and certainly not into identity politics? I have never lived in a 'safe space' on any subject and I find it impossible to believe that the intellectual life of a society can remain undiminished by designating no-go areas and restricting the boundaries of free speech.

I was once a professional organiser of campaigns and elections. Compared to my successors today, with the technology they have, data collection, analysis of electors and an ability to target them individually, I was in a Stone Age. Yet we managed far greater turnout of voters than is regarded as 'good' today. It is likely that young people today would probably see my generation as having also been in a social and political Stone Age. We would have been puzzled if anyone had raised 'identity' as a subject of concern. So, what can today's young idealistic generation, who want to change the world for the better, learn from my experience? How do I persuade them of the value of experience without being patronising or puncturing their idealism? That is the formidable challenge Joe Farrell has set me.

I hope that any younger person reading this book will realise that the lessons and critiques I am seeking to pass on from a long political life of sixty years are not meant to throw cold water on their belief that they can finally tackle and remove the injustices in our national society and internationally. This is meant to help them in that endeavour. I want them never to stop trying

But let me be candid. Any young person engaged in politics to change the world, requires more than idealism and passion. Gathering experience does count.

Here are examples from Labour history and my own life, where the lack of experience on the back of idealism has been a sobering corrective. In the 1930s, as Hitler began a massive German rearmament programme, Labour in Parliament voted against every UK government defence budget, all modest, on the grounds of an idealistic belief in internationalism founded on the League of Nations. Clement Attlee spelled this out at the October 1934 annual conference: 'We have absolutely abandoned every idea of nationalist loyalty. We are deliberately putting a world order before our loyalty towards our own country ... We want to put on the statute book an act which will make our people citizens of the world before they are citizens of this country.' The reality broke upon Labour only in 1936 with the German and Italian air and ground support for the fascist Franco in the Spanish Civil War. Attlee became Churchill's deputy prime minister as the Second World War compelled Labour to shed much of its international idealism. The final breach with that past came when Attlee, as prime minster of a Labour government, secretly decided to build the UK's own nuclear bomb.

In the early 1960s, young members of my generation were active in the Movement for Colonial Freedom. As British colonialism retreated from Africa, we rejoiced. We firmly believed that the newly free people would easily shrug off the effects of colonial rule and their prosperity would be the result. Instead, we saw the emergence of 'the Big Men', such as Robert Mugabe, naked power play and corruption. Hope is not extinguished, however, as a new generation of young people in the African states are starting to assert themselves and openly challenge mendacity and corruption.

Problems that were at the forefront during my time of political activity have been displaced with new priorities that claim the attention of the younger generations. Now the emphasis is on identity, politically correct speech and condemnation of historical figures for what they said and did in their times. I used to think 'woke' meant waking up from sleep. But there are things that do *not* change at the national and international levels and continue to confront and sometimes confound us generation after generation.

Within our own state, ideologies continue to frame attitudes that frame policies – vested interests still compete with each other in the struggle to exert influence on governments; the exploitation of labour by capital still exists; the role of the public sector and its claim on national wealth remains contentious; the size and proper role of the state is still unresolved; poverty levels are shameful; people still need to be fed and housed, and children educated; the 'big tent' characteristic of political parties is still in place, providing a constant source of friction within them. In the post Covid-19 crisis era, these will all become more demanding of priority attention and resolution.

On the international scene, the realist school (of which I am a member) has been proved right about the basic factors in state-to-state relations. State interests and spheres of influence are as dominant today as they have always been, as are the existence of Great Powers and the contests between them. Academics identify the practices of the Amarna civilisation (1550–1200 BC), in what we now know as Egypt, Syria, Iraq and Turkey, as the beginning of international relations. It was an age of kingdoms. The reality today of spheres of influence, alliances of weaker states with powerful ones, and changing alliances, would be recognised as normal conduct of international relations by an Amarna ruler or diplomat if he were to visit us today.

While the fundamentals are still there, improvements have been made in states' practices, the norms of international conduct and legal protections of people as individuals. Although I am in the realist school, that does not mean discounting the achievements, some of great significance, others on an incremental scale, of the idealist school that most of the younger generation adhere to.

However, it is necessary to explain that they will require resilience because the old verities are still there in operation and gesture politics, which appears to ignore them, carries as much weight for change as a butterfly.

Take, as an example, the Left's pursuit of an 'ethical' foreign policy – a call which I have heard at countless meetings. It is a chimera. Robin Cook, who was MP for Livingston, had a first-class mind and was a brilliant parliamentarian. Within weeks of becoming Foreign Secretary in 1997, he announced New Labour's ethical foreign policy. He was supremely confident at the press conference. The permanent secretary beside him looked pained. Robin, on behalf of the UK, signed the legal instrument setting up the International Criminal Court, explaining that, in doing so, he could not conceive of a British government or service personnel breaching any part of its statute. It was not long before he was lamenting and condemning his own government from the back benches for its invasion of Iraq.

The UN's power structures remain those formed in 1945, bearing no resemblance to the world that now exists. Defending their state interests has, so far, prevented the smaller veto powers, Russia, UK and France, from ceding their seats to others who, on the face of it, would more accurately reflect the new economic and political balances in the world.

Human Rights declarations and conventions are easiest to apply where it is easy to do so but are without meaning in places where they are most needed. The violence of war, whether by states or non-state entities, remains an instrument readily reached for. The International Criminal Court has no jurisdiction over the superpowers. The International Court of Justice has no power to enforce its decisions. This is as much the world of today's younger generations as it was for mine.

Then there is that whose consequences all generations must struggle with – power. Although, while seeking to exercise or constrain it, societies may use different political tools, institutions, conventions and rules, it will remain the main driver of human conduct. The emergence of Artificial Intelligence, far from altering that fact, will merely bring in new tools and new methods of pursuing, accumulating and asserting power.

So perhaps the experiences I relate and the views I have formed from a world that seems to have disappeared will not be redundant and will contain valuable knowledge for the younger generation to use as they meet their own challenges.

This book is the truth as I saw it during my time in politics from 1960 to the present day. 'The truth as I saw it' is an important caveat. This is my view of events and what shaped them, and what shaped me; but others will have different opinions not so much on what happened, but why it happened, and how the events were handled.

I have tried to avoid making this a self-serving justification of my political life and actions. It is an explanation, including acknowledgement of mistakes, of why I took the positions I did while in the Labour Party, later as an active member of the SNP and, even later, over the past thirty years. I have changed my mind on policy issues, believing that to be consistent, while a virtue, can also be a block on the mind when faced with new situations not hitherto encountered, or when previous positions are overtaken and changed by events. I have always been willing to reconsider policy, guided by a desire to be intellectually honest with myself and to be honest with the public.

A Difference of Opinion

This book is a hybrid – part memoir, part comment on a wide range of matters past and present as I saw and see them. It does not travel in a direct line from childhood to the present and I do digress here and there. I learned to touch-type as a radio operator in the Royal Navy and have built up my typing speed so much that, for more than sixty years, my thoughts have flowed straight from the keyboard. This book is as it came from there.

I was married to Margo MacDonald for thirty-three years and she will loom large in a number of these pages. It could not be otherwise. We were two halves of one whole. I am incomplete without her.

Jim Sillars
Edinburgh
July 2020

I

A Working-class Start

I was born on 4 October 1937 in Scotland, in a council flat at 6 White Street, Ayr. Shortly after my birth we moved to 35 Seaforth Crescent, another council flat nearby, where our family stayed until after I left primary school. Seaforth Crescent was working class. The Second World War started when I was two. My father was Matthew Sillars, a railway locomotive fireman at the time of my birth and later an engine driver. My mother was Agnes Sillars (née Sproat), a weaver at a carpet factory before her marriage. My brother Robert was four years older than me.

Also living in Seaforth Crescent were Grandpa and Granny Sillars, Aunt Peggy Sillars, Uncle Robert Sillars – disabled, he worked as a cobbler and went to his work each day, about half a mile away, on crutches – and two sisters of my mother and their families. In an adjacent street, there was another of my mother's sisters. A bit further away, about a twenty minutes' walk, lived my Grandpa and Granny Sproat and my aunt Nellie Sproat. In another direction, about ten minutes' walk away, lived my father's brother, Uncle Jock, and his family. His house had no electricity and was lit by gas mantles. This nearby extended family was not unusual in those days. We were not poor but not well off either.

The flat in Seaforth Crescent was an upstairs one in a block of four. It contained a living room with a fireplace, a bedroom with a fireplace, a kitchen and bathroom. The floors were covered in linoleum. We had a back garden in which my father grew vegetables. No one dreamed of owning a home. Paying rent was what you did. Over the back of our garden was a big area of allotments which were called 'the plots'. These had been abandoned, probably because the holders were involved in the war, and there were many thorn bushes that proved perfect for hiding in when we played soldiers.

The first event that shaped my life was the death of my mother in April 1942 from tuberculosis. I was aged four years and six months.

Her passing was devastating and, even today, it can cause me pain to think about it. Papers found by my brother's daughters, after his death at the age of eighty-seven, show that he mourned her to his last day. We shared the same view – we felt cheated by her death.

Young as I was, I knew my mother was not well as she was often in bed. I slept on a bed settee in the living room and I can remember waking up one morning and there she was out of bed, fully clothed, lighting the fire. I recall asking something like, 'Are you well now?' and she gave me a strange smile, something in my adult years I came to understand as enigmatic. My mother knew she was dying. I was oblivious to that. She moved into the living room in the last days of her life and I slept in the bedroom. I woke up one morning to find my brother in the arms of my father, crying. When it was explained to me that my mother had died, I don't think I took in what that meant. I didn't join my brother in crying.

But the day of her burial was different. I had been taken to one of my aunts in the Crescent. Why she did it I don't know but she picked me up and took me to the window to let me see my mother's coffin leaving our house. That's when it hit me that she was dead, gone forever. I went berserk, trying to tear myself away from my aunt to get out and stop them taking my mother away. I would not experience that level of grief again until my wife, Margo MacDonald, died. I sometimes think what I experienced that day enabled me, both at a personal and political level, to absorb blows and stay standing. On that day, the well of grief within me was almost emptied and it took a long time to refill.

I have been told that when she was finally succumbing to TB, my mother asked to see my brother and told him to look after me. That he did. The loss of our mother bound us as closely as twins. I was a small boy, it was rough on our street and there was a much older and much bigger boy who picked on me. My brother fought on my behalf. It wasn't that I was afraid of fighting – I would take on anyone my own size – but this one was way out of my class.

TB was a terrible scourge before antibiotics became widely available after the Second World War. In our extended family, in addition to my mother, three other female cousins died of the condition. Diphtheria and scarlet fever were killers of children. I can recall as if it were yesterday Mr Logan, a neighbour, standing in our kitchen, tears rolling down his cheeks, telling my father that his three-year-old grandson George, my pal, had died of diphtheria. Today, people do not expect premature deaths but it was different then and it was usual to see men walking around with a diamond-shaped black patch on their overcoats as a mark of mourning.

A Working-class Start

My father eventually married again and I had a lovely stepmother in Madge Duncan from Dundee. I had no problem, despite always missing my mother, of taking to her. She was exceptionally kind and I quickly came to love her. I was delighted when she gave birth to my sister Jean in our flat in December 1945. A sister – a wonderful Christmas present.

Money was tight and we lived from week to week with nothing to lay aside as savings. We had nothing with which to compare our position. The well-off people lived in the posh areas south of the River Ayr, in places where we never ventured. No one where we lived had a car. Coal and milk were delivered by horse and cart. The biggest local shop was the Co-op and it wasn't a supermarket in those days.

Wartime rationing, not only of food but clothing, was an austerity that we lived with as the natural order. Entertainment came via the radio and the cinema. We had a radio that plugged into the electricity supply but others in our street had ones run on large batteries, and it was usual to see people taking the batteries along for re-charging at the local garage. The local cinema, the Regal, showed what we called 'pictures' – a mix of British and American films. In the British war films, officers were all upper-middle class and the other ranks were from the working class. We thought that perfectly natural. There were films about Russian partisans beating the Germans. We all called Stalin 'Uncle Joe'. It was in the non-war American films that we could lose ourselves in a fantasy world before going back to the harshness of the real one. At the end of every showing, we all stood while the national anthem was played, a practice that began to break down only in the late 1950s. We were still in the age of deference.

We lived in the context of the war. Even as children we knew how important Franklin D. Roosevelt was and I remember the pleasure and relief among the adults in the Crescent when he won the 1944 US presidential election and the shock when he died before the war ended.

Among the things I remember from those war years was powdered egg. When my mother died and before my father married again, he would sometimes cook. He was typical of his time –men did not cook or do housework – and so when he put his hand to powdered egg it came out of the frying pan like a piece of leather. His lumpy custard matched his other non-existent culinary skills. Then there was the concentrated orange juice and cod liver oil. The former was OK but I hated the taste of the cod liver oil.

There were shortages all the time. I learned to knit and darn holes in my socks and jerseys. When I got a new pair of boots, my father would hammer steel tacks into the soles to make them last longer. Dead silence was required when the nine o'clock news came on the radio with the latest bulletins on the war. I checked with my brother and he confirmed that never once did we hear anyone in our street question that we would win the war. I knew who Winston Churchill was and of his importance.

We never went hungry. A piece of bread and jam, the 'jeelie piece', was always available. Neighbour helped neighbour. Mrs Kelly, who lived below us, was a great baker and we got our share of her efforts. Doors were either not locked or had the key kept on a string which could be retrieved by a hand through the letterbox behind them. The local policeman was Jimmy Alexander and, knowing our situation after my mother died, he would check up on my brother and me if he knew our father was at work and we were likely to be alone in the house, as was often the case.

A few years ago, I took part in a debate in Edinburgh about the merits or otherwise of Margaret Thatcher and, once again, her claim was trotted out that the Good Samaritan could not have been good had he not been wealthy. To counter this, I cited Mrs Kelly, whose family was as hard up as ours, yet who, time and again, gave my brother and me from the little she had.

Steam engines even to this day hold a fascination for people and, in my young days, having a father who fired and drove them was a reason for immense pride in him. We were a railway family. My great-grandfather, my grandfather and his brother were all railwaymen too. We talked about the railways at home. Railwaymen got free travel passes for the family every year and could go anywhere with them. We used ours once a year to holiday in Dundee with my stepmother's brothers. I loved the train journey, first from Ayr to Glasgow and then from Glasgow to Dundee, but I intensely disliked where we stayed, which was a room and kitchen in Lochee Road. My brother and I slept with one of the uncles. He was anything but happy about the arrangement and neither were we. There was an outside toilet, shared with everyone else on the stair, which I hated using.

My father was a strong supporter of Labour and the trade unions and greatly admired Nye Bevan, although he was not uncritical of him. He told me that Archie Manuel, a railway driver like him, who was MP for Central Ayrshire, lost his seat in 1955 because Bevan had called for the nationalisation of ICI in Irvine, by far the largest employer in the county. The other thing I remember from that conversation was that, on the morning after the election result, young Tories had hung a pair of railway overalls on Manuel's front door handle – my first lesson in how cruel politics can be.

I was just three months from my eighth birthday when I stood in the kitchen with my father the day that Labour won the 1945 election. It was joy unconfined. He rushed out, met our neighbour across the way, Mrs Logan, and they literally danced up and down in celebration. Even at that age, I knew something significant had happened in our lives. 'A Labour government' were the words I heard spoken with unmistakable satisfaction.

There was one incident during the 1945 election campaign which struck a chord in my young mind. All during the war, Churchill seemed to be placed just below God but above the king in importance. I had never heard one word of criticism against him. During the election campaign, my father had taken me with him on a visit to another railwayman. There were several men in the house. Churchill was speaking on the wireless, when one of the men, in a voice steeped in anger and contempt, made an attack on him. I heard it and was surprised at how different that was from normal. Years later, when Churchill died, I was in a meeting of Ayrshire County Council Labour Group agonising over whether, at the full council meeting, we should stand and engage in the one minute's silence. In that meeting, a lot of anger spilled out because of Churchill's past actions. As Home Secretary, he had sent the troops in against the Welsh miners and, as Chancellor of the Exchequer, had been the leading protagonist against the unions in the 1926 General Strike. These were unforgiven crimes against the working class. In the end, however, it was Danny Sim, the group leader, who laid it out – Churchill was a political lion, one we may have cause to detest, but a lion nonetheless, and his role in halting Hitler had to be acknowledged. We all stood for the minute of silence.

I must have had politics built in to me because, as well as picking up the importance of my father's friend's abuse of Churchill, I read avidly the two papers my father bought – *The Daily Herald*, a Labour one, and *The Daily Express*, a Tory one (because its racing section was the best, my father explained). In those days, the newspapers reported speeches of major political figures in detail and I was able to see how two sides could disagree on issues. I was in a local shop when the announcement of Gandhi's assassination came through on the radio and ran home to tell my father because I knew it was important. I remember surprising the dairy owner I worked for as a milk boy by expressing political opinions.

In January 1950 I went from Newton Park Primary School into a transition class at Heathfield Primary School, as entry to Ayr Academy was not until summer of that year. Because of the impending general election in February (which Labour won, narrowly), the teacher thought it would be a good idea to have a class election. I put myself forward as the Communist candidate. When my turn came to address the class, the teacher heckled me, which I thought was unfair as he had not done that to anyone else. I've no idea what I said that riled him. I got two votes (including my own). I was clued up about the general election and, among my schoolmates, kept repeating the slogan about the Labour leader Clement Attlee – 'Vote for Clem because he's a gem'.

I was with my father, again in the kitchen, when Labour's defeat was announced in 1951. It was as though the world had ended. He said something like, 'We're in for it now.' so dark was the picture he painted of what was to be delivered to the working class by the Tories. I left the house to play 'headers' with a pal in a state of dread, thinking the sun would never shine again. Of course, it didn't turn out as bad as my father feared. His view of the Tory Party was formed in the 1930s and he was not aware of how the likes of Rab Butler and Harold Macmillan had changed it.

My father was typical of our class. He brought in the money, did not even contemplate cooking or washing up and expected his dinner to be on the table when he came home. Not until he was sixty-five, with my stepmother ill in bed, did he deign to go to the shops. That was not his only working-class characteristic. My brother and I went to the selective Ayr Academy and, for my father, having got there was enough of an achievement. At that time, I was not university material but my brother was. He was quite brilliant at mathematics. In later life, he taught himself chemistry to pass his Fire Service exams, finally reaching Division Officer level. But the idea of either of us going on to further education would never have crossed my father's mind. I never heard the word university until I was in the Navy in Hong Kong.

That is not say he was not ambitious for us. He was anxious to get us into an apprenticeship in a trade but that was as far as it went. My brother became a bricklayer and I got an apprenticeship as a plasterer. He was immensely pleased when my sister became a nurse. I have been amused over the years when hearing middle-class socialists extol the virtues of the working class, as though we are a noble people with no faults. In reality, our class had its own inner-class system. White-collar workers, clerks, joiners, brickies, plasterers, electricians, engineers and railway engine drivers were at the top, with miners, labourers, postmen, bus drivers and conductresses below them. Keeping the differentials between the skilled, semi-skilled and unskilled was one of the prime functions of the craft unions and the reasons for the closed shop. (The closed shop, for those who do not know, operated on the basis that you had to be a member of a designated trade union or you didn't get a job. And you could only be a member of such a trade union if you were a skilled craftsman or an apprentice.)

*

I digress here. One day, in the tearoom of the House of Commons, a number of us were gathered round Left-winger Tony Benn as he spelled out another of his ideas – that the way to have a greater representation of the working class in the Commons was to restrict everyone to one parliamentary term only. It just so happened that I was the only working-class person present. Tony was surprised, therefore, when I said it wouldn't work and would be against our class interest. I cited his junior minister, Alex Eadie, as proof. Before entering Parliament, Alex had been a stripper in the pits. That was the most back-breaking underground job of all. If he came away to Parliament for four years, going physically soft, he could not possibly return to it and would have to find a job on the surface for lower wages. So, the Alex Eadies of the world would not come. Then I turned to my old man, by then the senior railway engine driver at Ayr sheds. Such was the speed of technological change in signalling that he would not 'know the road' after four years away and the only job available to him would have been in the 'shunting engine' category, which was usually kept for men no longer medically fit for the main line. With that potential loss of status, there was no way the likes of Matt Sillars could come to London for four years. But, as I pointed out, college lecturers, academics and lawyers would not mind a parliamentary stint on their CVs.

I had a great liking for Tony Benn and admired how he was willing to explore new ideas, and he had the most attractive and charismatic personality. But I thought he was in love with the perfect working class of his imagination – a legion of Jimmy Reids – and had a deep-felt need to be one of us. This view was, I believe, underlined when David Lambie and I, both MPs from Ayrshire, once went to see him in his ministerial office in Victoria Street about a local problem. Behind Tony's desk was a huge Transport and General Workers' Union (TGWU) banner and, while David and I drank our tea from good china cups, he took his from a big mug of the type favoured by lorry drivers. After the meeting, as David and I walked to the lift, I asked if he needed the big banner behind his desk to complete the working-class picture. He laughed.

*

A Difference of Opinion

On the railways most drivers and firemen were in ASLEF (the Associated Society of Locomotive Engineers and Firemen), describing themselves as 'the cream of the railway', while a small number of drivers and firemen were in the NUR (National Union of Railwaymen), which took in other workers such as guards, signalmen, shunters, wheel tappers and rail maintenance men. There was a separate union for salaried staff (the TSSA). My father was in ASLEF. My grandfather, an engine driver, told me he joined the NUR because he didn't believe in an elite and that, if every railwayman was in the same union, they would all be stronger. When, in later life, I wanted to wrong-foot Dad, I would ask him to justify being in ASLEF which seemed to be contrary to his socialist principles. He was generally good in debate but not on that issue.

My father was a gambler. Not an amateur gambler. He studied racehorse form and pedigree and pored over the football fixtures before he filled in the Littlewoods football pools coupon, from which he had several good winnings. I cannot recall my stepmother or us children ever getting anything substantial extra, like a new football – popularly known as a football tube at the time – football boots or ice skates, as a result of his winnings. Every September, there was a major horse racing meeting in Ayr and the big race, the Ayr Gold Cup, was run on a Friday. Just up the road from our street was a park where an annual fair was held at the same time. We called it 'the shows'. Whether my brother, sister and I had a good time on the night of the Gold Cup meeting depended entirely upon the horses my father had backed that day. A big win and we were on the roundabouts and the bumper cars and had shots at the shooting gallery. No win – nothing.

As I say, he was no amateur and sentiment played no part when placing a bet. In 1978, the Scottish football team went to Argentina with their manager, Ally McLeod, convincing the nation we would win the World Cup. I sat with my father and brother to watch the first match on television against Peru. When we lost 3–1, he greeted the news with, 'Och well.' The tone alerted me. I asked if he had backed Peru, to which the answer was yes – the odds had been terrific. Before the team departed for Argentina, we had lost 1–0 to England at Hampden. I looked at him and asked if he had bet on an England win, to which he said yes, for two reasons – first, we did not have a good team and, second, the odds had again been too good to ignore. He had wanted Scotland to win both games but the gambler in him could not ignore the odds. He had a peculiar attitude towards his winnings. Once, when he won a substantial sum – around £100 – and it quickly disappeared,

I asked him where it had gone. He told me the money wasn't really his – it was the bookie's – so there was no problem gambling with it.

I was too young to remember but my brother told me that, during my father's first marriage, he had come home one pay day without any money, having gambled the lot away, and that my mother's reaction had been to hit him hard over the head with a toy tin hat and take both of us off to Granny Sproat's house. It seems my mother was a very strong character and never again, while she was alive, did my father repeat that mistake. However, my stepmother was no match for him. He never brought home an unopened pay packet. The various experiences with my father and the bookies put me off gambling for life.

The man who most mattered in my life, after my father and brother, was my grandfather, Robert Sillars. A senior engine driver, he was forced to leave the railway after suffering a nervous breakdown. He got no help from my grandmother. She was cruel and, in front of me, often taunted him for his idleness. I was very young but remember being distressed at these scenes. It was an appalling level of domestic abuse. As I grew older, I came to detest her for the way she treated him.

He loved reading – books, papers, periodicals, anything he could get his hands on – and I was on the same wavelength. He was often banished to the kitchen and there he and I would talk for hours. Even though I was just a young boy, we would talk about Burns, the Bible and what the newspapers were saying. He explained why he changed from Liberal to Labour, why he and others went back to work when the 1926 General Strike collapsed (there was no appetite for a revolution) and shared his views on trade unions, football, golf (he was a low handicap player) and the railway. It was from him I learned about Gallipoli, for which he blamed Churchill. He had no gifts to give me, except an old encyclopaedia, which was like being handed a gold mine.

He had a prodigious memory and was able to recite very long poems from Burns. Later, when my grandmother died and he moved in with us, we would talk for ages and play cards, with me ensuring that he won with great frequency, something that delighted him. I remember one disagreement we had when, in my idealistic youth, I declared that, after the 1939–45 war, we would have no more. He replied, 'Jimmy, there will always be wars and rumours of wars.' – a view I dismissed. There have been almost 200 big and small wars since 1945.

I cared about my grandpa and admired his intellect, his self-learning, his love of books and his thirst for knowledge. He was reading ten minutes before he died suddenly at the age of eighty-seven. I regarded it a privilege to conduct his funeral.

*

On my mother's side, the Sproat family consisted of eight sisters, one son, and the illegitimate son of an aunt. My grandpa, Jimmy Sproat, was an engineer in the local ice factory. I have photographs of me with him and my Granny Sproat but no memory of them. My uncle, Sony Sproat, was in the 51st Highland Division captured at St Valery in 1940 and died later of cancer in a POW camp.

The Sproat aunts were important up until my mother died and my father remarried. They gave my brother and me a shock soon after my mother's funeral when, with my father out at work, they came and, laughing together, emptied her wardrobe, tried on her clothes and stripped the curtains from the windows. With wartime rationing, it was, of course, sensible for them to take her clothes but it was the way they did it – the insensitive way they behaved in front of two grief-stricken boys left us shaken. After that, I never really trusted my aunties on the Sproat side again and the episode caused a breach in the family, which became wider after my father married again.

The aunties were resolutely opposed to it and made their opposition clear to my stepmother. In a sense, my brother and I were put to a loyalty test – it was either them or our stepmother – and, although they did not cut us off completely when we took our stepmother's side, we were, from then on, definitely regarded as not 'one of them'. One aunt in particular, who I used to visit regularly, started keeping me at the door. My father used to tell me that blood was thicker than water but I found that was not true and preferred the idea that you can pick your friends but not relatives.

All in all, although my father and stepmother gave me a good home, my mother's death caused an underlying sadness. I wished so much that, when my brother became a senior fire officer and I was elected an MP, she could have seen how her two boys had got on. But it wasn't to be.

2

School

When I was five, I went to Newton Park Primary School – or, to be more exact, that was where I was supposed to go. I hated school. It ended my freedom and I saw it as a ten-year prison sentence, with a short parole each summer. That glorious Friday when we broke for the long summer holiday was better than Christmas. My brother Robert had to drag me to the school gates and I would hold on to the railings like grim death as he tried to prise my fingers free and force me into the playground. He was pleased when the railings were removed for the war effort. Once the bell rang, he went into school and I ran away to an aunt's. This went on for some weeks.

Eventually I did attend classes every day but my only interest was in English and history, which for me included the Bible. I remember being taught about Clive of India and that his magnificent victory at the Battle of Plassey was key to 'us' conquering India – apparently a beneficial event in world history. We were told of the Black Hole of Calcutta into which white women and children were thrown to die during the Indian Mutiny but nothing of the barbarity with which the mutiny was put down. As for the Opium Wars, I was left with the impression that they ware an altruistic act by the British to save the Chinese from the addictive effects of the drug. And the Boers were regarded as having stood in the way of Britain's right to rule in southern Africa.

I don't mention any of this disparagingly to gain approval from those who have a present-day need to mentally flagellate themselves in expatiation for their colonial ancestors' sins. The idea of the Empire and the British right to rule was taken for granted, seen through a very different lens from today, by all classes. Racism was deeply embedded in British society. Kipling's poem, 'The White Man's Burden', was an assertion of white supremacy over black and brown people, with the implication that the whites were their natural tutors who would 'civilise' them – over a long period of imperial rule, of course. Africa was described as having been the 'dark continent' before the Europeans arrived and we were totally unaware that Africans had their own long history of civilisations and achievements, the truths of which were smothered in colonial times. People today cannot claim to be so oblivious to this.

It was only when I began to read widely, after leaving school, that I discovered truths about colonialism. I don't blame my teachers. They were captives of the imperial zeitgeist and would have been incapable of questioning what was in the standard text books, all of which extolled the creation of the British Empire with its explicit superiority of the white over the coloured. That racist legacy of Empire lingers, despite the laws that have been enacted that seek to ensure respect and equality for people of all colours.

The only thing that I liked about school was the prospect of playing in the football team. In those days, the main interests of working-class youngsters were boxing and football. In our family, there was also golf. I had three boxing heroes – Jack Johnson, a previous world heavyweight champion, Joe Louis, then the current world heavyweight champion, and Bruce Woodcock, the British heavyweight. I was sure Woodcock was heading for a world title fight when he took on Joe Baksi, an American ranked third in the world. Baksi broke his jaw in knocking him out. That brought forth the Yankee gibe about 'horizontal' British heavyweights.

Boxing gave me my first lesson in the disgrace of racism. Live bouts were reported on the wireless. During a fight in 1946, I heard one commentator remark to another what a pity it was that the 'colour bar' would stop the obvious winner going on to fight for the British title. I was struck by how unfair it was. The British colour bar, preventing a boxer of colour fighting for the title in this country, was made in 1911 by the British Boxing Board of Control and not removed until 1947.

But, for me, football was king. I was very good at it, having converted from the usual one of 'best-foot' (the right) players to being equally skilled with both feet. This was achieved by kicking a small ball, about the size of a tennis ball, with my left foot all the way to school and back every day. When in Primary 6 and chosen for the team, I was in raptures. The night before my first match I put on the jersey (made of wool) and paraded in front of the big mirror in the bedroom. No political event or winning any election compares to how I felt the day I put that jersey on for the first time.

I wasn't the best player in my first year in the team. That was Jackie McInally, in Primary 7, who later played with Kilmarnock in the then First Division. But in Primary 7, I was the team's best player, out on the left wing. But I failed in the Mackie Cup Final against St Margaret's when we were beaten 1–0. That was the first time I had to face up to my own responsibility for failure. It wasn't that I played badly – I didn't perform at all. I didn't need the teacher, Mr Allan, and his look of disappointment in me in the dressing room to know that I had let the side down. I am not sure to this day whether it was nerves at taking part in a cup final – a very big deal – that was the problem, but I saw it as a failed test of character, that was never going to happen again. In the final games of the season, I played brilliantly and we won the league. But that loss in the cup final, and my self-assessment afterwards, proved to have great influence on me in the life that followed.

I warmed to Mr Allan, not just because he organised the football team, but because he never seemed to need recourse to the belt – the long leather strap used for hitting pupils over the hands. His class was the only one I felt relaxed in. Two things he said have stuck with and influenced me. I can see him now, standing at his desk telling us that one of the greatest things that happened in our society was the emergence of the age of tolerance, in which each of us learned to treat those who held different opinions or belonged to other religions with respect. This tolerance was the foundation of civilised conduct. The other was advice – to be our own most severe critic. That way, he explained, we would be immune to flattery and unfair criticism. If we knew we had done badly at something, no matter what praise we got, we would know it was not true and vice versa. I have passed it on to my grandchildren.

Whether we now continue to live in an age of tolerance is an open question. The right to speak freely, even if it is offensive to some other individual or group, no longer seems to apply. This is the thin-skin society, with some unable to endure opinions that are different from theirs. I have watched with astonishment as people have been coerced to make an apology when no apology should have been given. Of course, it cannot be claimed that there is an absolute right to say anything we want and we have libel laws to ensure that. Even in the United States, with its constitutional right to free speech, there is case law that defines a narrow unacceptable level of comment. But, whatever inhibitions we may place upon ourselves (which is different from the state doing so), in steering clear of language that some communities might find deeply offensive, our right and the right of others to speak our minds should be vigorously defended.

My worst school year was in Primary 5, which was an episode in purgatory. The teacher was Mrs MacArthur and her reputation came before her. She had a long thin wooden stick she hit us with when she was not using her fists. Once, when we doing long division, she looked over my shoulder and spotted a mistake. I got a hammering from the fists. I think I must have transferred my fear of her – and it was fear – to the subject itself as, even now, when I am presented with an arithmetical problem, I do it twice to make sure of the conclusion.

In Primary 7, we did not sit an English 11-plus. We sat the qualifying exam at age twelve, to determine whether we remained at Newton Park School, a junior secondary, or went to the selective Ayr Academy. I qualified for Ayr Academy, as had my brother before me.

If anything, I hated Ayr Academy more than primary school. It was clear that people from working-class backgrounds were not welcome. On my first day, the deputy rector, Mr Casells, called us out one by one to his desk. He asked me if I was a relative of Robert Sillars. I said yes, he was my brother, to which his reply was, 'You will end up a common labourer just like him.' I was angry – my brother was an apprentice bricklayer, not a labourer. That did it for me, on day one.

Just how much we were looked down on by the teachers was brought home on two particular occasions. Many of us who came from the Newton side of Ayr and the mining villages had been brought up playing football, whereas the Academy played rugger and cricket against private schools. We set up a scratch football team and challenged Newton Academy, the winners of the Ayr league, to a game on a Friday after school. They were a good team captained by David Dunsmuir, a schoolboy international. We beat them 3–1 and, chuffed, thought ,once the word got out, Ayr Academy would put together an official football team. Far from it. On the Monday morning after assembly, our names were read out and we were told to report to the gym master, Captain T.B. Watson. He lined us up in the gym and punched every one of us, first for playing the 'lower-class' game of soccer and second for engaging with what he called 'the dross' from the other side of the river, where of course most of us lived.

The other arose when the Academy held a boxing tournament in the gym. One fight was between the son of the local lemonade factory owner, who was in the audience, and a boy called Adam Truesdale. Adam came from a very poor family. He wore wellingtons not just in winter but in early summer. But he could box. Adam was knocking seven bells out of the other boy, then the bell rang and he was disqualified. It was outrageous.

The irony was that when Ayr Academy decided to send a team to the Scottish Schoolboy Boxing Championships in Glasgow, Adam and I were among those who went. I fancied myself but, in my first and only fight, I was walloped by a Glasgow boy, a real boxer. I hit him only once and was so surprised that I dropped my guard and got more punishment. Pride was at stake and I held on until the end of the fight. Adam Truesdale didn't lose. He demolished every opponent, to become the Scottish champion at his weight.

Only one teacher at Ayr Academy, Mr Inglis, who taught English, did anything for me. I bought into his love for English literature but only had him in the first year. I started to play truant – we called it 'plunking'. Another boy and I would leave home to catch the bus to school and then it was into a small wood to disappear for the day. In the last three months, I didn't bother hiding – I just didn't go except for the final week. The rector, Mr Cairns, called me and a pal into his office in the last day to show his displeasure and told us that we would never make anything of ourselves. One night, on an aircraft coming back from London, I met that pal. He was a senior engineer.

Years later, when I was MP for South Ayrshire, I met Mr Cairns at Ayr railway station. He came over to say how pleased he was to see an old boy do so well. I told him I considered myself not an old boy of Ayr Academy but of Newton Park School.

3

First Jobs

I can't remember ever getting pocket money from my father and I was desperate to get a job. I was ten when the first one came along, in the small local hardware store a couple of streets away from my home. It involved filling empty bottles, of all shapes and sizes with bleach (which the owner made up) and then delivering them, using a small wooden box on wheels, to customers. I had no protective clothing. The different bottle sizes meant there was spillage but I was oblivious to any danger. After the deliveries, I got my first pay – a sixpence. I went home full of myself but, when my father asked how much I had been paid, he went through the roof about exploitation and I was forbidden to go back.

My next job, at eleven years old, at Bryson's, the local dairy, was different. We milk boys worked mornings seven days week. It was the horse-and-cart age. Jimmy Bryson was a good man and I got on well with Betty, his daughter. Twelve shillings a week enabled me to buy all my comics and sweets. And a bonus – plenty of milk to drink.

In the harsh winters, it was agony delivering the day's milk and then lifting the empties that had been out on the doorstep all night in the snow or rain. Gloves were no good, getting instantly wet. My fingers would swell up and be very painful. One time, on returning to the dairy, I plunged my frozen hands into a tank of very hot water that was being used to wash the bottles and fainted with the pain. I remember, when my hands were freezing, asking myself how it was possible for scientists to create an atom bomb but not produce a pair of gloves that would keep a milk boy's hands warm. That kind of glove exists now for, among other things, use by golfers in winter.

We only got New Year's Day off, Christmas not then being a public holiday in Scotland, although schools were closed. To get that one day off, we made our usual delivery in the morning and then came back at 7 p.m. on Hogmanay and did another delivery. There were no fridges in

16

our area in those days, so the second delivery would remain outside in the cold overnight and not go sour.

I stayed with Bryson's dairy even after we moved to the other side of the town. But when the dairy changed hands, I looked for a new job closer to home. I did so because of the way the new employee who was in charge of my milk run treated the horse who pulled the milk cart. On his first day, he went into the stables, took out a hammer and started to hit the animal. The horse was terrified. So was I. As I stood there aghast, he told me this was to show her who her new master was. I wanted out and soon left and went to work delivering milk for another dairy.

My new dairy, unlike Bryson's, did not serve working-class areas. It was the posh Doonfoot and Alloway we delivered to (my daughter Julie lives in Alloway now). I was by then at secondary school and very happy with the change. When I worked at Bryson's, at Christmas I got a lot of tips – something like seven shillings in threepenny bits, which would be left in an envelope in the neck of the empties. My logic was that, if I gathered that much in working-class areas, where money was short, I was bound to cash in big in the posh areas. Mistake. Come Christmas-time deliveries, not even a farthing (one quarter of a penny) had been left in the empties. Milk boys were appreciated in working-class communities and would be rewarded from what little the people had. But, in well-heeled Doonfoot and Alloway, we were anonymous – milk appeared on the doorsteps and that was all that mattered.

*

On leaving school at fifteen, I got an indentured apprenticeship (a signed commitment to work for five years) with James Legatt, plasterer, in Ayr. I was cheap labour. In those days, to plaster a wall, the tradesman first put on a mixture of plaster, sand and water. Once that was dry, he put on the finishing skin, made up of plaster and lime. My job was to mix the first course of plaster on a big wooden board, with a shovel (it set fast), then fill a hod and carry it on my shoulder into the tradesman, dumping it on a flat table. I then mixed the finishing coat, taking it in, this time, pail by pail.

The first job I worked on was a group of shops in the Forehill housing scheme in Ayr, which are still standing today. Hugh Muir was the journeyman, Tommy Potts the senior apprentice and then me, labouring. I can claim to have mixed most of the plaster, the cement for roughcasting and the concrete for the floors. I was paid a first-year apprentice wage of thirty-nine shillings a week, I discovered from listening to the men at tea-break that the boss would be charging the client labourer's wages for me, a rate much higher than mine. This, I learned, was a normal swindle in the building trades.

The only break in the cycle of labouring came one week in every month when I attended a technical college. A labourer replaced me for that week. It was at the college that I learned how to put plaster on a wall. After the Forehill project was finished, we were sent to work on a house renovation. By this time, I was really fed up just labouring. When Legatt came to check on progress, I took the opportunity of asking him when I was going to start learning my trade. I doubt if anyone had ever talked to him like that before. He took umbrage and an argument started. I told him I was leaving and he warned me he would charge my father for the weeks I had attended college. That did it. I was raging, thinking how much he had made out of me at the Forehill shops and was still doing so in this job. I had just mixed a batch of first coat plaster. I dug the shovel into it and told him to take it in himself and walked off the job.

My father and stepmother were very good about it. My father knew I had been exploited and could not bring himself to criticise me, although he was concerned about me losing my apprenticeship. Within a couple of days, a letter arrived from the Master Plasterers' Association summoning me to an evening meeting in the County Buildings. My father came with me. There it was explained to me that I was indentured and therefore required to complete my time with Legatt, and had to go back to work the next day.

I was just fifteen when I faced this group of stern men admonishing me. There was not one word from them about how I had been exploited – not surprising, perhaps, as they too were surely misusing their first-year apprentices. I refused point blank to go back. Nothing they said about my indentured contract counted. My father had to tell them that he was not capable of making me return to work and I didn't.

So I was out of work with a black mark against me in the building trade. No more apprenticeship. My father got me a job at the Ayr railway engine sheds, where I started work as a cleaner, just like my father and my grandfather before me. I was very happy – the railway suited me fine and the money was a lot more than I got with Legatt.

In winter, a cleaner's job was to wash the engines using a cloth dipped in paraffin, which we drew in pails from the main store but we could earn extra money, at men's rates of pay, by working in the coal screes when there was a shortage of workers there, due to holidays or sickness. Wagons of coal were shunted up into the screes. We emptied them into big tubs, then pushed the tubs to a tipping point with the coal then going into the engine tender below, as preparation for the next shift. It was big money at the screes, earning me about an extra six or seven pounds a week, much of which I gave to my stepmother over and above what I gave for my room and board. The screes were hard work – back-breaking for a youngster – but, because of the money, I kept it up as long as I could.

In the summer holiday period, we cleaners became firemen and, once, I got the chance to fire the same engine my grandfather had driven. I was bursting with pride and he was delighted. We got firemen's wages and I loved working on the steam engines. It was quite skilled and responsible work, entailing more than just shovelling coal into the firebox, which itself required skill as you had to know where to place the coal to get the most combustion. The fireman worked the entry of water into the boilers through a steam injection system, and if he got it wrong, disaster followed. Every boiler had a brass plug which, if there was no water in it, melted and the engine would grind to a halt.

My shifts were mostly hauling empty wagons up to the Ayrshire pits and taking loaded ones back down to Ayr harbour for onward ship-ment to Northern Ireland. On one occasion at the pits, a lesson was burned into my mind about family responsibility. It was the last day of work in the pits before the start of the miners' annual holiday. My driver, who had witnessed it before, told me to watch what happened when the men came out with their holiday pay packets. I watched a tragedy. Not all but a number of men took a couple of coins and tossed for each other's pay packet – the loser went home to a family getting ready for the holidays with no cash.

This was the time I became an underage drinker. It is the Scottish male curse – the desire to show our manhood by the amount of alcohol we can consume. At the Butlin's holiday camp just outside Ayr, they ran a dance on Saturday nights during which lots of drink was on sale and no questions about age were asked. I was not interested in dancing – I never have been – and access to drink was the attraction. It was the same in the Bunch of Grapes pub in Ayr, where we young railway cleaners would gather and down our whiskies and beer. In the railway cleaner's bothy we would boast (exaggerate) about how much we had drunk.

Then came my first trade union experience. I had, like my grandpa, joined the NUR. It was 1955 and railway drivers and firemen wanted wages commensurate with the skills they had as locomotive footplate men. Anthony Eden, Tory prime minister, had just won a general

A Difference of Opinion

election on Thursday 26 May. ASLEF decided to strike for more wages on the 28th but the NUR decided not to strike. I was at home off work on the first strike day. My father wanted me to join it. I told him I was in the NUR and, as it had decided not to go on strike, I would be going to work the next day. There was a major row, as I dug in my heels. My stepmother made the clinching argument, telling me quietly that, no matter the difference between my union and my father's, the fact was that I would have to cross a picket line and, in doing so, I would bring shame on the family and forever be known as a scab and a blackleg which, in working-class circles, was the mark of Cain.

So I said I would join the strike cycled down to the strike headquarters in a church hall and signed up. There were strike meetings at which senior officials of ASLEF told us we were in a working-class struggle, along with the dockers who were also out on strike. The enemy was not so much the Railway Board as the Tory government, which had declared a state of emergency.

The little strike pay we got was handed over to my stepmother and I was flat broke. That strike taught me a lesson for life. I hadn't realised up to then that all I had to maintain myself was the ability to sell my labour and this was a vulnerable position to be in. As well as learning that fundamental lesson, which applies to everyone who has no inherited wealth, I learned something else too. I found out that it was a false idea to believe that the longer a strike goes on and the more skint strikers become, the more likely they are to cave in and return to work. Years later, when I was a Labour MP I tried explaining to John Biffen, a leading Tory MP, that, once people are out on strike, the union has difficulty getting them back in, no matter how hard up they may be. He couldn't understand. It seemed so illogical to him.

To bring the strike to an end, there was some arbitration with the drivers getting a wage increase but there was hardly anything for the firemen and cleaners. The men were not happy – they wanted a bigger settlement. The problem the ASLEF national leaders had was getting us to agree to go back to work. Those final meetings were stormy, with the men condemning the leaders for selling out. Finally, however, back to work we went, marching in a show of solidarity down to the engine sheds to sign on again, demanding no victimisation against the strike leaders.

So, between my experience as a milk boy in the richer parts of Ayr, my exploitation at the hands of the master plasterer and my experience of struggle in a strike, by the age of sixteen, I was well and truly embedded in working-class political culture. Now, with the benefit of access to

Cabinet minutes of the time, far from wanting to grind us into defeat, the government, desperate to get us back to work, seized on the idea of a 'referee' making an award the union would accept. We didn't know that was their position. We saw it as us against the Tory government, which men like my father still saw through the lens of the 1930s.

4

The Royal Navy

Although happy on the railway, wartime austerity had come to an end and my generation became more ambitious about broadening our horizons. Moreover and much more important, I would be called up to do my National Service once I reached eighteen.

Ayr was home to the Royal Scots Fusiliers. A number of lads I knew had been drafted into that regiment and the tales they told when on leave about the discipline and stupidity they encountered made me determined to avoid it. My brother had been called up to the RAF but I thought my chances of that were slim. My pal Bobby Etchells and I decided the best way to dodge the Army was to join the Royal Navy as regulars. That does not sound logical but joining the Navy to see the world seemed infinitely preferable to the picture painted of National Service in the Army. We joined up in Glasgow. As I had attended Ayr Academy, I was designated Ordinary Telegraphist – a radio operator. Bobby, who had gone to a junior secondary school, became a stoker.

I was seventeen and, when I went home and told my parents I had just signed up with the Navy and would get my papers in a few weeks, my father said I wasn't going. I said I was going. Rows followed but there was nothing he could do – I was going. The papers and rail tickets arrived in September 1955 and off I went to Glasgow, where a number of us were met by RN staff and put on a train that would, after a few changes, get us to Victoria Barracks (HMS Victory) in Portsmouth. My first problem was that I spoke Lowland Scots rather than the English as pronounced by the BBC. On our first weekend leave, I went into a newsagent's to buy a paper and was duly humiliated by the man telling me he didn't understand me and would I repeat myself. I knew damn well that he understood me but decided that I would need to master the 'English' way of speaking the English language.

After being issued with uniforms, we new recruits were marched to a store and given 200 cigarettes each – a free ration every month. Along with my brother and sister, I had never smoked but here they were for free. I tried a couple, didn't like them and gave them away. Later, I learned not to dispose of something valuable like that but to use them as barter with, for example, someone to do my duty shift when I wanted to go 'ashore' – the term used even when living in shore-based barracks.

Cleanliness was a naval priority. During a six-week induction course we were taught to *dhoby* (wash) and iron our clothes. Aspiring radio operators were given an aptitude test and we were all given lectures on the ethos of the Royal Navy, in which reverence for Nelson was unmistakable. We were told of the great battles won by various admirals and were required to remember them all because, at any time, we could be stopped by an officer and answer questions about them.

At the end of six weeks, our group went its different ways. The Ordinary Telegraphists went to HMS Mercury, the Navy Signal School, up in the Hampshire hills near Petersfield. Mercury was a big estate, where trained operators monitored Russian communications and the raw recruits were trained to read Morse code at twenty-five words a minute and touch-type at thirty-five words a minute. It was a nine-month course and included learning how to code and decode messages, develop skills in voice communication and master how the communications system of the Royal Navy was organised worldwide. Mercury was commanded by Captain Alexander Gordon-Lennox. When I entered Parliament in 1970, he was a retired Rear Admiral and the Serjeant at Arms of the House of Commons. We both found it amusing how our positions had changed – a bit.

Personalities and events from those training days have stuck in my mind. On one occasion, we had paraded in full kit and rifles as a guard of honour for Lord Mountbatten, the First Sea Lord. These guards of honour were regular occurrences but this one was different. Afterwards, Mountbatten stood on a small wall and called us to gather round. He explained that, in his early career, he too had specialised in communications and proceeded to tell us how important our role would be onboard ship and to the Admiralty in London. This unusual informal talk made us feel he was one of us. It was a masterful performance. He was a charismatic aristocrat with a common touch – a powerful combination.

I won the Captain's Prize for coming first in our class. All of us having passed the course, we celebrated in a pub in Petersfield. I got blind drunk. I had no memory of doing so but was told later by the officer of the watch I had challenged him to a fight when we returned to Mercury. Next morning the bugle call was followed by a message over the camp tannoy for RO2 Sillars (by then we were called radio operators) to report to the Guard Room. I was puzzled but down I went to be confronted by the officer telling me what I had done, which included vomiting all over the road outside. Threatening an officer with physical violence was a serious offence and I saw my career coming to an end with a stiff sentence in a naval detention centre.

But he didn't charge me. He had taken the trouble to get my personnel file during the night and told me that I had talent and a bright future but it would all come to nothing if I did not curb my drinking, which I obviously could not handle. He said he was not letting me off lightly (but he was). He pointed out what a fool I was making of myself and, to drive the point home, he made me clean up my vomit that was spread all over the road, at a bus terminus used by the civilian staff. There I was with a brush and pail, looking like death warmed up, cleaning up my own mess in front of a bus full of civilians arriving for work, clearly enjoying seeing me paying a price for my stupidity.

The lesson that officer gave me – exercising humanity when he didn't need to and not blighting a young person's life because of one stupid mistake – proved a valuable one in my later public life. The severity of his lecture about my drinking had an effect too. I didn't stop, but never again did I put myself in jeopardy. The irony was that I didn't actually like beer or whisky and only took them to conform to the image of the hard-drinking Scot. Later in life, when much more mature, I stopped taking any alcohol and have not done so for over thirty years. I have never missed it.

There was a history-changing event near the end of my training when, in 1956, the Eden government was threatening to and finally did invade Egypt after President Nasser nationalised the Suez Canal. In the Navy, each night at 9 p.m., an officer makes a 'round' of the mess decks, accompanied by a sailor, to make sure everything is clean and tidy. The night it was my turn to be escort, there had been a party in the wardroom celebrating the coming war and the officer was drunk. At each mess deck, he gave a little speech, a vitriolic attack on the Egyptians, whom he called 'Gypos'. Britain had to take back the canal because the 'Gypos' did not have the ability to sail merchant vessels through it safely by themselves. When I suggested that the Egyptians had been sailing ships for centuries, I was told to shut up and asked what did I know about anything.

Shortly after that episode I was drafted to HMS *Salisbury*, a brand-new frigate. We were engaged in working up to become part of the fleet, and so did not join the ships getting ready for Egypt. But Suez was all the talk. Our bridge wireless office (BWO) was where all communications came in and it was frequently packed with officers and petty officers getting the latest on the crisis. I was very junior so I just listened, until one day when they were all denouncing the nationalisation of the canal. I was prompted to say that I didn't see anything wrong with that, as we had nationalised the pits and the railways. Talk about swearing at the Pope in the Vatican! It quickly got round the ship that there was a 'Gypo-loving bastard up in the BWO'. I was unpopular for some time.

I spent seven months onboard *Salisbury*. She now lies at the bottom of the Atlantic, sunk for target practice. Our mess deck was solely for signalmen and radio operators. We slept in hammocks but other ratings often had to find a bed in an alleyway. During exercises in working up we did four hours on watch and four hours off. I was seasick most of the time and often did my watch with a bucket between my legs. I was, however, happy.

I was the favourite rum bosun. Every day at 12 noon, the rum bosun drew the rum and dished it out by the tumblerful. It was accepted that he would, when using the standard measure, put his thumb in it, thus getting more for himself. As I didn't like rum, I never used the thumb and so everyone got an extra share from mine. Many went back to work half cut. This practice was abandoned in 1970.

On our mess deck the hierarchy was interesting. At its head were the leading radio operator and leading signalman but the main influence came from an ordinary three-badge signalman, Dad Andrews, a Geordie. The three red badges on his uniform indicated that he had served at least twelve years and that his experience merited total respect for anything he said. He was the major influence on us all. He and I got on extremely well and he was a vital source of advice. He was the one who told me, after my pro-nationalisation intervention over Suez, that I should stay onboard for a while for my own safety.

The leading signalman was a fellow Scot. I cannot now recall his name but have never forgotten his description of the bravest man he had ever seen. It was during his time as a prisoner of the Japanese, who captured him when HMS *Exeter* was sunk in the Java Sea. He described the savagery of the Japanese guards who, every morning, would parade the prisoners and then pick out one for a vicious beating, while all the rest had to stand there and watch. One day they picked a man whom everyone knew would not survive. As this poor chap was about to step forward, a big Australian pulled him back, stepped out and punched a guard on the jaw. It was certain death and not a pleasant one, but this extraordinary man gave his life for the other.

Dad Andrews' stories were different. He revered the Canadians who he said were the best and most committed to fighting the war he had ever seen. But it was his views of the dockyard workers that were most revealing and bit of a shock to me with my trade union background. He and the older sailors detested them, saying they were lazy and swung the lead at every opportunity. Whether true or not, this was widely believed and trade unions were despised. That information I used later in life when, as a Labour MP, I was assailed going into a Scottish party conference in Aberdeen by a group from the far Left who were advocating trade union organisation in the armed forces. I asked one of them if they had any experience of life in the military, to which the answer was no. I then asked if the policy meant that sailors or soldiers who formed a branch would be entitled to implement their decisions. The answer was yes. I then asked, if the decision was to shoot striking dockyard workers, were they were entitled to do so? Utter confusion on his part.

*

I was posted to Hong Kong in 1957. That was the turning point in my life – when the politician within me finally emerged, as did the ability to take a lead position in a group, to take on authority and to write.

Before I knew of the new posting, HMS *Salisbury* was in dry dock and the radio operators were split up and sent to other naval establishments. I went to a naval air station in Devon to conduct communications exercises with pilots. I got on well with them. They were a different kind of officer from any I had met before – more personally friendly and willing to have a chat. While there, I was told to report back to *Salisbury*, pack, leave the ship, go into HMS Drake, the naval barracks at Devonport, and await transhipment to Hong Kong to join 3AOTRA. I had never heard of 3AOTRA. It obviously wasn't a ship. Dad Andrews knew. It was a combined Army–Navy operations unit – 3Amphibious Operations Troop Royal Artillery. In wartime, the unit would occupy different high points of land, concentrations of the enemy would be spotted, and co-ordinates passed to a naval ship, miles away, whose big guns would obliterate them.

Each troop needed Navy radio operators as the Army and Navy communications were not compatible (we sent and read Morse at faster speeds than the Army). So I was to become involved with the Army I had joined the Navy to escape from. But, as I found, being in the Army as a Navy man was not the same as being in the Army as a soldier and that difference could be played to my advantage.

This transfer came at the time I was going to be married to Anne

26

O'Farrell from Ayr. My leave had been arranged from *Salisbury* but could not be taken from Hong Kong. So when I left *Salisbury* and went to the naval barracks to await transit, we brought the date forward and had a one-week honeymoon in Dundee. My tour in Hong Kong would be for two-and-a-half years, which was standard in those days. As 3AOTRA was a shore-based posting, a naval rating was entitled to have his wife and children (if any) with him. But there was an age barrier and, as I was below it, I would have to wait until my last year in Hong Kong before Anne could come out. That was where my son Matthew was born. On getting married, I decided that, at the end of my tour, I would buy myself out of the Navy.

A mix of Army, RAF and Navy lower-deck personnel travelled out to Hong Kong on the *Empire Fowey*, a 12,000-ton passenger ship. We were in third class, in huge mess decks with bunks, while NCOs and their families were in second class and the officers and their ladies were in first. We passed through the Suez Canal, the first British-flagged ship to do so once it was re-opened after the Suez crisis. While docked at Port Said waiting to form up with a convoy, the Egyptians set up loud-speakers on either side of the canal and spent several hours hurling abuse at us. I was amused by the jingoist reactions of my fellow third-class passengers, all of them lamenting that we should have continued to give the 'Gypos' a pasting instead of withdrawing. We also had visits from the 'bumboat' men, who surrounded the ship in their little boats, trying to sell us souvenirs. What was memorable is that every one of them spoke in a broad Scottish accent, having learned their English from the Scottish regiments stationed there in the many years Britain controlled Egypt.

It was onboard that I first ventured into a 'leadership' role. It happened over the food. We lower-deck people ate in a large canteen area and an officer would come round at lunchtime and ask if we were satisfied with the meal. Everyone said, 'Yes, sir.' but actually thought it awful. It took a bit of courage but one day I replied, 'No, sir, it's rubbish.' The officer was startled and miffed because the complaint had to be looked into. Eventually I was called in front of the senior officer in charge and asked to state my case which, while standing to attention, I did. The food did not improve but the officers and senior NCOs had marked me out as someone to keep an eye on. My immediate mates were astonished by my temerity. One said he was so surprised because, until then, he had me marked down as a very quiet chap. I was. I didn't, and still do not, like confrontation but do not avoid it when it's necessary.

5

Hong Kong

I arrived in a hot and humid Hong Kong in July 1957 and spent the first night in HMS Tamar, the RN shore base that is now a Chinese People's Liberation Army barracks. Next morning, I went by boat across the harbour to Kowloon and on to Gun Club Hill barracks, where I joined five other Navy radio operators, a petty officer and about thirty soldiers within 3AOTRA. This is when I first started to understand the institutional mind and its severe limitations when confronted by the unorthodox. Basically, the Army encourages obedience, whereas the Navy needs people with the ability to think and act individually and take responsibility because that is the only way a warship can survive in extreme circumstances. This is a clash of cultures.

The other Navy lads explained how things operated but they were not a happy bunch. The troop lodged with an artillery regiment. We used their canteen, leisure and medical facilities and the navy petty officer had membership of the sergeants' mess but, for operational purposes, we were quite separate. We worked tropical hours, starting at 7 a.m. and finishing at noon. By the time I got sorted out, it was time to put up in the mess deck. That was a shock – it was dirty, with stuff strewn all over the floor. I waited for the corporal to get us all to clean up for the 9 p.m. 'rounds' and was surprised when my Navy mates said there was no such thing in the Army. I watched an army lad, wearing thick socks, get up from his bed, walk out on to the balcony, go along to the toilet, come back and lie on his bed. I couldn't believe his unhygienic ways.

I slept badly that first night. I found out why on waking up. My stomach was covered in blisters. I thought I had caught some dreaded tropical disease and made a beeline for the medical centre. The soldier in charge looked, nodded his head and said he would give me some calamine lotion to cool the bedbug bites. Bedbugs? He said they were a constant problem and that, if I lifted the mattress, I would see them. He was right. I asked others in the mess deck and they simply shrugged, admitting they were a problem. I decided they were not going to be for me.

When we paraded at 7 a.m. on day two of my army life, I had a run-in with the troop sergeant. There must have been special training in those days, teaching sergeants to behave like their film caricatures – terrifying the ordinary soldier by coming up close and yelling in his face. The Navy had a sensible dress rule in the tropics – No. 10s and 10As – and ratings could choose between them. Both were a blue shirt and blue shorts. For footwear, No. 10s was black shoes with blue stockings, whilst 10As specified sandals and bare feet. I went on parade in 10As. The sergeant did the nose-to-nose stuff, shouting that I would never appear on parade like this again. I told him I had opted for 10As, which he obviously knew nothing about. I compounded his amazement at not being in the least perturbed by his yelling by saying that immediately after the parade I wanted to see the CO to state a serious complaint.

When I went before the CO, a Major, he asked what the problem was. I lifted my shirt and told him that I had never experienced bedbug bites in my life and that I wanted an immediate transfer back to the Navy. A transfer on day two was impossible, he replied. I stood my ground and insisted that I had the right to go back to the Navy with its proper living conditions. As the argument developed, I realised that he was faced with a terrible dilemma. If I transferred back to the Navy because of the bedbug bites, the Army was going to look bad as it would not take long for the story to make its rounds. He said the fatal words, 'Can't we find a compromise?' I can still remember the look of puzzlement on his face when I said 'Yes, it's called paraffin.' I would stay provided two things happened. First, I would be given paraffin in order to burn the sailors' beds and kill the bugs and, second, that we sailors would have a separate space in the barrack room with only six beds, which we would be responsible for keeping clean. He agreed. I burned the beds and we got our special area. I couldn't demand the same cleanliness for the soldiers as I wasn't one but could for the sailors.

No soldier would have or could have done what I did. Most of our troop were army national servicemen and were frightened of the sergeant – never mind being able to face up to officers. But, when I had bested the sergeant over my sandals earlier, I realised that I had a Navy card to play. I have always had a quick mind and it was in overdrive that morning.

My third day with the Army was equally eventful. After lunch, I put on a pair of plimsolls, shorts and a plain white sports shirt to play football with some of my new army acquaintances. I was the only sailor there. We were having a kick at goals when there was an almighty roar from a small man accompanied by two others, marching smartly towards us. The Army lads said with dread in their voices, 'It's the provo-sergeant.' I found out later that the provo-sergeant was part of the internal disciplinary force within a regiment, quite distinct from the Military Police. Anyway, this man came along, carrying a stick under his armpit, obviously very self-important. The young soldiers were extremely nervous saying things like 'We're in for it now!' and some were shaking. It turned out that we were playing on an area of the football pitch that was out of bounds. We hadn't realised and had not done it deliberately.

We were ordered to line up and I went right to the back. Yelling at the top of his voice, the provo-sergeant made each soldier stand to attention and yelled, 'Name? Number?' and let loose a torrent of swearing. When my turn came and he yelled for my name and number, I asked him what his name was. He was dumbstruck, a man of a narrow institutional mind set, unprepared for anything that did not fit into his known pattern of thought. After a second or two to recover, back on form, he asked in a voice dripping with sarcasm and threat, 'How long have you been in the Army, lad?'

'I'm not in the Army,' I replied. More confusion. I did not immediately say I was in the Navy then, after I did, informed him that although I had not read the Army regulations yet, I was sure they were not essentially different from the Navy's and that I was going to report him for swearing at junior ranks. I then walked away and proceeded to the guardroom where, deliberately using naval language, I asked to see the officer of the watch. There was more confusion before, finally, the guardroom called the duty officer.

A young lieutenant turned up and could hardly believe I was making a complaint against the provo-sergeant. It was unheard of. He was relieved when I told him I was seconded to 3AOTRA from the Navy. We parted with him saying the complaint had been noted. I doubted there was any intention of following it up.

I waited a few days then asked to see our troop CO. I explained about the complaint against the regiment's provo-sergeant and asked whether it had been followed up. I was told it had, which I knew was a lie, and that I would hear back soon. A couple of days later, I was told that the provo-sergeant had been told off. I knew that was another lie and I suspected the CO knew that I knew it was a lie. However, I had enough sense and had won enough victories to know when to call a halt. Our troop sergeant's and I had a private chat at his request and, when I explained that I would always wear 10As and sandals, he agreed that I would not need to appear on morning parade again. We sailors had our own clean space, I had beaten the dreaded provo-sergeant and there was to be no more morning parades for me. I wasn't really a rebel but what, in the Navy, was called a 'lower-deck lawyer' who knew just how far to take things. That proved not always to be the course I took in later life, in politics. After these early episodes, the officers had accepted that I was more than just a name and number and we all got on fine.

It was with 3AOTRA that I learnt the importance of training and fitness. Each new batch of national servicemen arrived in July and were broken in by a fifteen-mile hike in the New Territories over a route known as Bride's Pool. Each had one full water bottle and a small pack. On my breaking in, I had drunk all the water well before halfway and the second half was torture. I was physically shattered, dying of thirst, staggering rather than walking. By the second year, with a lot of training, route marching and climbing mountains behind me (the mountains around Hong Kong are around 3,000 feet), I could do the whole hike and still have plenty of water left at the end.

I was very good at the job. On exercise, our troop broke up into small groups of five or six, each with a naval radio operator. Sometimes a group had no officer, with the sergeant or corporal in charge. Between us we carried a wireless set, large lead batteries, Sten guns, water bottles and full packs up to a mountain top from where we could spot the enemy and call in the gunfire of the heavy naval cruiser sitting offshore. I was doing forty laps round the football pitch every night before bed so, in terms of physical fitness and my skill as a radio operator, there were no complaints.

Among the regular soldiers I met was Tony O'Donnell, another Scot. He was a bombardier (corporal equivalent in other army regiments) and put in charge of the battery maintenance. Of the very highest intelligence, with a wide vocabulary, a mastery of mathematics and fully up to date on current affairs, he was a remarkable man. He was such a forceful personality that officers tip-toed round him, knowing he was more than a match for them. We became firm friends and collaborative colleagues within the first few weeks of me landing in the troop.

It was in a café-bar in Hong Kong that I got another lesson in racism. A US Navy cruiser was in harbour on a visit. A number of American sailors were in the café, when another came in alone and the Chinese waitress, thinking she was doing the right thing, took him over to them. Despite serving on the same ship, he was told to fuck off. They were

31

white, he was black. We, a small group from the unit, invited the black sailor to come and sit with us. The tale he told of life onboard his ship was extraordinary. Although President Truman had abolished segregation in the US armed forces in 1948, it was still very much in practice. His ship had not only segregated mess decks, but also segregated gun crews. We asked him if a white gun crew fell a member short, wouldn't they be forced to replace him with a black guy? He laughed and said no way. It was beyond stupid.

I had Tony O'Donnell to thank for guiding me towards reading Marx, Engels, Bernard Shaw, Bertrand Russell, R.H. Tawney and others of intellectual influence on the Left. He had a transcript of the famous BBC 1948 radio debate on the existence of God, between Bertrand Russell and Father Frederick Copleston. Reading that and other books by Russell saw the end of me as a Christian and I became an atheist. Unlike others on the British Left, Russell was not taken in by Stalin. His exposure of the true nature of Soviet Communism, written in the 1930s, ended any chance of me joining the Communist Party. We got a lot of reading material from the YWCA library (yes, YWCA), which was located in a hotel near Kowloon harbour. We also read *The South China Morning Post* and the UK papers *The Observer* and *The Sunday Times*, which arrived a few days after publication back home.

The Army had an excellent education service and a number of us enrolled in English and general knowledge courses for free. I passed GCE O Levels in both.

I should qualify becoming an atheist. Strictly speaking, given the limited knowledge that even the most advanced science can employ about how our planet came to have life, no one really knows. The Big Bang is still titled a 'Theory'. Pushed in a philosophical debate, I would be able to go no further than declaring for an agnostic. However, in relation to those religions that stake out their beliefs in God, I am an atheist, a sort of working definition of where I stand.

I am not a militant atheist. I am aware of atrocities committed in the names of various religions but also acknowledge the crimes against people that took place in the atheistic Soviet Union and in China under Mao. I am acutely aware of, and grateful for, the influence of Christianity on British culture life, with so many people inspired by it to write the most powerful and moving music. My favourite piece of music is 'Jerusalem'. Yes, I know it's about England but it is a beautiful piece. The Sermon on the Mount cannot be bettered as a guide for a community to live in harmony and working with my Christian friend

David Thomson, who I shall mention later, and with Muslims in the Arab world has taught me just how important a religious faith can be for people. So, while I cannot share their faith, I respect the people who have it. The only problem I have with the religions practised today is that some believers think they have the email address of their god and can therefore act in his name against others, however atrocious the action.

As well as Tony and me with our advocacy of socialism, there were two English public school national servicemen, Chris Rudkin and Peter Banks, both well able to take us on in a debate, making for a very political atmosphere in the troop. Peter Banks was particularly resentful of America and it was from him that I first learned of the 1944 Bretton Woods agreement that led to the dominance of the United States in the world economy after 1945. In Peter's view, America took advantage of Britain's growing economic weakness, due to spending our national wealth fighting Hitler, to bully us into a submissive junior position. Years later, in discussion with Tory MPs, Peter's bitterness was widely shared within the Tory Party.

Far from being concerned with the overtly political atmosphere, our CO decided that one session a week would be devoted to a current affairs discussion, with him leading it. He only lasted two sessions as Tony and I challenged him successfully on imperialism and colonialism – at the time the British government was facing trouble in Cyprus and elsewhere. At the next session there was a military padre who contested the godless views of Bertrand Russell. We reckoned we had beaten him in that debate because he left shouting that Bertrand Russell, like all atheists, would turn to God on their last day. But we were not finished with God. We had a special visit from a Bible-bashing member of the Church of England who claimed to have been a sinner but had been saved one night in Gibraltar and had come to save us. He wasn't as well versed in theology as Tony and me and left after a verbal mauling. There was more God to come. Next, we were paraded down to a hall above the NAAFI, where another army padre came to tell us about Jesus the carpenter boy. At the end I waited behind and very politely told him that what he had said was absurd, that outside our barracks were millions of people living in poverty, and could he tell us what Christianity was doing for them. He thanked me just as politely and said he would think about it.

The next week he opened by acknowledging that one of us had raised doubts about how he should teach us Christianity but he did think it best to start when Jesus was young. So, we got another load of tripe.

A Difference of Opinion

At the end, I waited behind and told him we would not be back. I told the CO the same and our troop's intelligence was never again insulted.

The result of all our open debates was that our troop had two spheres of influence – one was the authority of the officers, which was never directly challenged, and the other was the influence which Tony and I exerted, not just over our fellow lower rankers but also those areas into which the officers were prepared to enter discussion and debate with the lower ranks on non-military matters. A good example was Captain Powell. He was in charge of a group of us on duty out in the New Territories one night, manning a searchlight which we were meant to shine upon refugees coming over the border. He, the officer, had a three-ton wireless truck to stay in. A canvas tent was attached to it and, inside it, a canvas bed and bowl for washing in. The rest of us, six, shared a one-ton truck which had no amenities.

I was regaling the lads with my views on the need for them to support the Labour Party after they were demobbed and got back home, when Captain Powell called me in to the big truck for what he called a 'man-to-man' discussion, something officers should never do. He started off by saying he too was a Labour supporter and wanted to put me right on some things, citing his admiration for Ernest Bevin, who had been Attlee's Foreign Minister. After telling him Bevin was an arch Right-winger, I proceeded to get stuck into him, pointing out that, whilst he was comfortable in his big tent, the rest of us were sharing more cramped conditions with no amenities. How could a Labour man justify that? That was an unfair, underhand debating point from me because that kind of distinction between ranks was normal. It was, however, a telling debating point which, on purely political grounds, he had no answer to. He was a very well-meaning man, well liked by the men and a good officer who could get the best out of us on exercises.

It will be difficult for many readers, especially any who have served in the military, to believe the dominance that Tony and I exercised in that small unit but it was the case. We were more than the intellectual equals of the officers, gaining in self-confidence and expressing our views in a way seldom, if ever, done by junior ranks. We were never in any danger of military discipline as we never sought to undermine the officers' authority on how the troop conducted itself as a military unit. We were both actually quite proud of the special status of the unit.

It was with 3AOTRA that I learned to play tennis and five-a-side hockey when we moved from Gun Club Hill to the barracks on Nathan Road. Chris Rudkin was a county-level tennis player and helped me get into the game. I found I was just as good at hockey as I was at football.

We played five-a-side hockey within the tennis court, which was surrounded by a small wall. Our routine was out at 7 a.m., play five-a-side hockey, get showered, have breakfast and go to work. We finished at noon and played tennis or hockey in the afternoon. It was a good life.

It was also with 3AOTRA that I learnt to admire the work done by the Salvation Army. Our CO had the idea of the troop 'adopting' a Chinese child from a very poor family. All of us agreed to chip in, including the national servicemen, whose pay was very low. Tony and I were given the task of explaining our troop's purpose to the Salvation Army and seeking their assistance to find a child from a single-child family, in order to provide the parents with money, a good part of which was earmarked for the child's clothing and education. This was not lightly done. The Salvation Army people were thorough in testing why the troop was doing this. Was this something that would give the family stability for a prolonged period or just a passing idea that might be abandoned? Tony and I learned a great deal – not only about the plight of refugees but also about the quality of the Salvation Army's hard-headed understanding of their problems and the compassion and commitment shown. The fund continued to operate after I left Hong Kong and all the time the troop was there.

Tony O'Donnell took seriously ill just as I was about to be demobbed and we had been told he did not have long to live. This proved to be false. Thirty years later I landed at Bahrain and there, walking along one of the airport corridors, was Tony wearing a hard hat – he was chief engineer in charge of the airport's expansion. He had recovered, left the Army, gone to university and now occupied this senior post. When he came back to Scotland he lived with his family in Livingston. I was able to visit him for the last time when he was in a hospice in Edinburgh.

*

During my time in Hong Kong I grew to appreciate the inner strengths and dynamic of the Chinese and their depth of feeling about the Japanese, which continues to manifest itself from time to time.

Three people in particular opened my eyes in this respect. The first was the big Chinese man in the Army canteen who took our plates and scraped them into a large trash can. We learned that he was a medical doctor from northern China and, while he acknowledged that the nationalist regime under Chiang Kai-shek had been a corrupt disaster, he and his family could not live under the Communist system and, with little cash, had made their long way to Hong Kong. Like many others, he lived in a shack. With his qualifications not recognised in

Hong Kong, he was studying to qualify. The plate-scraping job was all he could get as a newly arrived refugee. That this cultivated man kept his dignity in the most menial of jobs and was studying under the most difficult of circumstances showed a depth and strength of character that no one could fail to admire.

Then there was Mui Ying, our amah. When my wife Anne arrived in Hong Kong, we, like some other service people, did not take military married quarters but a flat in a civilian area. Our flat, in 9 Hanoi Road, Kowloon, was owned by a Chinese woman. The Navy gave us a rent allowance plus an allowance to hire an amah, a servant. Mui Ying was highly intelligent and spoke good English, and I asked her what she was doing working as an amah. She looked at me as if I was daft – this was the only work available. Her husband had a poorly paid job and she used what she got from us to give her small daughter an education. Amahs were expected to work seven days a week and be at the beck and call of the 'master' or 'missy'.

My wife did not like the idea of having a servant but she quickly came to understand that Mui Ying needed the job and they became friends – a relationship that lasted long after we left Hong Kong, with them always keeping in touch. We paid Mui Ying above the normal rate and she got the weekend off, plus holidays at Chinese New Year. For me, what was admirable about Mui Ying was her strong character and her determination as a Chinese woman facing adversity, to exercise courage. That courage was revealed in what I call 'the Japanese incident'.

My wife was a member of a coffee-morning club, with each member taking it in turn to host the get-together at home. From the information network the amahs operated, Mui Ying knew that the wife of the manager of a Japanese airline was among the members of the coffee circle and was due to be invited to our flat. A day or so before the coffee morning, Mui Ying explained that under no circumstances would she open the door to the Japanese woman and, if Anne let her in, she would not serve her coffee. Mui Ying was prepared to get fired even though her pay was vital for her daughter's education. She explained the reason – the atrocities Japanese soldiers had committed against the Chinese after their invasion during the Second World, including men being picked up at random and used for live bayonet practice. She stood her ground, expecting to be sacked. We told her to take the day off.

Then there was the confrontation with army neighbours. One day, I came home at lunchtime to be passed on the stair by two Chinese Hong Kong policemen heading for the exit. At a door on the floor below us was a bundle of belongings – the sign that an amah was being dismissed.

When I got into our flat, Mui Ying said her friend downstairs needed help. She had called the police but they would do nothing because a serviceman was involved. It turned out that a British Army corporal and his wife had borrowed money from the amah (which, strange as it may seem, was not an unusual occurrence as some spent well beyond their means). When she asked for it back, they sacked her and threw her out. I went downstairs, banged on the door and asked if this was true, only to be asked what business was it of mine and be addressed as a 'Chinky-loving bastard'. I persisted and eventually around about 70 per cent of what had been lent was thrown in our faces. I told the amah that this was probably all she was going to get.

From what Mui Ying told us, officers treated their amahs well but that was not true among some of the other ranks who, for the first time, found themselves in a master–servant relationship.

Word of my intervention on the amah's behalf spread swiftly and I found that, on my next visit to the local shops, I was greeted as a friend. Thereafter, I had many a conversation about how families had come to Hong Kong as penniless refugees and were carving out a living in the most difficult circumstances. One family I passed on the way to work lived under a stairwell from which the man sold plastic combs. People were crowded into shacks up the hills and in the slums, where running water came from a single tap serving a whole neighbourhood. There was no welfare system, only help from the likes of the Salvation Army, yet these people had a dynamic that was impossible to miss.

I found this dynamic missing on a business visit to mainland China in 1988, when I met an Indian who owned a textile factory in Dalian. He told me the 'iron rice bowl' instituted by Mao was a real problem because there was no 'get up and go' among his workers like there was in Hong Kong. If he had orders for Christmas, he told the workers that the deadline was July, knowing it would not be met but he would get them in time for Christmas. He was not exaggerating, as I saw myself when visiting factories. But the reforms of Deng Xiaoping have released the dynamic that I saw decades before in Hong Kong.

After some time with 3AOTRA, I was taken back to HMS Tamar and worked in Headquarters British Forces, where we handled all Navy and Merchant Navy communications (the Merchant Navy used the Royal Navy worldwide communications system). After what had been a free and easy life with 3AOTRA, I found life in the Navy irksome. There were formal parades, snobbish officers who thought we on the lower deck were inferiors. Accurate word. A few years ago, in a second-hand bookshop, I found an official booklet issued by the Navy during the

1939–45 War for officers recruited from civilian life. On one page, it explained they had to keep their distance from their 'inferiors' on the lower decks.

I am sure the officers doing 9 p.m. rounds got a shock when they passed my bed as my bedside locker was piled high with books on communism and socialism, as well as history and theoretical works, including essays on Mao Zedong. We worked twelve-hour shifts from 6 a.m. to 6 p.m., and 6 p.m. to 6 a.m. The operator manning the local network for our flotilla of gunboats had the job, every four hours, of checking and signing for the confidential code books which were kept in the office safe. One night, when I was on that duty, I was about to check the code books when the petty officer told me I didn't need to, as he had already done it. I kept my eye on him. Four hours later, I went to get the safe key and again he told me that he had already checked and signed for the books. I challenged him as to why he was doing the checking rather than me and he explained that he had been told that I was not to be allowed near the codes for security reasons. I laughed not because the officers thought I might steal them and hand them over to a foreign power but because the petty officer was from the Irish Republic – not even a British citizen.

Not long after that spat with the petty office, out of the blue, I was sent back over to 3AOTRA to help with the conduct of an exercise of target spotting practice, between the troop and a Navy cruiser. I found that strange – it was just a routine one-day 'shoot' at Port Shelter in the New Territories that had been done countless times. There were RN radio operators in the troop so there was no reason for me to be involved. I did the exercise and found myself being driven back to Kowloon in the CO's jeep, during which he asked if I fancied coming back to the troop. I said yes and, by the time I got back to the Tamar, I was told to pack and return to the Army. No one had ever been transferred back before and I never had any explanation as to why this happened to me. After my brush with the petty officer over the code books, I put it down to being regarded as a security risk. As the Army troop had no information that could be used by an enemy, I suppose it was the safest place to put me. The 3AOTRA officers knew me and were quite happy with a socialist they trusted.

As I had decided after getting married to try to buy myself out, I saved up the cash (£150 or £3,322 in today's money) to do so. Once I had it, I made an appointment at HMS Tamar to meet a Lt Denny, the officer nominally in charge of my social welfare. It was the first time we had met and took an instant dislike for each other. He treated me with contempt, making it clear that I really was his inferior and he ended the meeting by telling me that a simple request for discharge by purchase would not be enough – I would have to give him my reasons in writing. I got the impression he thought this was beyond me.

A week later, I sent him a four-page memo, analysing what was wrong with the Navy, making them the reasons I wanted out. These are some salient points:

The Royal Navy Objectively

If we are to believe the propagandists . . . of naval recruiting, the service offers good prospects . . . On examination prospects are poor, pay inadequate . . . living standards are atrocious . . . cramped mess-decks, where privacy is unheard of and impossible. Even in performing the basic body functions one receives only the bare minimum of privacy. [HMS Salisbury's toilets for the lower deck only had 'half' doors so you could be seen on the throne.]

Good pay is the clarion call of all recruiters . . . But how good is it? When we consider the abnormality of naval life . . . it is like so much in the R.N.: inadequate . . .

A civilian lives in, and is part of, a form of democracy; whereas naval ratings are subject to arrogant aristocratic rule.

In its punishment of lawbreakers, the naval system shows itself to be vicious and stupidly near-sighted. Vicious, because not only does it punish the offender, but also, and to a greater extent, his family . . . Take the case of an acquaintance of mine who was jailed for fourteen days. He lost his liberty and his wife and child lost their income . . . This, I contend, constitutes a punishment of the rating's family.

The memo went on to attack the class division within the Navy, citing an episode when I was due to report to the mess for rounds in Tamar. The mess deck was a Nissen hut with two entrances. Every night the duty officer came in by door A so that is where I stood. But on this particular night, the officer came in by door B and gave me a dressing-down for not being there. I tried to explain that the duty officer always came in by door A. Arrogantly and unwilling to listen further (and with a drink in him), he gave me another dressing-down. The point I was making was that, because he was an officer and I a junior rating, I didn't dare ask him for an explanation as to why the routine procedure had changed or point out the fault was his not mine. I had to stand to attention like an idiot while this fool lectured me, without being able to answer back.

Lt. Denny told me what I had written was libellous and, if it went in front of the captain, I would find myself doing time in a Navy detention centre. I reminded him that he had asked for written reasons and now he had them I wanted to proceed to make the formal request to the captain of Tamar, on the grounds I had set out.

In due course I was given a date to attend Captain's Requests. The drill was that you stood in line and, when your name was called out by the master-at-arms, you stepped forward, stood to attention and took your cap off. In answer to questions from the captain you explained the reasons for your request.

I was all ready for an argument in order to justify what I had written. I expected the captain to reject my request and demand that I withdraw the so-called libellous missive or else. Instead, he directed a question to Lt. Denny, 'Is this him?' to which Denny replied, 'Yes, sir.' And then, without asking me any question at all, the captain said, 'Granted.' Once my tour was up, I would be on my way out. My Navy mates were astonished. One of them had tried three times to buy himself out but was told no because there was a shortage of radio operators. The conclusion I reached was that the Navy didn't want me any more than I wanted to continue to serve.

I still had a year to do in order to complete my two-and-a-half-year stint and I would finish it with 3AOTRA. I had also reached the age when Anne was permitted to join me and we had a very pleasant year in Hong Kong. With the tropical routine in the Army finishing work at noon, we led more of a civilian life than a military one.

I bought a portable typewriter and used it to engage in the correspondence columns of the *South China Morning Post*, citing my civilian address, omitting my naval rank and signing myself just 'Jim Sillars'. I learned a great deal from drafting letters, particularly how to dig up facts and how to marshal an argument. One particular debate was about capital punishment, with me on the abolition side and a Colonel Harrington, a former Inspector-General of Prisons, on the other. It lasted two weeks. He never had reason to suspect his opponent was from the lower deck of the Navy. The space given to letters by the editor was enormous. One-thousand-word letters were not unusual.

Hong Kong has a tendency to get under the skin of those who have lived there. I kept watch on it long after I left and, as soon as I had an official position again, this time as an SNP MP, I went there to find out from Hong Kong Chinese leaders what safeguards they were seeking as the UK government set about transferring the colony back to China's sovereignty.

Hong Kong Revisited

In 1988, a month after the Govan by-election, during the Christmas parliamentary recess, Margo and I travelled to Hong Kong at our own expense. I particularly wanted to meet Emily Lau, a member of the Legislative Council of Hong Kong who was campaigning for the UK government to give all Hong Kong citizens a full British passport and right to abode in the UK, when the territory was transferred to China in 1997. She was also concerned about just how democratic and autonomous Hong Kong would be when China's Basic Law for Hong Kong was eventually published (that came in April 1990). She was a formidable personality. 'Who paid for you to be here?' was her opening question, explaining she was fed up with HK government-sponsored visitors swallowing the official UK line that everything would work out fine in future.

The point about the passports was not have the five million Hong Kong Chinese permanently enter the UK in 1997 but to give them a bargaining position with China if Beijing became oppressive. At that time, Hong Kong was very important to the Chinese economy and China would be vulnerable to any threat to empty it of the businesses and professionally managed investment channels, so vital to mainland development. What the people got was a British National Overseas passport, of no value, as it allowed entry to the UK for a limited visit only. The full passport campaign failed. The Tory government and Labour opposition seemed terrified the people would actually come. There was more than a hint of racism in their attitude.

My chance came to confront the Prime Minister about Hong Kong when my name was drawn for a PMQ on 27 April 1989. When I began, all assumed the question was about Scotland:

> Is the prime minister aware of the indelible stain on her reputation from the rejection of democratic fundamental rights for a small but nevertheless important group of people?

There I paused while the Tory and Labour benches groaned with derision, certain I was on about Scotland, only to be silenced.

I refer to the Chinese population of Hong Kong. Does the Prime

Minister accept that it is only if they get British passports and resident rights in the United Kingdom that the people of Hong Kong will have any real bargaining power with the Chinese government?

Before she answers, will she reflect upon the paradox of the way in which human beings are being disposed of there is more akin to Stalinism than Thatcherism, which is supposed to be about fundamental human rights and libertarianism?

All Mrs Thatcher could reply, having prepared for answers on Scotland and not Hong Kong, was that the standard of living there was higher than in China, which was totally irrelevant to the point I was making, and that I could seek to amend the British Nationality Act.

The next time I drew a PMQ was on 4 May. Mrs Thatcher was again fully prepared for questions on Scotland, but not on Hong Kong:

May I refer the prime minister to her earlier remarks about the increased overseas aid given by Britain? Is she aware that does not apply to the colony of Hong Kong? Will she acknowledge that there has been a serious breach of our moral obligations to the Chinese people of Hong Kong? Will she and the government seriously take onboard a review of the present policy, which denies those people the fundamental right of a vote in a democratic country?

Her reply showed how totally unprepared she was and that even Margaret Thatcher, after ten years in power, could flounder:

PM: I am delighted that the Hon. Member seems to think that in Scotland there is much greater faith in the United Kingdom.

Me: That is not a reply.

PM: Ah, but it is a reply. The Hon. Gentleman did not say that Scotland lacked faith in the future of the United Kingdom, and I quite understand why, because Scotland has benefitted enormously from a higher standard of living. I am so glad to recognise that on this our tenth anniversary.

At the end of this wander in irrelevance, she did finally get to Hong Kong, claiming that the agreement she had made was 'much welcomed in Hong Kong'.

As the future of five million people was involved, I decided to pursue her with a letter of 12 May:

> I refer to our recent exchanges at Question Time about Hong Kong ... you did not respond to the basic point I was making: that the people of Hong Kong, through being denied the right of abode in the United Kingdom (and therefore ultimately in the European Community) will be left in an extremely weak position in trying to ensure adherence to your agreement by the government of China ... [I]t is one thing to transfer territory, but quite another to transfer people and provide them with no cast-iron guarantee to protect their forward position. The day the United Kingdom formally hands over sovereignty of the territory in 1997, you and I know full well that any breach of your agreement will see the UK quite impotent, without remedy to face any adverse reaction by China.
>
> If you have misjudged the value of your agreement, and breaches occur, then it is not you but the people of Hong Kong who will pay the price. No-one knows that better than these people themselves, and for you to suggest that the agreement is 'much welcomed' in Hong Kong is the reverse of the truth ... You must be aware that when people in Hong Kong argue for right of abode here, they are not expressing a wish to actually exercise that right. They want to remain in Hong Kong and make your agreement work. But that is more likely to happen if the Chinese authorities know they are dealing with a population that has an alternative. I cannot believe that you and the government do not fully understand the strength of that argument.

The strength in that agreement, the 1984 Sino–British Joint Declaration, lay on one side – China 'resumed' sovereignty and stated clearly that it would exercise it through the National People's Congress.

In 2020, the British government claimed that China breached the Joint Declaration when imposing new security laws on Hong Kong. I set out the falsity of that claim in an article in *The Herald* on 29 May 2020. It made the point again about the transfer of people and the denial of passports but demonstrated that the Joint Declaration, by its terms, gave the sole right to China's National People's Congress to write Hong Kong's Basic Law. It went on:

UK ministers give the impression today that the Declaration is a tablet of stone. But it is hollow: no British monitoring rights, no consultation or intervention rights ... An international legal instrument it may be, but its terms allowed China's policies to be translated into the Basic Law of Hong Kong in 1990, seven years before the hand-over. That date is important.

Important because a Sino-British Joint Liaison group worked on the details of transfer from 1985 to 1999. The UK didn't object to the Basic Law's Articles 23 and 18 and Annex III and hasn't done so since. Or has it? The Liaison group's records are sealed under the 40-year rule. Perhaps an MP can seek to have them published now? [Mhairi Black did – nothing doing. What is there to hide?]

It is Article 18 and Annex III [that] Wang Chen, of the People's National Congress, invoked last week justifying Beijing's right to impose new laws on Hong Kong. Article 23, dealing with secession, subversion, and foreign interference, and unity of the homeland, has never been activated after the Hong Kong people objected to it in 2003. It is coming now, with China's security apparatus with it. [That Article is now redundant, having been replaced by a new security law imposed by the PNC, with the added factor that China's security apparatus now operates in Hong Kong for the first time.]

The UK has falsely claimed that Hong Kong was guaranteed autonomy until 2047 and accuses China of a flagrant breach of that obligation. Article 18 and Annex III ... clearly show that autonomy was always conditional and based on Hong Kong posing no threat to China's perception of its sovereignty, security or unity.

Two different demonstrations were relevant to how Beijing reacted to events in Hong Kong. I noted that the 2014 Umbrella Revolution, calling for a democratic vote on who should be HK Chief Executive, was peaceful and, while condemning the civil disobedience and alleging a US hand in it, China did nothing else. But the demonstrations in 2018–20 were violent, with loud calls for international help and independence – the very threats Article 23 was meant to prevent.

In that *Herald* piece, I went on to describe how a Greek tragedy was unfolding in Hong Kong:

Western encouragement to demonstrators, and US law asserting a right to monitor China's conduct, plays into the hands of
Beijing allowing it to claim further justification for its new laws.

We do Hong Kong's young people no favours with these
tactics. Pitting Hong Kong against China is no contest . . . The
demonstrations will continue, but they will not stop China's
new laws. The future for the young protesters? Either the bitter
pill of knuckling under, or seeking political asylum as refugees,
elsewhere.

The young people have cause for anger. Just 1,200 people out of a
population of 7.3 million were permitted to 'elect' Carrie Lam, the person
nominated to Beijing for approval. Although Article 45 offers the prospect
of a wider electoral base, it also stipulates that until then, a date never
given, the method of selecting the Chief Executive will continue. I always
doubted there would be a move to democracy. How could we expect the
Chinese Communist Party, fundamentally opposed to the democratic idea,
to contemplate granting democracy to Hong Kong's people, thus giving
them legitimate ground from which to challenge China's role in their lives?

The demonstrators were young, brilliant organisers of civil disobedience but there does not exist in Hong Kong the kind of mature
politically experienced older group with influence on them, who can
point to the realities they face as part of China. Emily Lau's generation
seemed to have no role. I have been distressed to hear her on BBC radio
lamenting the situation, distancing herself from the violence, yet not
being able to offer any sense of direction on how the problems may be
resolved. The young were on their own.

There is no one to tell them that the greater autonomy they seek is
moderated by the fact ultimate power is held in Beijing and that, as well
as addressing the problems of today, they have to consider how they can
use the next 36 years to negotiate a renewed autonomy when Beijing
will be under no legal obligation to do so. That is the conundrum they
seemed unaware of.

The situation in Hong Kong will continue to be fraught with difficulty – it is the price the people are paying for Margaret Thatcher
transferring them along with territory. The present British government
has offered to extend the time Hong Kong British National Overseas
Passport holders can stay here from six to twelve months and describes
it as a 'pathway' to citizenship. There is also talk of renewing the BNO
passports that three million have allowed to lapse. I shall be surprised
if that comes to pass.

6

Civvy Street and into Politics

When I left the Navy in 1960, I was a different person from the one who entered it. Those advertisements you see on television – the young man saying he comes from Blyth but was made in the Royal Navy – is true about me. I have a love–hate relationship with the 'Andrew' as we sailors call it. I owe it a great deal and, despite the objections set out in my memo, I am glad of the experience. However, its hierarchical organisation was at odds with a developing socialism that was leading me to challenge authority. To leave was sensible as I was bound to get into serious trouble by staying in. The first thing I did at home was join the Labour Party.

My first job in Civvy Street was at the 'big stamp works' (there was a separate 'wee' one), in Ayr, where they bashed out axles and other parts for the motor industry. The job I was given was in the 'down-time' office – the system for monitoring the efficiency of the stamping machines. There was a code for every part of them and I had to post faults on a code board as they occurred, submitting a report at the end of every week to the works manager. Having learned Morse code, this other one was no problem.

But I ran into trouble on day one. Work stopped at 5 p.m. but work-ers packed up ten minutes before to wash up. They then all gathered at the front gate, waiting until the hooter went before leaving. I was at the front and asked the gates man why we were all standing there when everyone was ready to go? He explained about the hooter. I thought this was ridiculous – scores of grown men waiting until a horn blew when they were all ready to go home. So, I clocked out there and then. No one followed me. When I got to work the next day, I was summoned to the managing director's office and asked for an explanation. I challenged him to justify the logic of us standing there when we were all ready to go. It was workplace timekeeping, he explained, and waiting for the hooter was an essential part of it. I asked him if we were all supposed

46

to stand outside waiting for it to blow before coming in to work. He hadn't thought of that. The upshot was that, in future, I could come in and leave by the clerical workers' gate, where we didn't have to wait for the hooter. I said that was fine but privately decided that this place was not for me. It is the only job I have ever had where I dreaded Monday mornings.

By this time, my brother Robert had done his National Service and was in the South Western Area Fire Brigade and knew of a vacancy at the Kilmarnock station. On applying, I was lucky to get the job. Lucky because, at the interview with the firemaster and his deputy, the latter took a dislike to me. He complained that not once had I addressed the firemaster as 'Sir'. My reply was that I had just left the Navy and did not see the fire service as an equivalent where 'Sir' was compulsory. The firemaster wasn't put out by this, and gave me the job as a fireman. He was later to regret it.

At Kilmarnock, I joined the Fire Brigades Union and quickly filled the vacant shop steward post of chairman of the area committee. No one else wanted it.

Along with men from other brigades, I spent three months of intensive training at the Scottish Fire Services College in Gullane, East Lothian. One of the things senior fire officers were addicted to was training men on the hook ladder – something the FBU was opposed to, on safety grounds, because men in the London Brigade had been killed on it, during exercises. The ladder had an iron hook (with teeth) attached to the top rung. Using it, a man could, in theory, scale a tall building from ground to top floor, going up window by window. Once you reached the first floor, you leaned out of the window, hooked the ladder on to the window sill above, then stood out into mid-air, feet on the bottom rung holding a higher rung with arms out straight to keep the ladder perpendicular and climbed into the next window and so on, ever upwards. If you did not stand with arms outstretched, the ladder swung about dangerously like a mad thing. It wasn't even needed as we had turntable ladders that could do a far more efficient job. I think senior officers saw it as character building.

We trainee firemen practised using the hook ladder on a tall tower with open windows and wooden sills, which got wet when it rained and made the hook on the ladder slip. I never flunked the drill but no one liked it and some were terrified of it. We were in the middle of a drill when the commandant came along and asked each of us if we liked using the hook ladder. Everyone said, 'Yes, Sir.' except me. I told him I did not – it was a dangerous piece of training equipment which had no relevance at a fire (none were carried on fire engines) and the FBU opposed its use in training. He didn't argue with me but, in the end-of-course report he sent to the firemaster, he said I lacked 'moral fibre'. That was pretty damning about someone in a job like a firefighter. When he showed me the report, the firemaster just laughed.

*

I was an active shop steward. Labour controlled Ayrshire County Council also had a majority on the Joint Fire Board, whose other members came from Ayr Town Council, Dumfries and Galloway. The union had matters of concern that were being ignored by the Joint Board and we felt that the Ayrshire Labour group members on it had forgotten about their responsibility to us, a section of the working class. Although I was in the Labour Party, I was very much a new member and knew nothing about its structures in Ayrshire or its main personalities. The FBU area committee decided to take its complaints to the full county Labour group meeting. I was deputed to present the case and, as they say, did not miss them and hit the wall, verbally flaying them for failure to adequately back the union. It was the bravery of the ignorant. The leader of the group and county convener was a giant in local government, Danny Sim – a miner, a sea-green incorruptible and a man feared by many because of his intellect and natural authority. I knew nothing of him. At the end of my verbal assault, he told me that the group had never been addressed like that before.

When I told the area committee how I had torn into the Labour group, I expected praise. Unhappy would not accurately describe their reaction – they all reckoned I had ruined our relationship with the group. They were wrong. Danny Sim was a big man. He must have realised that I would never have spoken the way I did if I had known the power structures and personalities of the party in Ayrshire. So he did not hold it against the union and instructed the group members of the Joint Fire Board to take up the issues I had raised. As I was to discover later, he did not hold it against me either.

Danny Sim came from Kilmaurs, a village in Ayrshire. He left school to go down the pits and was self-educated. He had the peculiar habit of describing the minutes of the county council as the 'minuets' but I never heard anyone, including those in the Tory group, laugh at him. The county clerk told me that, if Danny had been born in to a middle-class family, such was his intellectual ability that he would probably have ended up a judge in the Court of Session. Danny ran the council and devoted every hour to the service of the people. The usual Right-wing gibe about Labour – that they are irresponsible spenders – did not apply to him and his group. Frequently, he would remind us at meetings that we were dealing with the people's money, not our own, and had to be careful about how we spent it. Danny's expenses rules, which applied to councillors and officials, said a third-class ticket was all that was needed if going by rail. The county clerk often had meetings in Glasgow and had to pay the difference from his own pocket if he went first class.

He had tests for invitations to conferences, which then and now flood into councils and other public bodies. Test 1: was it really necessary to attend? Test 2: would you spend your own money to go? If, in either case, the answer was no, then you shouldn't go. People like him are difficult to spot in today's public services.

Danny Sim, in the landward areas of the county, built quality housing and invested heavily in education and public health, including the supply of good clean water. He told me that, when he was first elected to the council and went along to inspect the local source of water, he had found a dead sheep in it. It was from him I learned much about Labour's history in Ayrshire and the struggles they had, when in a minority on the council, to improve working-class life and the emotional toll it took when they failed. One episode involved the efforts to get free school milk for children, to help counter rickets, then widespread in working-class communities. The motion to supply milk was made by Clarice Shaw (née McNab), who later became the MP for Kilmarnock in 1945. Danny described how the tears flowed down her cheeks when the Tories rejected it.

My membership of the county Labour group came through being a councillor on Ayr Town Council (how I shall explain later). The connection between Ayr Town Council and the county council was the Education Committee and the Joint Fire Board, on both of which the town had representation. At one of my first meetings of the county group, I challenged Danny Sim in the chair on a point of order. He declared it a point of interruption. I persisted and he let me in. He was not pleased. I thought that with my previous FBU assault, I would be persona non grata with the great man. Not so. I noted earlier that Danny, although he didn't like to be challenged, respected those who did so. He took a shine to me and I was often invited into his office for a cup of tea and a talk. During those chats, he taught me two principles – a councillor or any elected person should never criticise or insult any official, as the official cannot answer back. Also, while it was important to be guided by one's ideology, it was equally important to be fair and reasonable in dealing with people who had a different view. In that, he was consistent, being meticulous in recognising the rights of the minority Tory leader and making sure the Tory group was adequately represented on any county council delegations. Above all, he drummed into me that socialism was not the soft-touch system that some seemed to think.

At a time of full employment, that last point was illustrated by two different policies about eviction for non-payment of rent. Ayr Town Council Tories (the majority) were not hard-hearted. When it came to a family in rent arrears, they avoided early action to evict. The result was that the arrears mounted until, finally, they were forced to issue an eviction order. In Ayr, around twelve families a year lost their homes. Ayrshire County Council had many more houses than Ayr Town Council. Danny Sim made it plain, in public, that Labour saw people as having a right to housing. The rent had been set at a payable level and it was the responsibility of the tenant to keep a roof over the family's heads by paying it and, if they did not, they would be evicted in short order. He balanced having the rights to a council house with responsibility to the wider community. The result was that, in the whole county landward area, there were, on average, only three evictions a year. That point of balance between rights and responsibility is often forgotten today.

*

I was enjoying life in the fire brigade – proud to be part of a vital public service. The wage was not high but the shift work enabled us to do other work to supplement our incomes, untaxed. One man in my shift in Kilmarnock delivered coal on his days off. The favourite was window cleaning. My brother worked with a firm that did house removals and I worked with him. Helping to lift a piano up a couple of flights of stairs was the worst part of the job.

I made my mark in the union when attending my first FBU national conference in 1962, moving the resolution against the UK's possession of nuclear weapons. I discovered an ability to speak and hold an audience, won the debate overwhelmingly and was reported prominently in the FBU newspaper's report on the conference. John Horner, the general secretary, made sure, thereafter, that I was a student at the union's national political schools. These were not casual affairs. We attended lectures by university professors, economists, sociologists and politicians and were subjected to tough questioning on what we had heard. It was at one school that I first heard an argument in favour of the UK joining the European Economic Community (EEC). Horner's lecture was toughest of all. His insistence on the application of intellectual rigour when addressing any policy issues reinforced that imperative hammered into me by the socialist leadership in Ayrshire.

Back then, in the early 1960s, political education was offered in Labour circles. J.P.M. Millar ran the National Council of Labour Colleges from his home in Tillicoultry. This was an informal set-up funded by the trade unions and it involved correspondence courses on understanding company accounts, the role of the stock exchange, labour history and economics. His work was supplemented throughout the country with experienced councillors and MPs taking sessions on Sundays. Those who participated were expected to work hard and open their minds. For example, at the end of a session, we would be told that, the following week, we would debate whether wages policy was essential for a socialist economic policy or if it was possible for a millionaire to claim to be a socialist. The whole idea was to make us think and see things from different perspectives. I doubt if anything like that exists today and the Labour movement is the poorer for it.

John Horner was a member of the Communist Party, leaving it in 1956 over the Soviet invasion of Hungary. Two other FBU men were instrumental in shaping me. The UK national president, Enoch Humphries, another ex-Communist, from the Lanarkshire brigade and Alex Napier, the Scottish regional secretary, a fireman on the east coast. Enoch was dynamic, could turn on the anger and thump the boss's desk when the situation required it but he could also turn it off just as quickly when he had won. Alex was different – thoughtful, calm and a source of good advice. Both were masters of negotiations – analysing the other side, assessing the point beyond which an employer could not go and balancing that against the point beyond which the union would not budge, thus identifying the latitude available to both, from which an agreement might be achieved. They taught me how to negotiate, the importance of having fall-back positions that had been thought out beforehand and how, sometimes, it was necessary to show strength by walking away. It is a pity Theresa May never had anyone teach her those lessons.

Then disaster struck – a knee injury at a fire incident. This required surgery and time off work. All seemed to go well with the operation and recovery and I came back to the Ayr brigade, to which I had been transferred. One night, we got a call out about midnight to a chimney fire in a three-storey tenement building. It was my turn to go up on to the roof with the small hose, put it down the chimney and extinguish the fire. Halfway up the roof, my knee gave way and locked. I was able to crawl up the rest of the roof and put out the fire. Then I had to shout to the lads below that they would need to come up and lower me down with a rope.

Another operation was followed by a medical examination to determine if I could continue as a fireman. No was the doctor's answer. The union did not want me out of the service and paid for a second opinion from a specialist in the Royal Infirmary in Glasgow. His opinion was the same.

The union then asked the Joint Fire Board to give me a job in the control room, manning the telephones, or in the fire prevention department. By then, however, the firemaster saw me as a thorn in his side, able to circumvent him on issues by my ability to go straight to the Labour members of the Joint Fire Board. When the Board, with a number of my political friends on it, discussed my situation, the firemaster explained that he was sympathetic but the rule was clear – everyone who was a member of the service had to be a fully functioning firefighter. As this was an operational matter, the Board deferred to the firemaster and I was out. I did not get the chance to pick up my P45. It was delivered to my door by the Ayr station officer at 8 a.m. the next morning.

*

By the time I left the fire brigade, I was secretary of the Ayr Constituency Labour Party as well as the local government election agent, both voluntary. I didn't need to look for another job as the Ayr party executive asked me to go full-time as election organiser. I was happy to do so and found myself a round peg in a round hole.

Within weeks of me leaving the brigade, one of our councillors had to demit office and I was first co-opted and then elected to Ayr Town Council, becoming one of its appointees to the County Council Education Committee and the Joint Fire Board. Far from getting shot of me, the firemaster now had me as one of his bosses – and one who had first-hand insight into how he ran the brigade. I didn't abuse my position. The Board made policy and the firemaster had sole charge of brigade operations but my presence meant that his written reports, especially those on trade union relations, did sometimes take us into a mix of policy and operational issues, such as whether the men should move to a shorter working week, the shift changes that could entail and what the financial implications might be.

One matter brought before the Joint Fire Board confirmed, if I had ever doubted it, that the firemaster used my knee condition to get rid of me. The chap who got the job I vacated had a piece of bad luck. During a routine surgical procedure, an infected swab touched one of his eyes, rendering it blind. As a consequence he was unfit to be a fireman. The union asked for him to be accommodated in the fire prevention department. At the Board meeting, I pointed out that neither I nor anyone I had served with knew of anyone from fire prevention department ever being called to a fire as an active firefighter. Despite what he had said a few months before about me, the firemaster concurred and the man was transferred to fire prevention. He went on to become an officer in the brigade, never having to attend a fire but doing excellent work in preventing them.

Ayr Town Council had always been run by the Tories but, shortly after I became a member and after a tied election was followed by the toss of a coin, Labour group leader, Charlie O'Halloran, became provost and, with his casting vote, gave us a majority. Convener of the Cleansing Department, employer of the dustmen, was allocated to me. We had not been in power for even a month when the men decided to strike. No warning, no submission of demands – just a sudden strike. I felt it was a bit rich – all those years under the Tories and no action then a lightning strike against a Labour administration. The men had a fair complaint about their conditions and negotiations were soon concluded – my first experience of negotiations as an employer.

It was as a member of the Town Council and Labour election agent that I made the first blunder of my political life – a blunder which cost us the subsequent election and helped return the Tories to power. I was proving a good writer, with a 300-word article each week on the back of the Tote result sheet – the Tote being our fund-raiser. So, I got to write all the election material. One election leaflet was a telling satire on the opposition candidate in a key marginal ward. He was a railwayman who had been a Labour councillor, then an independent and, currently, in all but name, a member of the Tory group. My leaflet followed his career from cloth cap to bowler hat and then top hat. It went down a storm. I then got carried away and wrote a second leaflet which went well beyond that invisible but very real line of what is acceptable in a personal attack. It proved a disaster. The Tories reprinted and distributed it widely. It contributed to our defeat. It was my first experience of hubris – a lesson learned and a mistake admitted.

*

The first general election I was involved in took place in 1964 with Alex Eadie, a miner from Fife, as our candidate. We had raised the money for the election fund and my wages by operating a tote, which entailed recruiting members at £1 a week with a money prize of £100.

The Labour Party nationally was on the up and it was easy to enrol the necessary numbers. The Ayr constituency party had also bought a building using a loan from Usher's Brewery to open a big social club, with another part of the premises given over to party offices and meeting rooms. The club gave significant contributions to the election fund. Alex reduced the Tory majority but we lost.

The tote was associated with the only bribe I have ever been offered. Robert Maxwell was the Labour candidate in Buckingham. The tote idea was his and it worked. He sent his agent round the country explaining how to set them up. A couple of years later, at my house, Maxwell's agent emerged from a big expensive car. I was by then also secretary of the Ayrshire Labour Federation. Maxwell was standing for the Labour Party National Executive at conference and the agent had £200 to offer if I would deliver the Ayrshire vote. I turned him down flat. But I had learned something important about Maxwell – he was a crook. His agent's bribery tour failed – there was to be no seat for Maxwell on the NEC.

We were over the moon when Labour won in 1964 but we knew that another election was near. At that time, I had a serous falling-out over money with the constituency executive. Before going on holiday, I had asked for a pay rise of £1 which would have taken me to £19 a week – not much considering the money flowing in from the tote and the club. When back at work, I was told they would raise my wage but only by ten shillings. Flabbergasted that a committee, many of them shop stewards, were acting like capitalist employers, I resigned and got a job as a teleprinter operator (one of the skills I learned in the Navy) at the air traffic control centre at Prestwick Airport.

No one else was employed in my place. I remained active in the party and, when the general election was obviously coming in early 1966, I was asked to be the election agent. I did so because the candidate was Charlie O'Halloran, a close comrade on the Left. It was a difficult election for me as I could only be a part-time agent. But I did a lot of pre-election planning work during my night shifts, when it was relatively quiet, so everything was ready for the off.

By common consent it was a good campaign, with the activists enthused. In the course of it, I had a private run-in with the Foreign Secretary, Michael Stewart, over Vietnam. Ayr was a marginal after the 1964 result so we had a high-profile senior Cabinet minister come and speak. That required booking the Dam Park Hall and doing all the organising for what would be a huge meeting with over 1,000 attending. On the day, I double-checked everything. I had the stewards well briefed, the transport was laid on and a meal arranged for the speakers afterwards. A couple of hours before the event, I walked over to the Town Hall where Charlie was giving tea to Stewart and his wife, in the Provost's room. I was introduced and Charlie asked if everything was in order. I said yes but I would not be there or at the meal afterwards. When asked why, I told Stewart that it was because I so profoundly disagreed with him and his support for the Americans in Vietnam and I didn't want people to see us falling out in public. He probably thought I was one of the mad Left. Charlie, who had joined me in drafting anti-USA resolutions on Vietnam, said nothing. I wasn't surprised.

A couple of days before the big rally, Charlie and I were in the campaign office when the *Daily Express* rang and asked him, given he was to share a platform with the Foreign Secretary, if he accepted his line on Vietnam, which was supportive of the US position. I expected Charlie to say he didn't, so was shocked to hear him say he was a hundred per cent in agreement with it. My belief in him vanished in a moment. Having heard him sell out on what was a fundamental moral policy position, I now had a candidate I no longer respected. It didn't stop me trying to win the election for him but it was a real blow. Elections provide a unique insight into human character because they exert enormous pressure on people. If there are any cracks in character, elections will expose them. Theresa May's woeful performance in the 2017 general election is an example of that truth.

Sir Alec Douglas-Home, Foreign Secretary, had been chosen as Tory Prime Minister, by the Cabinet, when in the House of Lords. Tony Benn had fought against going to the Lords automatically when his father, the 1st Viscount Stansgate, died. He got an Act through Parliament that allowed peers to disclaim their titles and so Lord Home became Sir Alec Douglas-Home, able to stand for the Commons in a by-election in Perthshire in 1963. The original candidate, George Younger, gallantly stepped aside for him. He was the 1964 Tory candidate for Ayr. Sir Alec owed him a favour and up to our town he came, to campaign. When it was announced he was coming, I was delighted. His image on television was dreadful, his years in the House of Lords had blunted any debating skills he once had and, week after week, Harold Wilson made mincemeat of him at Prime Minister's Questions. The new satirical television programme *That Was the Week That Was* regularly made him look a complete fool and it didn't help that he admitted finding economics difficult and had to resort to counting matchsticks to help work out the figures involved.

A Difference of Opinion

As I saw it, Sir Alec was God's gift to Ayr Labour – so inept that, once people had had a gander at him, he would deflate the Tory campaign and up would go our vote. How wrong I was. He spoke to a huge crowd at an open-air meeting outside the railway station, then went walkabout in the High Street. That night, after teatime, going back to the campaign rooms on the bus (I didn't have a car then), what I heard alerted me to my error. In a town like Ayr, word spreads quickly and, once in the rooms, the activists were telling me the same – Sir Alec's visit had been a triumph for the Tories. People were saying, 'He's a very nice man, not at all what he looks like on television, and some of the things he was saying are worth listening to.'

The people read him accurately. He was one of those aristocrats who can be as relaxed with the dustman or bricklayer as with the Queen because he had nothing to prove to anyone. Being snobbish was beneath them. He *was* a nice man. What the people in Ayr saw was a very different person from the figure savaged weekly on television and derided by Harold Wilson. He nearly won the election and it was widely believed that, had the fall of Khrushchev in the USSR been announced the day before polling, rather than the day after, he might have done so, as people, nervous of what Khrushchev's fall might mean in the Cold War, may have opted for no change in the UK government.

On polling day, the turnout from the Tory areas in Ayr and Prestwick was the highest ever – even the dead must have voted. The overall turnout was 85.32 per cent. Labour lost by 484 votes. I called a recount not because I thought there had been a mistake but because it would make our defeat look better and would set the party up for a bigger fight next time. George Younger asked me if I thought we would win on the recount and I told him to relax – he had won. I explained why I had called for it and, seeing the logic, he was good humoured about it. George Younger was one of the most charming people I ever met and, when I was MP for the neighbouring constituency of South Ayrshire, we worked well together on issues that were of importance to the people in our part of the county.

Once the election was over, the constituency executive asked me to come back as the full-time agent, at a higher wage than previously. I took up the job. It was expected that full-time party agents would support the Labour government and all its policies. I adhered to that, often defending what I did not agree with at constituency party meetings. That is until one debate, in which I took on the local miners' agent, who had tabled a resolution condemning the general policy of the 1966 Labour government. My debating skills were far superior to his and he made a stupid mistake in calling for the nationalisation of the Bank of England, which the Attlee government had done in 1946. That mistake alone enabled me to demolish him. But I had, privately, actually agreed with the general thrust of his criticism and, on my way home, thinking over the debate, I was thoroughly ashamed of myself. I resolved never again to be a party hack, backing my government or party, right or wrong. There are many party hacks around today, especially in the SNP, with its iron-fist discipline, who show blind allegiance to the party. I often wonder if, in doing so, they ever consider the damage they are doing to the health of democracy.

7

The SNP Breaks Through

The constituency of Pollok in south-west Glasgow had long been held by the Tories when young Alex Garrow, a Glasgow councillor, unexpectedly took the seat in the 1964 general election with a majority of fewer than 300 votes. In a snap general election called by Harold Wilson in March 1966, Garrow won the seat again with a slightly increased majority of just under 2,000 but, in December of that year, after disembarking from an aircraft at Glasgow Airport, he dropped dead, aged only forty-three.

The Labour candidate in the by-election that was called following Garrow's death was Dick Douglas and standing for the Tories was Professor Esmond Wright. The SNP put up George Leslie, who proved to be a formidable campaigner. The Communist Party also put up a candidate, Alex Murray, whose working-class message was well received but attracted few votes. Along with other full-time agents, I was drafted in to work on the campaign. The result on 9 March 1967 was a Tory victory which was not a shock but the SNP's 10,884 votes, constituting 28.16 per cent, was. A big chunk of that came from Labour. I thought we had lessons to learn from that result.

Later in 1967, Tom Fraser, Labour Cabinet minister and MP for Hamilton, resigned his seat to take up the post of chairman of the North of Scotland Hydro-Electric Board. Two of us who had been organisers in Pollok were attending an agents' course in Dorset when we heard. We told Labour National agent, Sarah Barker, that we could lose to the SNP. She was incredulous. Sarah was a unique figure in the party's history. Virulently anti-Communist, determined to keep fellow travellers becoming candidates and then MPs, she kept extensive files on many and knew who to put the black spot on. When she retired, Ron Hayward, the new general secretary, took the files and burned them. MI5 wept.

The Hamilton by-election campaign took place in October 1967, with polling day on 2 November. It was one of the most historic days in Scottish politics. So confident was Labour HQ in Scotland of winning Hamilton, no full-time agents were called in to organise. There was no call for workers to pour in from other constituencies. When Charlie O'Halloran and I went up on polling day to help, everyone in the main Labour committee room was totally relaxed. When we asked for polling slips of Labour voters to start knocking doors, we were told to sit down, have a cup of tea and a sandwich because 'we weigh the votes here'. Complacency does not begin to describe it. Labour owned Hamilton and, although the SNP candidate, Winnie Ewing, had fought a sparkling campaign, with the press entranced by her freshness and vitality, the party was convinced she was no danger. Her slogan, 'Stop the world, Scotland wants to get on.', had a huge impact but the local Labour Party was blind to its positive effect on voters.

When Charlie and I eventually got the polling slips, he started at one end of the first street and I at the other. When we met in the middle, we knew Winnie had won. Tory voters were telling us that, this time, they had us and the supposed rock-solid Labour voters on our slips were telling us it would be the SNP because Labour needed a shake-up. There was no point in us rushing back to the committee room with our findings. Like Sarah Barker, they would have thought us stupid. We did our stint and then left for home and waited for the political earthquake we knew was coming. The result:

SNP 18,397 – +46.10% on 1966
Labour 16,599 – -29.66% on 1966

It put the SNP firmly on the map and meant they would be threatening to challenge Labour territory.

The Hamilton result knocked the Labour leadership and the party off balance. The SNP had no right to take a Labour seat. They were usurpers. There was fury. In one private meeting in Ayrshire, Willie Ross, Labour Secretary of State for Scotland, referred to Winnie as 'Mrs Spewing'. Oliver Brown, a notable nationalist and brilliant writer, produced the famous quote that, when they heard the Hamilton result in the House of Commons, 'a shiver ran along the Labour benches looking for a spine to run up'.

In my capacity as secretary of the Ayrshire Labour Federation, I wrote and sent a paper to all our affiliated groups, dated 9 November 1967, about what we had to learn from the Hamilton by-election. Here are relevant extracts:

A Difference of Opinion

There have been predictable reactions to Hamilton, the Nationalists seeing it as the first step to an independent Scotland, and one or two Labour spokesmen said the reverse was a temporary revolt (*sic*). Both are wide of the mark . . .

Let's look at the Nationalists, first in the light of the reality which now faces them – the need to start spelling out in detail exactly how they will disentangle Scotland from the British economy. They will be able to rely less and less on slogans and emotion, and be forced to come through more and more with clear-cut statements on the ways and means by which they will achieve independence. The signs are that they will not be able to carry out this complex and difficult exercise. They lack experience of government, and have only sketchy knowledge of the problems involved. It is significant that faced with the responsibility of being an M.P. (and not merely a candidate), Mrs. Ewing could only remark on Friday morning that the question of getting more jobs in Scotland was a very difficult problem . . .

Another reason for them not being able to carry out a successful independent policy is that they lack intellectual honesty. They take refuge in fantasy when the facts belie their beliefs . . . For instance they will not get away with claiming to get complete independence when, in the words of their own document, *SNP & YOU*, we will have 'mutually satisfying arrangements with the Bank of England to control our balance of payments' [shades of the SNP position in the 2014 referendum].

It went on to show just how important UK expenditure in Scotland was, cited the superiority of the Scottish NHS to the English health system, which had and still has a different structure, although it operates on the same principles, and pointed to the success of our comprehensive education restructuring. It ended:

Now to the question of a 'temporary revolt'. If the Nationalists are as wrong as I make out, why did they poll such a high vote, and why is there a growing feeling in Scotland that we need a bigger say in our own affairs? The Nationalists were bound to get a very very high vote whatever Labour said or did at Hamilton, because at the moment they are the only means open to people to register what is a genuine and legitimate feeling in Scotland (and Wales) that we should handle much

60

more of our domestic life, and would do so for the better of our nation.

The real lesson of Hamilton is that Labour must recognise this as fact. There is much in Scottish life that could be and should be dealt with here. We have our own laws, local government, education system, and other matters distinctly Scottish. And it is a nonsense that changes in these should wait their turn in the queue for legislative time at Westminster.

This was recognised in many Labour circles well before Hamilton. The result there will now act as a spur towards a greater degree of devolution. The Labour Party will not ignore the obvious feelings of our people and new measures are bound to be forthcoming. They will, however, be in the interests of economic sanity not go to the lengths of 'independence' advocated by the Nationalists (*sic*).

Devolution is, of course a unionist position, with some powers, but never full sovereignty transferred from Westminster to Edinburgh. Even today this is something some people cannot understand.

It is evident, from all that Winnie Ewing said and wrote in the weeks and months after the result, that she felt the full force of Labour's displeasure when she took her seat in the Commons. She was on her own and was made to feel Labour's pathological resentment both in and outside the chamber. This had its negative effect on her and, as a result, she had a negative effect on me for which I take full blame. She toured Scotland, speaking to large meetings. She came to Ayr, to the Racecourse pavilion, and Alex Neil and I went along. At the meeting, Winnie trashed the Labour Party in Ayrshire, condemning our councillors as 'self-serving, useless failures'. This was the group led by Danny Sim, selfless in the cause of the working class and successful in meeting our people's needs. I left the meeting seething and told Alex Neil, 'I will get her.'

The SNP message of independence had no meaning for me. I was brought up in a household where our heroes were British Labour leaders, like Attlee, Stafford Cripps and Nye Bevan, and I was a product of the trade union movement which was pan-British. That the SNP was a threat to Labour was obvious. I undertook a speaking tour in all parts of the country to whichever Labour branch would have me. My purpose was to restore self-confidence by providing reasons for attacking the SNP. I got a lot of media coverage and became known in the party as 'the Hammer of the Nats'.

After much private discussion among a number of people, including MPs, Alex Eadie, then MP for Midlothian, and I wrote a pamphlet aimed at attacking the SNP and shoring up the position of the Labour Party. 'Don't Butcher Scotland's Future' was published in 1968. It pointed out that the Scottish economy had become 'fully integrated' with that of the rest of the UK and 'to separate them now would be as difficult as extracting the original acorn from the giant oak'. It went on:

> We believe the difficulty of such a task has been demonstrated, paradoxically, by the SNP itself through its inability to produce detailed plans of how they intend to carry out the business of dismembering the U.K. economy . . .
>
> A separate Scotland would be competing against the rest of the present U.K. for projects floated by U.K. or overseas capital. Scotland would not, as is the case now, be a specially favoured Development Area but an independent 'foreign' country depending entirely for attracting investment on her own resources and prospects.

It criticised the SNP's comparison with Scandinavia, pointing out that the countries there had a very different industrial development to ours and, in the case of Norway, though it had been occupied during the war, it had not been bombed and devastated and that Sweden, having been neutral, had profited from it. The 'comparisons were not valid', we wrote. It did recognise a need for change: 'reform of government to help British regionalism work, and to give the people a feeling of genuine and active participation in decisions which affect them'. The pamphlet did what no others had done up until then – it placed the issues of internal UK government structures in the context of the post-empire era:

> Britain has no Empire now and our politics are entering a period of intense domesticity. Those who have for years urged the nation to attend more to the barren slum areas of our cities than to the barren rocks of Aden, have suddenly found the whole country converted to their outlook overnight.

A Scottish parliament was denounced as a 'bogus proposition' because we had to keep the Scottish seat in the UK Cabinet and send a large number of MPs to Westminster. So reform should be in the Westminster setting. In addition to the Scottish Grand Committee and Scottish Standing Committees on legislation, we urged the creation of a Scottish Select Committee, drawn exclusively from Scottish MPs. We advocated a Scottish Ombudsman. But the real reform within Scotland should be in local government, for which we advocated a two-tier system based on regions and districts, with the regions given membership of the Scottish Economic Planning Council assisting the secretary of state. Culture was not omitted, with a recommendation for the creation of a Scottish Council for Culture and Leisure with wide powers to make a 'real impact on Scottish life'. The pamphlet was popular within the Labour movement and sold like hot cakes.

At that time, it wasn't difficult to hammer the SNP. After Hamilton, its membership soared as naive people joined expecting more success immediately but it was pretty ropey on policy. I took on a number of debates with SNP people in Ayrshire and found them easy to deal with. The most difficult debate with a nationalist was when I clashed with Oliver Brown, one of the founding members of the National Party of Scotland in 1929. He had challenged Alex Eadie to debate but was ignored and so then he challenged me. Old hands advised taking the same stance as Alex, as I was nowhere near ready to take on such an experienced opponent, known for his able mind and sharp wit. But you cannot write a pamphlet and refuse to debate. Plus, running away from a leading nationalist would intensify, not solve, Labour's main problem at that time – the loss of confidence and conviction. The debate took place, before a packed house, mostly nationalists, in the McLellan Galleries in Glasgow.

As I went into the hall, I heard Annie Welsh, SNP organiser in Cumnock, say she had brought a busload with her because they wanted to see this over-confident Labour so-and-so thumped. When it came to it, I didn't find Oliver Brown too much to handle. I liked him, admired his style, but I never gave an inch in my attack on the SNP. His nationalism seemed to be based on Scotland having been subjugated to England in 1707. To me, the examples he cited about how England has treated us badly showed that his nationalism was actually not defined by being Scots but being anti-English. One of the absurd examples of bad treatment was the claim that, during the war, Churchill knowingly sent up punctured barrage balloons to Clydebank. The much-expected slaughter didn't happen and the mood in the hall turned ugly. It was a very angry and unhappy audience I had to pass through to get out, kindly helped by Oliver.

What I learned from that experience, and since, is that some are what I call big N nationalists who are convinced that, under the Union, England has a deliberate policy of treating us as second class, of being of no account and, moreover, is instinctively anti-Scottish. 'Anti-Scottish', in protest at a policy or action by the UK government, constantly tripped off the tongue of Alex Salmond and that refrain, if not the actual words, marked Nicola Sturgeon's campaign against Brexit, once the result was declared.

*

I take the view that the UK is a fiction and is, in reality, an English state with Scottish, Welsh and Northern Irish appendages and that, if a choice has to be made on policy, then the English state interest will prevail. That does not mean there is a malign anti-Scottish attitude in English policymaking – at worst, they simply don't recognise that there is a separate Scottish position to be considered. I am not a 'big N' nationalist. Indeed, I doubt if I qualify as a nationalist at all. My conversion to independence was on the view that Scotland would be better off economically and, therefore, socially if we were.

My anti-SNP campaigning and my growing reputation as an organiser started to make me a nationally known figure in the Labour Party. With many all over the place after Hamilton, I was giving a clear lead in the fight back. My efforts, however much they heartened the party, were of little account against the forces at work and the change of mood in the national scene, where the SNP's assertion of Scotland's need for change was getting through, aided by the Labour government's economic failure.

The Labour leader, Prime Minister Harold Wilson, thought he could deflect and then smother that mood, by a typical Whitehall manoeuvre. Wilson once described Royal Commissions as 'taking minutes and spending years'. So, with that in mind, he appointed a Royal Commission on the UK Constitution. It started work on 16 April 1969, with Lord Crowther in the chair. He died in February 1972 and was replaced by Lord Kilbrandon, a Scottish judge. The Kilbrandon Commission did not report until 31 October 1973. While it was sitting and taking evidence, it did appear to reduce the nationalist pressure but, as with many a clever ruse, it came back to bite with a vengeance called Margo MacDonald.

8

A Union Man

In 1966, Willie Ross, Secretary of State for Scotland, appointed Enoch Humphries and me to the Western Regional Hospital Board, which oversaw hospital services to Glasgow, the rest of the west of Scotland and Dumfries and Galloway. The board had been Tory dominated and we were there to replace two of them whose term was up.

At the first meeting, I experienced how lay people can feel it necessary to shut up, instead of joining in a discussion, due to the fear of appearing ignorant in front of experts. Sitting beside me was Simpson Stevenson, Labour Provost of Greenock, who had been a board member for four years. The officials and medical people were using medical terms and, not knowing what they meant and not wanting to show my ignorance, I asked Simpson, in a whisper, to enlighten me. He whispered back that he didn't know and had not wanted to expose his ignorance either. On that, my attitude changed and I said plainly to the experts that I had not understood and would they now and in future use language a lay member of the board could understand. They found no difficulty in doing so. The lesson learnt was never to be afraid of saying you don't know because experts can use language to bamboozle, rather than inform lay people.

Enoch and I worked closely together and made our presence felt. I became chairman of the Medical Staffing Committee, which appointed consultants, senior registrars and hospital matrons and approved overseas secondments. The chairman had to be a lay member of the board, given the infighting that went on in the medical profession. I learned a great deal about the medical profession. Although we were responsible for a wide geographic area and handled a large budget for both capital and revenue expenditure, the board had only one press officer – marked contrast with the position today.

Nye Bevan said he had to stuff the consultants' mouths with gold to get them to sign on to the NHS. He did not exaggerate. At that time, NHS consultants worked a week divided into eleven sessions. Many, at that time a large number, worked nine sessions in the NHS and kept two for lucrative private work. However, as they entered their last years of service, they opted into the full eleven NHS sessions because their pensions were calculated and paid on the final-year salary.

The transfer to eleven sessions had to be agreed by the Medical Staffing Committee, and, on each occasion, a case was presented by the board's medical officer and the applicant consultant, on the basis that more consultant sessions was good for the NHS. I never refused any transfer except one. Before this particular meeting, Joe Wright, an old and very senior doctor at the Western in Glasgow and a member of the committee, took me aside and said that there was something I should know that would create difficulties for him, as a member of the profession, if he raised it. He explained that the man shortly seeking transfer to eleven sessions was currently working only five sessions, all of them at the Isle of Bute hospital. He did not live in Rothesay but in Glasgow and, if travel time to and from the island was taken into account, he would not be doing much in Bute. His other six sessions were in a private hospital in Glasgow, where he was known to be making a fortune. Everyone in the profession knew this and many disapproved but could do nothing about it. Joe Wright hoped I would. In short, I was to do the profession's dirty work.

In came the board's medical officer and the doctor and we got the usual stuff about how him shifting to eleven sessions would benefit the hospital with nothing said about the pension element. To the surprise of the medical officer, who expected the usual agreement, I took the committee into private session and told them that it wasn't going to happen this time and that, if they used their majority against me, I would go public and reveal the whole racket. I then reconvened the meeting and, to the visible anger of both our medical officer and the consultant, told him the answer was no and that he would stay on five NHS sessions. They stormed out of the meeting.

A vacancy had arisen at the Scottish Trades Union Congress for the head of the Organisation and Social Services Department when Jim Craigen (much later, Labour MP for Maryhill) left for another post. Enoch Humphries, a member of the general council and chairman in 1968, wanted me to apply. The general council was dominated by the Left – a combination of Labour Left and the Communist Party. I was duly appointed in October 1968 with a salary of £1,350. That appointment did not mean an exit from Labour politics. Then as now, trade

union affairs were entwined with internal Labour Party issues and personalities and I remained active on the political front.

The general secretary was Jimmy Jack. We were joined later by
Jimmy Milne, a member of the Communist Party from Aberdeen, as
deputy general secretary. The other full-time senior official was Robert
Mure, in charge of research.

Jimmy Jack hated his predecessor, George Middleton, for whom
he had done all the background research and drafting of articles that
Middleton had placed in newspapers and prestigious journals – all
without a word of thanks or acknowledgement. So much did he detest
Middleton that he could not bring himself to use the general secretary's
office when he took over, preferring to keep to his own small one at
the top of the stairs. I had the big office, as had Jim Craigen before me.

Jimmy Milne was an interesting man – not at all a Communist Party
apparatchik. When we hosted a delegation from the USSR and they
started to criticise the UK political system, they were a bit surprised
when their Scottish comrade explained that it had its merits, not least
of them being allowed to freely express dissent without anyone getting
shot. Jimmy said he was in the Communist Party despite, not because
of, Stalin.

In those days, the STUC was a powerful body. Its general secretary
was a household name, as were several members of the general council
like Enoch Humphries, Alex Kitson, Bill McLean, Alex Donnett, Ray
MacDonald, and Ben Smith. Jimmy Jack was unusual for a leader of the
trade union movement. He had a diffident personality, could not avoid
the limelight but did not seek it, and was not a forceful speaker. He was,
however, intellectually gifted, shrewd and thoughtful and a good economist, able to master the most complicated subjects, and it was from his
mind that the idea of the Scottish Development Agency and the Highlands
and Islands Development Board (HIDB) emerged. Under his leadership,
the STUC was a leading policy-making group. He was meticulous when
examining an issue and was able to go right to the root of any matter that
presented itself to us. That was the standard he set for our office.

*

Readers may be surprised about how I, a non-Communist, should
bother to spend time here with a party now defunct. But it was in its
time, from the 1920s to 1980s, a major force in the trade union movement and also an influence on the Left in the Labour Party. It was
certainly an ideological influence within the general councils of both
the STUC and TUC.

A Difference of Opinion

We socialists and communists could not avoid each other. We met at trade union branch meetings and conferences, had a pint together, argued, discussed and spoke on the same platforms. The CP members were tough interlocutors, well versed in socialist history and Marxist theory. The party produced able people, such as Mick McGahey, Bill McLean, Lawrence Daly, the last a working-class intellectual and brilliant speaker, and, of course, Jimmy Reid, a giant, the finest mind to have graced the movement. We democratic socialists could not help being influenced by the communist party members in our industrial and political activity. Nor, as was proved when Lawrence Daly, Jimmy Reid and others left the CP, were they immune to the severity of the criticism we levelled at them and to the faults evident in the Soviet Union.

In the Labour Party in Ayrshire, the Communist Party made no headway. We were solidly Left wing – a potent mixture of Marxism and Keir Hardie's famous claim to 'Burns and Bible' socialism. But that was not so in other parts of Scotland or the rest of the UK, where the Communist Party was a part of the warp and weft of industrial communities.

After being consistently rejected as an affiliate of the Labour party, its only MP defeated in 1959 and its membership falling steadily after the heady days of 1945 when it reached 60,000, the CP directed its efforts to penetration of the trade unions, at full-time officials level, and especially the shop-steward movement. At union national and regional levels, the Communists were fiercely contested by the Right and this led to Left versus Right contests, often vicious, within unions. Controlling a union mattered because all unions cast a bloc vote at the Labour Party conference. Bert Ramelson, one of the CP's most effective organisers in the trade union movement, boasted in 1973 that the CP could develop a policy in the spring and by autumn it would be adopted by the Labour Party at its annual conference. I think this was a bit of vainglory but through the trade unions, even although Communist union officials of a union could not from part of a delegation at Labour Party conferences, the CP was nevertheless influential.

No Labour leader could ignore the power of the trade unions. In 1967, TUC membership was 10 million and, by 1979, it was 12.6 million. They were the main source of funds. The annual STUC and TUC Congresses could dominate the front page of what we called the 'pink liar', *The Financial Times*. The Labour Left was not naive. We knew about the CP's slavish adherence to the Kremlin line but there were trade-union and political issues and ideas on which the Labour Left and the CP converged to oppose the Right – the role and autonomy of shop stewards, against single-union agreements with employers, government intervention in collective bargaining, prices and incomes policy and public ownership, to name but a few.

The importance to the Communist Party of its role within the trade unions, and the need for it to retain that role, led to corruption of union democracy. Where they were entrenched at the top of a union, they were determined to remain there even if it meant ballot-rigging. Eventually, this was exposed in the electricians' union in a court case in 1961 brought by its members, some of whom, like Les Cannon, were former Communist Party members. The ETU was expelled from the TUC and the Labour Party. It was only readmitted in 1962 after a clear-out and a new non-CP leadership, led by Les Cannon, had been installed.

An important link and uniting factor between the Labour Left and the CP was nuclear disarmament. Labour Party division on this was bitter. At an infamous meeting in Glasgow, the then leader, Hugh Gaitskell, and young socialists, hurled abuse at each other. We on the Labour Left, whatever our differences with the CP, saw it as essential to mobilise the maximum strength of the anti-nuclear movement, and co-operating with the CP we justified on that basis.

Our Left alliance was not an easy one. One of the great anxieties about the nuclear weapons programmes of the US, USSR and UK was testing in the atmosphere, with evidence that it was endangering the health of millions. The pressure for these to stop was not confined only to those who to 'Ban the Bomb'. The Soviets made this a big moral issue and the CP newspaper, *The Daily Worker* (later retitled *The Morning Star*), was up there in the lead, reporting speeches and carrying articles on banning testing. Then the Soviets started to test again in the atmosphere. Assuming we were all idiots who saw the nuclear issue purely in class terms instead of a matter that concerned all humanity, *The Daily Worker* declared that there was a difference between the workers' bomb and the capitalists' bomb, so the Soviet testing was OK. The hard-line Kremlin group toed that line, the rest of us treated it with contempt. Afterwards it took some time for the Left alliance to form again. For me personally, it simply confirmed my decision years before not to join the CP.

9

Donovan and *In Place of Strife*

Two publications had an effect upon the Labour Party and its relations with the trade unions in the late 1960s. One was the report by The Royal Commission on Trade Unions and Employers' Associations (the Donovan report), the other a Labour government White Paper, *In Place of Strife*.

Both came in the context of British economic failure – the 'sick man of Europe' era, as the 1960s and '70s were dubbed. No matter which government was in power, the failure to export more than was imported, creating a massive current account deficit year after year, placed an enormous strain on sterling's fixed link to the US dollar. At the 1964 election, that current account deficit was the big issue, standing at £800 million (equivalent to something like £15,360 million at 2017 prices). Who was to blame? The Right-wing press, in a sustained vitriolic campaign against the trade unions, especially the shop steward movement, asserted that British industry was failing to perform because of 'wildcat' strikers. The Tory opposition joined in the attacks.

With the increase in power of the trade unions and industrial disputes on the rise, blame for the economic state of the country was pinned conveniently on them. It is indisputable that British industrial relations were deplorable and blame, in certain instances, lay on both sides. The Communist Party, with its influence deep in the shop steward movement, was able to indulge its belief in the 'struggle' to keep a strike going when it could have ended sooner. There were, to be fair, passing references in newspapers and by industrial reporters about just how bad British management was. But, while TV cameras were not allowed inside private boardrooms to record the labour relations policy decisions of managers, they were given unrestricted access to the mass strike meetings of workers, with every militant speech recorded. The truth was British management got the trade union militant shop stewards it deserved.

Bending to unrelenting pressure from the press, with calls for 'something' to be done, Wilson, in 1965, set up the Royal Commission (chaired by Lord Donovan) on Trade Unions and Employers' Associations. The reference to employers kidded no one. All knew it was about the trade unions. It did not report until 1968. In those three years, the economic situation had worsened and there could be no doubt about what was to blame – not the unions but government policies in 1967, the effect of which led to a build-up of working-class frustration and anger that helped to shape trade union attitudes, not to the Donovan report, but to *In Place of Strife*.

*

Those damaging policies had their roots in the failure to devalue the pound immediately after the March general election in 1966. Today, in this 'floating currency' era, internationally traded currencies are devalued, mostly by fractions, on a daily basis. It is the market's decision not the UK government's that sets the pound's value when you exchange it for euros or dollars when go on holiday. For those doing international business, the floating rate matters a great deal.

That was not the position when Labour won the 1964 election with a majority of only four seats. The pound was in a 'fixed' relationship with the US dollar at £1 = $2.80. The bane of the UK economy was the balance of payments deficit of £800 million, due to imports being much greater in value than exports. In the election, Labour focused on the £800 million as indicating a crisis in the economy and being a measure of Tory government failure over 'Thirteen Wasted Years', the words chosen and repeated time and again to drive the message home. Given the state of the UK economy, the pound was overvalued, making British exports on the international markets too expensive. A lower pound to the USD, a devaluation, was the obvious answer.

Although, under Bretton Woods, it was not possible to uncouple sterling from the dollar, it was possible to devalue to a lower 'fixed' level. There were two problems associated with that in 1964 – both political. Labour had devalued sterling in 1949, allowing the Tories to glue the 'devaluation party' label to them. Then there was that four of a majority, which meant Wilson faced another election fairly soon and dared not fight it after a devaluation because, with dearer imports, the cost of living would be adversely affected. But those reasons disappeared when labour won with a 98-seat majority on 31 March 1966. There was no obstacle now to the badly needed devaluation. Surely the Harold Wilson the Left believed in, with his reputation as a brilliant economist, would act. It took time for some of us, who had so admired him when elected leader, to realise that this political god had big feet of clay.

In the 'fixed-link' age, prime ministers appeared to view the pound as an economic virility symbol, with devaluation an admission of government failure. Despite his majority, Wilson kept the pound in that currency prison, leading to a crisis in 1967, when we got the infamous 'July measures' – retrenchment, cuts, rising unemployment, a six months' standstill on the level of wages and dividends (later in October a wage freeze), a prices and incomes policy policed by a Prices and Incomes Board. To the anger of many trade unionists on the Left, the TUC backed the wage pause. That July was probably the seminal moment in the life of the 1964–70 Labour government

The pain inflicted upon the working-class, more than any other, proved to be in vain. On 18 November, a 14.3 per cent devaluation (from \$2.80 down to \$2.40) was announced. Interest rates rose from 6.5 per cent to 8 per cent. Wilson either lied or blundered when, in a TV address to the country, he assured us that the pound in our pockets was not devalued. With interest rates up and imports costing 14.3 per cent more, our pound would shrink in purchasing power as prices rose. It was a humiliating shambles.

Roy Jenkins replaced Jim Callaghan as chancellor and made a pre-Christmas TV broadcast explaining we would now all have to tighten our belts. As we watched his explanation with its political-economic jargon, my wife asked, 'What does all that mean?' I said that our daughter Julie, who was born in 1963, would now only get an ordinary doll, not the more expensive walkie-talkie one she wanted, to which Anne replied, 'That is not going to happen.' And it didn't. There was, and is, a lesson there for economists and their models. If they miss the human factor, their policies will be undone. There were millions of Annes whom the models missed.

That was the toxic atmosphere into which the Royal Commission report was published in June 1968. If, when set up, it was meant to conclude that the trade unions were the cause of Britain's economic woes, as we on the Left suspected, it proved otherwise. 'Donovan', as the commission and report were known, had conducted extensive in-depth research, thoroughly investigated the state of industrial relations, considered the case for and against the intervention of law in trades disputes, looked at international comparisons, and listened to and carefully probed witnesses. The result was a report that was fair and balanced and which did not find the trade unions guilty of wrecking the British economy.

As well as recognising that there were serious problems between employers and unions, it also drew attention to major internal issues and weakness within the trade unions and that these affected production in large industrial plants. There was a division of power between the shop stewards and the full-time officials and, in addition, there were tensions between shop stewards and union national executives. Plant bargaining by the shop stewards had a disruptive effect on the union national executives' role in setting wages and conditions.

Among its recommendations was the idea of creating a new Commission on Industrial Relations (CIR) that would foster constructive discussions and promote new ideas to improve negotiating practices for both sides of industry. It had considered submissions to make agreements between employers and unions legally enforceable but rejected the idea in the firm belief that involving courts in industrial relations was not sensible. The wisdom of that advice was proved later as was the cost for the government who ignored it.

There was no trade union knee-jerk reaction to Donovan's criticisms and proposals. June was the start of the holiday period so there was a time gap between publication and it being read and studied properly. The first mention of Donovan in the minutes of the STUC was on 6 August 1968, when it was noted the general council had not yet discussed it. On 14 October, it was recorded that no formal general council decision had been taken. From that meeting, an invitation was sent to Barbara Castle, Labour's Secretary of State for Employment, to address the annual congress in Rothesay in April 1969.

The TUC and STUC organised meetings, as did individual unions, to discuss the report but these were not decision-making affairs. We called them symposia, with attendees exploring this long and detailed document. The Department of Employment and Productivity sent out a consultative document, to which the TUC replied, in late 1968, with a 48-page booklet, 'Action on Donovan', which was a measured response to the main chapters of the report.

In December, the STUC general council decided to devote an away weekend, 18–19 January, at the Allan Water Hotel, Bridge of Allan, to its first formal examination of Donovan. Added to the agenda was *In Place of Strife*, the government White Paper on industrial relations, published on 16 January 1969, by Barbara Castle. Ken Alexander, Professor of Economics at Strathclyde University, STUC economic adviser, joined us. He was prominent in improving industrial relations in the shipbuilding and engineering sector on the Clyde and in Glasgow. An insider, he was one of us. As secretary of the General Purposes Committee, I took the main notes.

A Difference of Opinion

The meeting, being held in private, provided no gallery for anyone to play to. It was a serious objective examination of the Donovan recommendations and *In Place of Strife*. Jimmy Jack and I anticipated strong objections to Donovan from the CP members in particular but that proved not to be the case. The faults in the trade union movement were admitted. As well as acknowledging the detrimental effects that pitting the shop stewards against full-time officials had, it was conceded that there were other shortcomings such as the problems between the craft unions and the general unions. Not every Donovan recommendation was accepted but the general council response was positive and they were seen as making significant constructive contributions to improving industrial relations. But *In Place of Strife* got a different reception, with highly critical opinions from both Left and Right on the general council. All noted that, while some of its proposals were advantageous to the trade unions, the White Paper implicitly held them and the shop stewards responsible for the country's economic problems. *In Place of Strife* did not reflect an objective read of Donovan and came to different conclusions so a number of its key proposals were deemed unacceptable.

Once back in the office, Robert Mure and I drafted a resolution in the name of the general council, based on the notes of the meeting. Jimmy Jack approved the text and placed it on the agenda for endorsement by the General Purposes Committee on 4 February 1969. The resolution made reference to the welcome given to Donovan in general and noted support for some of the proposals put forward by *In Place of Strife* – such as appeals against dismissal and trade unions having the rights to recognition and negotiation – but then stated:

> Among the proposals which the General Council decisively rejects are those to introduce compulsory ballots before certain strikes; the enforcement of a cooling-off period; the imposition of fines on both workers and trade unions. Congress, therefore, calls on the Government to abandon these particular measures.

It went through on the nod. I remember Jimmy and I looking at each other in surprise when there was no discussion. The committee seemed satisfied that it accurately reflected the conclusions of the weekend meeting.

Then all hell broke loose. By 25 April, 42,000 copies of *In Place of Strife* had been sold by HMSO. Trade-union branches and individual members had copies. The objections to it were growing by the day. The temperature rose when it became known that Barbara Castle, as Secretary of State, was preparing a Bill giving the government power to enforce settlements in unofficial disputes (all led by the shop stewards), and disputes between unions and issue penalties for non-compliance.

I came to work with Barbara in the Commons and liked her but, whereas we trade unionists were grounded in the day-to-day workings of the shop floor, she was purely a political socialist. Her Left-wing credentials meant nothing because she, like a number of others, only saw us in the abstract – good theoretical material – while we workers lived in a reality of which she appeared to have no understanding. This dichotomy was evident in the difference between the opening words of *In Place of Strife* and the rest of its contents. It began well – 'There is necessarily a conflict between capital and labour' – but then contained missiles aimed at organised labour. While it did reference the failures of British managements to consult more genuinely with workers, its compulsory measures were aimed straight at the shop stewards. Four proposals – the enforcement of strike ballots, an imposed 28-day pause to prevent a strike taking place, fines for any trade unionist who ignored the 28-days' 'cooling-off' period and attachment of wages for any who refused to pay fines – were anathema to the unions' members.

Strike ballots were not new. The NUM, at that time, required a two-thirds majority to strike. But whether a union adopted ballots was for the union to decide, based on the special industrial circumstance it faced. Miners worked in pits and it was easy to organise a ballot for a regional or national strike but the engineers' 1.2 million members were to be found in different industrial sectors and in variety of sizes of companies, with local disputes suddenly arising that called for immediate strike decisions by the shop stewards.

The imposed 28-day pause, widely practised in the USA and Australia, was proved to be against the interests of workers because it prevented them taking action in an immediate situation, such as the alteration of a working practice without consultation or warning or the sacking the union rep. No comparative pause was proposed for any management who staged a lockout, which was still a weapon in use at that time.

The attachment of wages proposal was fatal. This would be achieved by a court order operating through the pay system of the very management that had caused the workers to strike in the first place. On top of that, it could land a person in jail for non-payment. In a Commons debate, a report was cited which showed that, out of 1,000 court orders in England for attachment of wages in child maintenance cases, 34 per cent ended in jail sentences. The idea that a worker taking strike action against an unfair employer could end in court and lead to jail was dynamite. It was contrary to Donovan's desire to stick to what it called the 'British tradition of keeping industrial disputes out of courts'.

All of us in the movement knew we had a problem with so-called unofficial strikes (95 per cent of all strikes). A strike called by shop stewards was rarely made official by a union, which would then have been committed to paying strike pay without any control by the executive. There were around five million days lost through strikes in 1967, some of them caused by inter-union disputes about which union would represent workers in a factory. The press launched attack after attack on the shop stewards, calling them 'wildcat strikers' and claiming they were a 'running sore', that they caused 'chaos' and, ipso facto, were responsible for the dire state of the economy.

As was frequently pointed out by union officials but generally ignored, no one could get workers to lose money through strikes if there was no reason for it. The reason was appalling industrial relations caused by many managements treating workers as simply having no rights. There was also more than a suspicion, especially in the vehicle industry, that, when sales were not going to plan, the management would slow down production by provoking a strike, through changing work practices on the assembly lines without consultation.

The strike-prone Linwood car plant near Paisley was a case in point. Shop stewards often came to the STUC office to complain about this practice. The men did not want to strike but the only alternative was to knuckle under to a management that treated them like dirt. The management's appalling attitudes to workers could also be seen at Leyland Bathgate, where there were different levels of canteens. The managing director had his dining room whilst, at the shop-floor level, there were separate canteens for the different groups – foremen, white-collar workers and blue-collar workers. On top of this, the managing director's wife would swan up in her company car, like Lady Muck, and expect to be kowtowed to.

But it was not the same everywhere. I paid a visit to an American-owned high-tech factory just outside Ayr, where my niece, Mary O'Farrell, worked. The American manager couldn't believe it when, after he had put the catering contract out to tender, the boss from one of the catering companies came with two menus. One was standard canteen fare – pies and beans, fish fingers and chips, the other a good range of quality meals. The manager said, 'We will have that one,' pointing to the better menu.

'No, no,' said the caterer, 'you don't understand – that is the management one, the other is the workers' menu.'

'We all eat in the same canteen and have same menu here,' said the American.

'You will regret that,' were the caterer's parting words.

It will come as a surprise that the most effective case against blaming the workers for the state of the economy came from Tory Right-winger Enoch Powell in a Commons debate on *In Place of Strife* on 3 March 1969. Powell demolished the argument that five million strike days were a national catastrophe. He was no champion of the trade unions and his speech, as one would expect, was based on his free-market beliefs, which included workers selling their labour or withdrawing it if they did not get their price. Having pointed out that five million strike days was 1 per cent of total working days – hardly enough to have a devastating effect on the economy – he went on to acquit the workers by explaining that 'one of the surest ways to drive men to frustration and anger' was to subject them to income restraint and for the government to feed them to the press as culprits for its failures. Exactly what the Wilson government was doing.

*

I was in the House of Commons when Enoch Powell was a member. A total free-market man, a journalist once asked him for a comment in the Members' Lobby, and he said 'Yes, for a tenner.' Both he and Michael Foot could hold the Commons spellbound with their oratory but, if you read the speeches in Hansard the next day, Powell's was the one with more substance.

He had a Rolls-Royce mind – a wide and deep range of knowledge (he became a professor of Greek in his mid twenties) – and could build a case and articulate it like no one else. But, if he started with the wrong premise, he could be so logically illogical and damagingly wrong. He could also hate beyond reason, as was the case with Ted Heath, whom he despised. Shakespeare is apt: 'The evil that men do lives after them; the good is oft interred with their bones.' His deliberate choice of words in the 'rivers of blood' speech was racist white supremacy. Disastrous for race relations at the time, it continues to have a malevolent influence. In some Conservative quarters, Powell remains a hero for his views on economic policy, whereas I view it as a tragedy that a man of such a towering intellect proved capable of sinking to a judgement on his fellow human beings on the ridiculous basis of skin colour.

The House of Commons vote on *In Place of Strife* was 224 Labour MPs in favour and 62 against. That was a false reading. A number of Labour MPs voting with the government did so with strong reservations and, ominously, most of the 62 were from the trade-union group. There were 175,000 shop stewards and 3,000 full-time officials back then. They weren't having *In Place of Strife* and mobilised. MPs among the 224 started to peel off from the government – as did a number of Cabinet ministers, chief among them Jim Callaghan who, unlike Barbara Castle, came from the trade-union movement.

At the STUC, the turn of events created by the strong reaction to 'In Place of Strife' immediately affected the General Council members' attitude. Jimmy Jack had sent out a draft agenda for the annual congress to unions and in it was the carefully worded, balanced, General Council resolution that had been approved by the General Purposes Committee. But, such was the furore, no general council member now wanted to own it. Despite all disclaimers they made of 'It wasnae me!', no one turned on Jimmy Jack, Robert Mure and me because they knew that we had put in the resolution – only what their thoughts were at that special weekend get-together. By the time congress met in Rothesay, the General Council, having long abandoned its own resolution, recommended acceptance of the Scottish NUM's outright rejection in total of *In Place of Strife*. The Royal Commission might just as well never have met or bothered reporting. Donovan was dead.

Just before Barbara Castle rose to address congress, I had a bet with David Martin, a BBC producer, who forecast a standing ovation. There was no chance of that. I won the bet. She was applauded out of politeness but the atmosphere in the hall was ice cold. One of the things that we held against her was that, by giving credence to the idea that the trade unions had to be shackled by government and court orders, the way was being paved for the Tories to mount a full-scale attack if they won the next election. That is what happened in 1970. In the debates on that Tory government's industrial relations Bill, Robert Carr, the Secretary of State for Employment, frequently quoted what Barbara had said and written in promoting *In Place of Strife*. That Tory legislation was the next big battle for the movement and I was in the thick of it.

10

Labour MP for South Ayrshire

Emrys Hughes was the Left-wing Labour MP for South Ayrshire. MI5's official history claims he was a KGB agent, perhaps because he was often in the Soviet Union. The reason for many of his visits was two-fold. Firstly, he had collaborated with Samuil Yakovlevich Marshak, a noted Russian poet, in translating the whole of Burns into Russian before Marshak's death in 1964. And, as it was a best-seller, Emrys had lots of roubles in a Russian bank. So, whenever he travelled the world, as he did, at his own expense, to attend anti-capitalist and anti-nuclear rallies, he went via Moscow, paying his fare in roubles to the Soviet airline. He could not have been much use to the Kremlin as a spy – the Labour leadership never let Emrys near policymaking and he had no contacts in the security services or defence departments. He never punted the Soviet line in Ayrshire. His rebellions against the whip on defence spending were something many of us agreed with.

In early October 1969, he was struck by a car when out for a walk. He lingered in hospital but died on 18 October, the very night the South Ayrshire Labour Party had arranged a social evening in Cumnock at which Willie Ross, Secretary of State for Scotland, was the main guest. Those organising decided to go ahead with it. Of course, with Emrys hardly cold, the speculation was about his successor. Everyone assumed it would be John Pollock, a major figure in Scottish politics. John went on to become general secretary of the Educational Institute of Scotland but, that night, he told us quietly he did not want to be an MP. That threw the net wide open. Willie Goudie, a miner from New Cumnock and a senior councillor and chairman of the constituency party, saw himself, as did others, as the next in line after John. But he made a mistake that night by starting to ask people to support his nomination. Willie was a good man and a nice one but that went down badly. I was approached too but said this was not the night to talk about it and neither it was.

As a miner, Willie was bound to get the NUM nomination and, as the NUM had the biggest number of delegates to the constituency party, he was the favourite. The problem was that he was measured against Emrys Hughes, who had been a national figure, a leader of the Left, a fine writer and a man who had taken on Churchill in the Commons and bested him on occasion. Willie was a councillor, albeit a good one, but that was as far as his talents lay in many eyes.

Later, John Pollock and others urged me to stand and told me that the NUM delegates were split, even if Willie was their union's formal nominee. Willie Paterson, another miner, who became county convener when Danny Sim retired, told me to stand and said he would support me. I would have lost the selection conference but for the fortuitous intervention of a Glasgow councillor who had relatives in the Girvan Labour Party. I shall never understand why a Glasgow councillor, not known in the party in Ayrshire, thought he could get the seat. But he did persuade the Girvan branch to nominate him and, in deference to them, was on the short list. Girvan sent four delegates to support him at the selection conference – otherwise, they told me afterwards, they would not have bothered being there, believing it was sewn up for Willie.

The NUM delegates were split but I lost on the first ballot. The Glasgow man fell out and, on the second ballot, his four Girvan votes came to me and I won by one vote. The ballot result had been left on the table so I saw it when I came in to make my victory speech. It was not only awkward speaking to a divided party but I was in a worse position than that, as I found out later. After the ballot result, the chairman had asked the meeting to make my adoption unanimous, which was the usual thing to do. A good number refused.

However, I was the candidate and the by-election was fixed for March 1970. The Tories had no chance of winning but the SNP fielded a formidable candidate in Sam Purdie, a miner who was then studying on a union scholarship at Ruskin College, Oxford. Sam had been Emrys Hughes's election agent in 1966 and was well known. He was articulate and a socialist. The SNP had high hopes and Labour was nervous. Probably, my record of fighting the SNP won me the nomination.

I was well received at public meetings in the villages of Ayrshire and the towns of Cumnock, Maybole and Girvan. But these were not easy meetings. The NUM had a very good programme of political education and the general public in the mining areas was well read and many knew their Marxist theory. The question-and-answer sessions were taxing. The journalists, who came into south Ayrshire to report on the campaign, were impressed by the people.

Sam Purdie ran a good campaign and we debated via letters in the local paper, *The Cumnock Chronicle*. I then took a personal decision about which the full-time organisers, who had been drafted in, and the local party members were not happy. I challenged Sam to a debate in Cumnock Town Hall. Some argued that I was defending a big majority and that it was folly to jeopardise it. What if I lost the debate? Of course, it was a risk. But I had read the SNP campaign material and had fought and debated with them up and down the country so I knew that, far from being a strength, Sam's socialism was their weakness in South Ayrshire. The SNP did not believe in class politics. Every Scot was a Scot before anything else and, in their elections, they sought votes from every social and political quarter. I knew that Sam, as their candidate, would be required to follow the party line and fish for votes not only in the northern mining Labour areas but also in the south, in Maybole, Turnberry, Girvan and Ballantrae, where the Tory vote lay.

At the debate in a packed Cumnock Town Hall, Sam was very good. He asked me how I could justify there being a Labour majority in Scotland but accept a Tory government elected in England. I could answer that from the class position and my internationalism. What he could not answer was the question I put to him time and again in front of a mining working-class audience – whether he was still a socialist and, if he was, did he want an independent socialist Scotland? I knew that was what Sam wanted but also knew he could not say so and could feel the audience turning against him. If he had been free to be himself and spell out his own vision of a socialist Scotland, I would have been in trouble. But he couldn't and I won. My supporters, however, had a last-minute fright when, in my winding-up, I said they would shout, 'SNP! SNP!' – 'Sillars Not Purdie! Sillars Not Purdie!' – all over the constituency. From that night on, I was on my way to a big majority. In 1966, Labour got 23,495 and the Tories got 11,442 – there was no SNP candidate. This time, for the by-election held on 19 March1970, the votes were:

Labour	20,664
Tory	9,778
SNP	7,785

It is worth recording that another significant meeting was held in that town hall, again before a packed audience. On the eve of poll, Willie Ross responded to a question on the EEC. As a member of the Cabinet applying to join, Willie gave the government's reasons for doing so. Being opposed to entry, I then got up and openly disagreed. Neither Willie nor anyone in the audience took exception to this. There is a lesson there for today's politicians. Candidates are party nominees but the public must also know that they are individuals and have minds of their own.

*

I wasn't nervous or overawed going into the House of Commons. During my time as a full-time agent, I had met many MPs who came to campaign in by-elections and, in Ayrshire, we met our MPs and debated with them frequently. You have to take the oath, swearing allegiance to Queen Elizabeth II. I didn't quite do that, stopping short at 'Elizabeth'. Unionist I may have been but I resented that title – there never having been an Elizabeth of Scotland or of the new state, the United Kingdom, formed in 1707.

It is forgotten now but, in 1953, there was an almighty row in Scotland over the Queen's choice of title. It was held to be an insult and showed that we were seen by the new monarch and her advisers as no more than a northern bit of England. The title was legally challenged in the famous court case, *MacCormick v Lord Advocate*. Wendy Wood, a famous campaigner for independence, was suspected of being behind a bombing campaign in Edinburgh, in which postboxes bearing the E II R symbol were targeted. To this day, E II R does not figure on Scottish postboxes.

On my first working day, an old Labour member took me aside and advised me to sit in the chamber for a few weeks and listen to the debates before speaking myself. There were a lot of very able people in all parties worth listening to and learning from but there was also dross. If I did what he advised, I would benefit from it. It was excellent advice and I passed on the same to Mhairi Black when she became an MP in 2015.

I was not long there when Harold Wilson called a general election in June 1970. Opinion polls forecast a Labour victory. At the end of the first week of the campaign, the newspapers were describing the 'black days' suffered by the Tory leader, Ted Heath. On the last weekend, Labour was 12 per cent ahead in the polls. The balance of payments was still very bad and Heath hammered away at this as evidence of Labour economic failure. He seemed to be getting nowhere with it until the Monday before the poll, when the balance of payments figures came out. They were worse than the previous month. He also made what was regarded as a desperate, reckless promise to 'cut prices at a stroke'.

On polling day, the constituency tour began in Girvan. I got on well with the Girvan Tories and we chatted away for a time. Although they knew they were not going to win South Ayrshire, they were in a chirpy mood. I missed that signal. That evening, a bit after the polls closed, I left our committee room in Auchinleck, on the cheery note that we would have another Labour government – our count was the next day. By the time I had driven the half-hour journey home to Ayr, the Tories were winning the election. Next day, we had a big majority again with Labour getting 23,910 votes and SNP votes dropping down to 3,102 – over 4,000 fewer than in the byelection. But, after my victory speech, Sam Purdie, again the SNP candidate, said he didn't know what I was so happy about as Scotland had again voted Labour and ended up with a Tory government. I privately acknowledged that truth and Sam's words never left me.

*

As the trade unionists feared, *In Place of Strife* had paved the way for an all-out assault on the movement by the newly elected Tory government. It published a Bill creating a National Industrial Relations Court, which could impose financial sanctions on unions and penal sanctions on their members. The trade-union group of MPs came to the fore and dictated how the parliamentary party would conduct the battle. There would be full-scale, unambiguous opposition, using every procedural trick in the House of Commons book – late-night sitting after late-night sitting and lifting the mace to bring the place to a standstill – all coordinated with the TUC and the STUC's campaigns outside Parliament. Such tactics could not now be used in our family-friendly parliament with its timetabled legislation and early-bed nights.

With my trade union background, I was heavily involved, speaking at huge demonstrations of workers, as well as taking part in the parliamentary debates. Eventually, of course, the Bill became an Act but that did not stop the campaigning. The trade union leaders, Hugh Scanlon of the Amalgamated Engineering Union (AEU) and Jack Jones of the Transport and General Workers Union (TGWU), said they would defy the new National Industrial Relations Court, as did shop stewards all over the country. The movement would make it unworkable.

Instead of being able to use the law to shackle and corral the trade unions, the Heath government discovered its limits if people believed the law to be malicious, unjust and directed against the working class in order to weaken their bargaining power. The Tory government policy crashed in 1972 when five shop stewards from the dockers' union were jailed for not obeying a court order. They became known as the 'Pentonville Five' after the prison they were sent to. Massive strikes looked likely but then, as though from nowhere, the Official Solicitor – a court official few had heard of and whose role is to represent people who are unable to represent themselves – got the men out. The anti-trade union act was on the statute book but it was inoperable.

With trade-union agitation at high levels, the government faced the miners next in the first UK national miners' strike for a generation. Towards the end of the strike, the NUM negotiation team was in Downing Street and the media was full of rumours that it would end or that it wouldn't end, that the government's final offer was adequate or that it was inadequate. I had been asked to appear on an open-ended STV evening programme alongside the Right-wing Tory MP, Jock Bruce-Gardyne, with a number of miners in the audience. Jimmy Gordon (later Lord Gordon, Baron Gordon of Strathblane) was the interviewer. As there was no word of any outcome from Downing Street, the programme finally had to end. Inviting a final comment, Gordon asked me what I thought would happen. I said I was quite convinced that, by the time we all woke up the next day, the strike would be settled and the NUM would have won. Bruce-Gardyne said the government should starve the miners out, as had happened in 1926. There was an angry roar from the miners in the studio, who then advanced on him. The programme was cut at that moment. I learned later from Alex Eadie, who was part of the NUM delegation, that they had agreed to settle with Heath but decided to make him sweat for a couple of hours.

That strike was when Arthur Scargill first became prominent. I remember telling Dennis Skinner at the time that I was not impressed by him – too egotistical and reckless. Later, during the years 1984–85, Scargill, as president of the NUM, with his ego in full flight, tried to bounce every mining area into a national strike without a ballot. Nottinghamshire and the Midlands area wanted a ballot so there was no unity and that was a fatal error. The threat against mining communities was real – pits would close and thousands of jobs would go. The Thatcher government had prepared for a strike and the coal had been piled up at the power stations. A wise leader was needed because it was not going to be easy to fight this battle to save as many jobs as possible. Scargill was a raging bull, devoid of wisdom.

I kept quiet about my view of Scargill. The Scottish miners were out and I could see no point in public criticism. So, along with the SNP activist Kenny MacAskill, I did all I could to help, with our efforts being directed towards Fife. The miners were relying on strike pay and funds gathered for them around the UK. As the strike took its toll on the finances of the Fife families, Kenny, a lawyer, dug into the law and came up with a Scottish social welfare Act that, he believed, could get financial help to the families. He took a test case to a tribunal, held in Kirkcaldy, and won. It was reckoned the benefits obtained would be worth around £1 million for all Scottish miners' families. The government appealed the tribunal decision and sent one of its senior solicitors up from London. Kenny was unable to attend but sent me along – a non-lawyer could act in this tribunal – as I knew the case. I cannot claim to have socked it to the Londoner. Kenny's original deployment of the law was watertight. The government lost. When the good news was phoned over to Fife, it was Gordon Brown who made the announcement to the media, with not a word about Kenny's role in what should have been a common effort.

I was not alone in my view of Scargill being a disastrous leader but we saw nothing to be gained by a public attack on the head of the union when the miners were fighting for their jobs and communities. That was not the case with Jimmy Reid. He let rip in a Channel 4 broadcast:

> Arthur Scargill's leadership of the miners' strike has been a disgrace. The price to be paid for his folly will be immense. He will have destroyed the NUM as an effective fighting force within British trade unionism for the next 20 years. If Kamikaze pilots were to form their own union, Arthur would be an ideal choice for leader.

It was a brilliant demolition of Scargill – every word was true – but it didn't help the increasingly skint miners because there was no way out for them from Scargill's leadership. Jimmy being right about their leader altered nothing. That analysis should have waited until the strike came to an end, as it did on 3 March 1985, in defeat.

*

I was active in the Left-wing Tribune Group and became its chairman for one year in, if I remember correctly, 1974. Dennis Skinner was vice-chairman. There were many formidable personalities – Michael Foot, Tom Driberg, whom everyone knew was gay, but none knew, as MI5's official history claims, that he was a paid KGB agent, Ian Mikardo, Eric Heffer, Stan Orme, Neil Kinnock, John Prescott, Renée Short, Frank Allaun and others. Along with Mikardo and Allaun, in July 1972, I co-wrote a pamphlet on Labour Party democracy. It made interesting re-reading in the Momentum–Corbyn era. It was titled *Labour: Party or Puppet?* It looked at the role of MPs and the parliamentary party and the oft-repeated claim that neither could be bound by conference decisions when constructing the election manifesto and implementing policies when in government. This we contested.

We sought to give activists a guaranteed say against candidate selection meetings being 'packed' by supporters of the MP seeking re-nomination – people who never attended at any other time or did election work. It was also quite common for such people to be marched in by trade unions:

> On the take-up of the Selection Conference we recommend that there be a party rule which states clearly that no delegate may attend a selection conference and no organisation should be represented at it unless they have chalked up a reasonable proportion of possible attendances at a GMC over the previous two years.

The most radical proposal was that, instead of the party leader being elected by the MPs alone, as was the case then, he or she should be elected by the whole annual conference. It took a long time for that seed sown in 1972 to bear fruit many years later.

A Private Memorandum

Throughout the 1960s and 1970s, with the UK economy was mired in constant crisis and the British establishment was gripped by a pervasive sense of failure. US Secretary of State Dean Acheson's quip, 'Great Britain has lost an empire and has not yet found a role', seemed apposite. This economic predicament was in stark contrast to the six-member-state EEC across the channel where growth was around 5 per cent a year. Joining it was seen by many political leaders, who were bankrupt of ideas, as an economic lifeline.

Not everyone agreed. There were deep divisions in the Labour and Tory parties. The EEC split the Labour Party on a Left–Right basis as it had been by *In Place of Strife*. The Right, led by Roy Jenkins, was in favour and the Left against. The Left saw the EEC as a capitalist club whose rules, together with a loss of sovereignty, would prevent us making Britain socialist. At a special Labour Party conference held in April 1975, two months before the EEC referendum which was to take place that June, I declared my opposition from the rostrum – for me, 'the EEC encapsulated the ethic of capitalism'. That line in my speech was picked up in a *Guardian* leader, as it expressed the root of the Left's apprehension of what the Common Market actually meant.

I had been having difficulties with more than the trade union Bill and the EEC. In 1972, only two years after my election as MP, my experience of seeing how Westminster actually worked began to erode my belief in the Union as it then stood. I faced a dilemma – pretend to myself and the Scots that what I believed before going to Westminster was still the same or admit that I might have been wrong in hammering the Nats. Following the SNP victory at Hamilton, should I have advanced my ideas on devolution instead of just turning a stony face to independence? It was not easy to admit that I might have been mistaken on such a fundamental matter – especially one so instrumental in my rise towards the top in Scottish politics – but it had been drummed into me in Ayrshire that, without intellectual honesty, you were a sham. I had to face up to my mistakes. Sam Purdie's words about Scotland voting Labour but ending up with a Tory government were not ones I could continue to dodge.

On 8 February 1972, I did what I have done several times since when self-challenging long held beliefs – I sat down and wrote myself a private memorandum, thirteen A4 pages, setting out the problems with my position on Scotland and the possible solutions to them. The memo looked at the condition of the UK and the fact that Scotland was in difficulty because regional policy was breaking down. Hitherto, the English midlands and south-east had been relaxed about restrictions placed on them, while incentives were offered to investors to move north. However, when those English regions decided they were no longer willing for that policy to continue, it meant Scotland lost the ability to attract so much inward investment. The extracts show what I was wrestling with:

There seem to be three courses open to Scotland. One is to remain as an integral part of the UK. One is to achieve a measure of devolution. The third is to set up as a separate state.

Arguments for a measure of devolution are attractive, of course. They offer the best of both worlds, or appear to. But if devolution means no more than that we can achieve a marginal extension of our present limited powers to strengthen the Scottish part of the UK economy, then it would add little to our ability to overcome our deep-seated problems . . .

If the desire is to exert a massive degree of Scottish control over Scottish economic life, then devolution is not the solution we can seek. Devolution would give us the form but not the substance of economic control. Centrally taken decisions at the UK level would still be the crucial decisions . . .

If devolution is set aside, we are left with the two extremes, continuing in unity with England as we are, or becoming separate . . .

This paper's analysis of Scotland's future as part of the UK shows it to be bleak. It may well be that the coming outline analysis of attempts to run Scotland as a separate entity will show a similarly bleak outlook; or possibly a worse outlook . . .

If that proves to be the case, then Scots are faced with a cruel dilemma. They will have to consciously choose between remaining a poorer part of the UK, or becoming (or remaining) a European nation with slower rates of development than others.

Paragraph 26 reveals that I was about to submit independence to an objective set of tests – by no means rejecting it outright. Indeed, most of the paper was concerned with a careful, detailed examination of the possibilities and difficulties associated with the idea of independence at that time. It reads:

> No-one can argue intelligently that a nation of five million people cannot go it alone. The case to be looked at is not whether it can become a separate entity, but what the consequences might be, and then to judge if it is worth separating from the rest of the UK.

What the memo then did was examine, extensively, independence as I saw the issues at that time – particularly our relations with England and the integrated nature of our economies. It ended:

> The whole point being underscored is that, while Scotland would be independent in the academic sense, there would be definite limitations on the degree of freedom that she could exercise.

I drew no specific conclusions other than that the status quo was not the answer to the Scottish people's problems. This was probably as far as I could go at that time. I recognised the defects in devolution but I also realised that, while the arguments for independence could not be ignored, the problems inherent in separating were daunting – investment competition with England, borders, defence, foreign affairs and nationality, none of which had been properly thought through by the SNP. I was no more capable than they were at solving them but I had at least taken a look. Although I was changed by the exercise, it was not a road to a Scottish Damascus. I was in an intellectual and political fankle and needed time to think my way through it. It took a while.

In those days, we Scots MPs travelled south on the sleeper on a Sunday night and back on a Thursday night. Willie Ross and I both lived in Ayr. We alighted at Kilmarnock on the Friday morning and walked to the bus station. I had given him my memo as we boarded the sleeper at Euston. When handing it back in Kilmarnock, he said he didn't know what I was worrying about because the SNP were no threat – they had only one seat and that was the Western Isles. I tried to explain that I was not worried about the SNP but Scotland's position per se but he wasn't listening. No one else ever saw the memo.

*

In a debate on the EEC, on 3 May 1972, the influence of that memo came out. The day before, the local elections in Scotland had been a triumph for Labour and a disaster for the SNP so I knew nothing I said would be seen as a panic response to an SNP advance. Although the memo had made no reference to the EEC, the UK moves to join it fuelled the 'nationalist' dimension of my thinking, as I started to see no logic in a situation where policy produced in Scotland would then be required to pass through London, only to be watered down again in Brussels.

Speaking last in the debate, I set out my evolving thoughts for 45 minutes, ending at 11 p.m. With no journalists in the press gallery at that time of night, the speech – a remarkable one from a Labour MP known as 'the hammer of the Nats' – was not reported in the next day's newspapers. The speech was in the House of Commons chamber, with the whole house constituting a committee at that stage of the EEC Bill, whose debates were under a guillotine timetable. Here are relevant extracts:

> The time may come when people in all quarters of the committee, especially those who voted for the guillotine, will very much regret that we did not take time to examine what will become, whether it takes 10 or 15 years to manifest itself, an acute problem for all the people of the United Kingdom . . . I am reminded of a speech in the early stage of this Parliament by Michael Foot who warned the Government that the course of their policies would have serious effects on the constitutional unity of the United Kingdom in so far as the people of Scotland and Wales reacted to them . . .

I traced the history of Scotland since 1707 and the Westminster response to the Scottish desire for more control through the creation of the Cabinet post of Secretary of State for Scotland and the Scottish Grand Committee. I went on:

> I should say that I do not regret that we have had the Union. We have had a mixture of Scotsmen, Welshmen and Englishmen in

the Labour movement. I have always thought that it would have been a tragedy if the wonderful genius of Aneurin Bevan had been locked up, as it were, in a tiny separate Wales, and we had never had the benefit of his views and his philosophy in the mainstream of the British Socialist movement . . .

One of the changing circumstances that we must take into account is the immense feeling now abroad in Scotland about Scottish nationhood. Many people may regret this, and I know some people do. But people will ignore it at their peril . . . It will become more difficult than it has ever been to hold the Union together . . .

The Treaty of Union was made, from the Scottish point of view, for economic reasons. The reason why we are here at Westminster is that this is where major economic decisions are taken on the English economy which ultimately affects the Scottish economy, and the crafty Scotsman says to himself, 'If that is where the decisions are to be taken, that is where we shall locate ourselves.' That is why we have a Secretary of State in the Cabinet . . . But if the European Communities pursue the Werner plan for economic and monetary union, the logic which brings us to Westminster may take us to Brussels, because certain Scottish interests which would be termed regional interests in the context of the United Kingdom would be converted to distinct national interests if Scotland were represented in Brussels . . .

If we think about the implications of that and a shift of the decision-making centre from Westminster to Brussels, we realise that there is some validity in the argument for some direct representation from the northern part of Britain. It may be to our distinct advantage.

It may seem strange that, having set out that position, I didn't develop it, repeat it and campaign for it. But that would be to misunderstand where I was at that time. It was not a rallying cry for nationalists or an attempt to bring the matter into Labour policy discussion. Rather it was meant as a warning to the Tory and Labour Parties of the danger they were putting the Union in by joining the EEC. It articulated what I thought could happen, not what I wanted to happen. Only Norman Buchan, MP for Paisley South, more thoughtful than the others, saw it in that context and spoke to me afterwards about the 'apocalyptic' version I had spelled out. My other Labour colleagues were different

– they didn't understand where I was coming from. But, while I had not intended it to be a call for independence in the new European setting, I had planted the seed in my own mind.

As well as being in a fankle over Scotland's position within the UK, I was having other difficulties at that time and I came to regret leaving the STUC for Parliament. I could handle myself in the House of Commons and in committees but I didn't like the place and missed frontline trade-union work.

When Roy Jenkins resigned as deputy leader of the party in April 1972 over disagreement on EEC entry, he and a number of his acolytes quit the Finance Bill Standing Committee. They were an arrogant bunch and thought that, bereft of their talent, the party would learn the lesson that they were indispensable.

Denis Healey, Joel Barnett and two or three others who were experts took over the opposition to the government. I was drafted in to make up the backbench numbers, and not expected to make much of a contribution. The one I did make stunned them all – it was a question about how the Bill affected feu duties in Scotland. The government ministers, their civil servants and our front bench had never heard of them.

It was the habit of MPs, not involved in a debate, to sit at an outside table dealing with the mail. That was where I was, apparently not looking happy, when Alex Kitson of the STUC came by and asked what was wrong. I told him I had made a mistake in coming to Parliament. He asked if I would fancy coming back to the STUC as deputy general secretary to Jimmy Milne, by then general secretary, with the idea of me eventually taking over when Jimmy retired. He was serious so I said yes.

A meeting was arranged with the Left group on the General Council at a pub in Glasgow, when it was agreed that I would resign my seat and return to the STUC. Then Stephen Maxwell of the SNP (who later became a good friend) won a stunning victory in the Wester Hailes regional by-election in Edinburgh, a mini-Govan, overturning a huge Labour majority. It looked like the SNP was on the rise again. The upshot was another meeting and a decision that I should stay in Parliament as I was needed to fight the nationalists.

From the South Ayrshire by-election onwards, it was forecast that I would one day become Secretary of State for Scotland, but that was never more than a possibility, and I have never regretted losing that 'opportunity'. But I have always regretted not going back to the STUC, where it would not have been a possibility, but a certainty, that I would have become the general secretary.

12

Devolution on the Agenda

The Heath government elected in 1970 suffered bad luck, at the personal and political level, right from the start. Iain Macleod, who had prepared for the job of Chancellor of the Exchequer while in opposition, died a few weeks after the election. Heath appointed Tony Barber in his stead. Barber was unprepared, out of his depth and a total failure. On one occasion, Enoch Powell asked him a technical question that a chancellor should be able to answer but on which Barber tanked and Powell slapped his knee in cruel glee at having exposed how inadequate he was. Powell could generate and show utter contempt for someone. A characteristic never mentioned by his many admirers on the Right.

I am convinced that, had Macleod lived, the Heath government would not have floundered the way it did. He was a politically courageous man and one of the best parliamentary debaters there has been. His early reputation was made from the backbenches with a searing attack on Nye Bevan, whom most Tories were afraid of in debate. I learned from Macleod about debate. On one occasion, he was on his feet making an attack on Labour Chancellor Roy Jenkins when one of our side shouted, 'Cheap!' Macleod stopped, turned and said something like, 'I am never cheap because I seek to go right to the heart of the opponent's case and, if I can take it apart, then the rest falls automatically.' Those are not the exact words but they capture what he said and they have guided me in debates, written and spoken, ever since.

Macleod had left a mark on me, before I was an MP, when I saw him on TV at a Tory Party conference, delivering what struck me then and remains in little doubt in my mind even today the most destructive attack on socialism I have ever heard. He eschewed the usual attacks on socialists wanting to level things down, spend other people's money, rule by bureaucracy and restrict freedom. He said simply that 'socialism is a good idea; the problem is that it doesn't work'. However, that didn't make me abandon my socialist belief. This was founded on the need to contest a capitalism that is in a stronger position than, and is exploit-ative of, labour and which, due to its inherent contradictions, creates its own crises, with labour paying the heaviest price. But it did make me look more critically at how some Labour policies actually worked in practice, such as nationalisation that, in reality, was state capitalism without one of the benefits of capitalism – the spur of competition. The state nationalised companies did not so much create a 'corporate' mind in its management, but a 'corporation' mind, that was not conducive to innovation and change.

Donald J Trump took over ownership of the golf courses and hotel at Turnberry in Ayrshire in 2014 and renamed them Trump Turnberry. However, this should not detract from me citing the Turnberry Hotel as an example of the kind of mismanagement I mean. Under the 1947 Transport Act, the UK's railway network was nationalised and the run-ning of Turnberry Hotel, Gleneagles Hotel, Central Station Hotel and the North British Hotel at Glasgow's Queen Street Station was trans-ferred to British Rail's hotel division. From then until it was sold to a private company, Turnberry Hotel closed for six months of the year. The village of Turnberry has one of the mildest climates in Scotland – palm trees grow there. The hotel's property has always included world-class golf courses. As the local MP, I met the London-based managing direc-tor of the British Rail hotel division. Dull. Not a spark of imagination. In his mind, there was a summer season when people came to the hotel and a winter season when they would not come. So, while the palm trees grew all year and the golf courses remained open, the hotel shut in winter, putting its workers on the dole.

Once Turnberry passed into private hands – quite a few – the owners seized on the assets of the climate and the golf courses. It has never shut in winter again. That Turnberry example was repeated all over a number of public-owned enterprises. Those of my generation who had to wait in a queue for a telephone and were lucky to have a shared line, before BT was privatised, will know what I mean.

*

But back to the post-1970 world. More bad luck came Heath's way with the threat of Rolls-Royce going bankrupt. Before and during the election, the Tories had trumpeted a new market-driven industrial pol-icy – no more Labour bailouts like those for Upper Clyde Shipbuilders and the car industry. The discipline of the market was to rule. But Rolls-Royce was not only a big employer, it was a key technology company and it would set British industry back years to lose it. Heath had no option but to put it in to public ownership. It was a correct and courageous decision but one of the greatest U-turns ever – and a huge humiliation.

He was unfortunate too in his choice of Industry Secretary, John Davies, who had been Director General of the CBI. Plucking an industrial heavyweight from his position and putting him in the government had worked in Churchill's wartime coalition, when Ernie Bevin became Minister of Labour, but that really was an exception. When Harold Wilson made TGWU general secretary Frank Cousins a Cabinet minister, he flopped. It was the same with Davies, so inept at the dispatch box that even on the opposition side we stopped baiting him and, instead, cringed in embarrassment.

Heath had made a mortal enemy in the trade-union movement and his economic policy was a mess. The NUM went on strike again and there was industrial unrest everywhere. In January 1974, with Heath claiming the strike as justification, he put the country on a three-day working week, television closed down early and, in the House of Commons, some of our debates were by candlelight. The government's blaming of the NUM, supported as it was by other unions, appeared to work. There were debates within the Cabinet on whether to go for an early general election on the question 'Who governs Britain, the elected government or the trade unions?' Heath hesitated and then called the election in February 1974. That hesitation came to matter.

But I have to step back a little in time here to set the scene of that election and what followed. In October 1973 came a double whammy. First, the Royal Commission on the Constitution reported in favour of devolution and a Scottish assembly. Second, as if perfectly timed, came the Govan by-election with Margo MacDonald, 'the Blonde Bombshell', as the SNP candidate. The nationalism that Harold Wilson thought would be kicked into the longest grass when setting up the Royal Commission was back. And Labour had a problem in Govan – their chosen candidate was Harry Selby, a Marxist councillor in Glasgow, who was out of time and place in a changing world.

When I went up from Ayrshire to canvass for him, I was given a handful of canvass cards and told where to go – a tenement area in a depressing state, with a burned-out car on the street corner. The first woman I met started talking about problems with the rats. I was dumb-founded – not only by the rats but by the casual way she talked about them. She took me down to the back-door area shared with her neighbours. Planks of wood were laid on bricks so they could walk over the stagnant water to hang out their washing. It was the same story a few doors down. People had no confidence in the Labour-controlled

Glasgow City Council and were unhappy with the Labour Party in general. I went straight back to the main committee room and asked to talk to Harry in private where, in a back room, I asked for an explanation for what I had just encountered. He was sanguinity itself. My breaking point was the burned-out car. He told me that he and others stood on it when speaking against rent increases. I left. I knew that Margo, whom I had never met, would win because Labour deserved to lose. My despair was compounded when I went back on polling day. Around teatime, Willie Ross was being driven round in a car belting out through a loudspeaker: 'Now's the day and now's the hour to kick out Tory power.' There was hardly a Tory to be found in Govan. We had been in power from 1964 to 1970. Glasgow City Council was in Labour control. Yet here we had people living in terrible circumstances. Surely we had responsibility for that.

Margo's victory rocked the political scene. She was stunningly beautiful – Willie Ross described her maiden speech as the nicest he had ever seen – but, more importantly, she was a natural communicator and obviously blessed with an original mind. Before Christmas, the SNP was back as a problem for us in the Labour Party.

But, as the year turned in 1974, we thought the threat would diminish. The miners' strike and the three-day week were hitting working-class pay packets. Labour was sure the February general election was all about class. In Left-wing Scotland, that would wipe out every other consideration and the SNP would be irrelevant. But the first UK-wide polls were not good, showing a rising Tory lead.

I was called to London to participate in a UK-wide party-political broadcast. Neil Kinnock was there, as was Ann Mallalieu, daughter of a Labour MP, who herself later became a peer. The producer was the actor Stanley Baker, a party member, with the filming done in his penthouse overlooking the Thames. We were told that, with the bad polls, the real challenge was not to win the election but to get enough seats that Labour could maintain a viable base from which to recover. Neither we nor any commentators, at that time, expected the Tories to lose. Heath's question about who should govern a democracy appeared to be clinching it for the Tories.

Back in South Ayrshire, I went canvassing in Minishant, a village near Maybole, and discovered it wasn't going to be all about class. At the first door, a woman came out, said something like 'Oh, it's you' and went on to tell me that she and a number of neighbours had met the night before to talk about the election, which in itself seemed unusual, and that, although they were going to vote for me, they believed the

SNP were saying things that were relevant about Scotland, especially with its slogan, 'It's Scotland's oil.' In later years, I learned the slogan was the brainwave of the SNP's deputy leader, Gordon Wilson, and it came to him while he was digging in his garden.

I got the message, which was reinforced by my brother-in-law, Billy Heron. A member of the electricity board's emergency response engineering team, he moved around the country a lot. He phoned to say he was seeing forests of SNP posters in windows. I phoned Willie Ross to alert him to this unexpected development. Again, thinking I was concerned about losing my majority, he told me South Ayrshire was safe and to stop worrying. I tried to tell him the majority wasn't my worry – it was the rise in support for the SNP that was troubling me. But he persisted in thinking I had election jitters so I gave up trying.

Ted Heath's claim that the miners were responsible for the three-day week and plunging the country into early darkness was undone when a BBC camera crew flew over a power station where there was lots of coal. That was the turning point. Heath lost the election. Labour didn't win it but we were the largest party.

After the election, in the members' cloakroom, I met Jim Prior, who had been a member of Heath's Cabinet. He told me there had been a debate about when to hold the election and, on the day Heath hesitated, Tory opinion polls were soaring but, after that television picture of stockpiled coal, they starting falling like a stone.

The UK result was:

Labour   301
Tory   297
Liberal 14
SNP   7

But it was the Scottish results that rocked the scene. There, the result there was:

Labour   40 – 36.6%
Tory   21 – 32.9%
Liberal 3 – 7.9%
SNP   7 – 21.9%

The SNP had almost doubled its percentage of the vote since 1970. Labour lost three seats to the SNP, one being Dick Douglas, but won back Govan and one to the Tories, John Mackintosh.

Heath attempted to form a coalition government with the Liberals but failed. A minority Labour government took office, with another election certain in the autumn.

When Margo MacDonald lost Govan I was delighted. She had only been in the Commons a short time but I realised what a formidable opponent she was to the Labour Party. Out of the Commons, denied that platform, she would disappear. I didn't know her then. Margo was not out of politics. In or out of Parliament didn't matter. She had arrived. Now deputy leader of the SNP, a charismatic national figure, she was free to campaign all over the country, drawing big audiences. The US embassy, which was monitoring the Scottish situation, was very impressed by her. Jack Binns, a US diplomat, told me Margo had one of the best minds he had encountered and she would be a constant problem for the Labour Party.

Chatting at that time with some of the new SNP MPs, it became obvious that Margo was a problem for them too. There was jealousy. They had been elected and she had lost so why was she on television so often rather than them? Margo was one of those rare people in politics who do not need 'MP' or 'MSP' after their names in order to command attention. Take 'MP' or 'MSP' away from most, they become anonymous. Not so with her.

*

It was self-evident that, if Labour in Scotland did not respond to the nationalist sentiment that was now on the rise, there would be problems in fending off the SNP in the October election. My personal self-examination memo of February 1972 made it easy for me to see the need for devolution to fend them off but, by then, it was not just an expedient for me – I saw it as essential if Scotland was going to be governed better. My experience in the Scottish Grand Committee, with uninterested English Tories sitting in to make up the numbers (they dealt with their mail and took no part in the debates), was that we discussed but could not actually decide on Scottish business. Now and again, we on the Labour benches would emphasise our Scottish majority by demanding a vote at the end of proceedings and would sometimes win it when the English Tories sloped off early for lunch. But nothing happened. The Grand Committee still reported to the House that it had 'considered the matter' with no reference to the government having been defeated.

The Standing Committees that dealt with the detail of Scottish legislation also had add-on English Tory members so, no matter what argument we on the Labour benches deployed, we were sure to be outvoted. This was obviously nonsense and, when combined with the problem of getting time for purely Scottish legislation in a crowded House of Commons agenda, it meant that the needs of Scotland were often in a long queue. A devolved administration would be able to deal with that situation better.

Then there was also Royal Ascot. On the biggest Ascot day, we Scots had the House of Commons chamber to ourselves to debate the Scottish economy. This was no prize allocation of time – it was a convenient arrangement for the English Tory members to go off to races, enjoy the parties, then come back at 10 p.m. and vote down the motion or amendments tabled by the Scottish Labour majority.

Both in meeting the pressure from the SNP and on its own merits, a devolution policy was now required, with a Scottish assembly equipped with sufficient powers to let us tackle Scotland's problems. Although I had written that memo in 1972 and aired the idea of Scotland in Europe in the House of Commons, the British part of my personality was still present. In 1974, I was still seeking a solution that would reconcile my 'nationalist' leanings within the context of the UK and the 'internationalism' that implied. It is a conundrum that many in today's Labour Party in Scotland still struggle with.

However, on devolution, there was a problem – the party in Scotland. It didn't want it. Leading, influential figures like Tam Dalyell, Robin Cook, Allan Campbell McLean and Brian Wilson, spoke for the majority, utterly opposed to an assembly. The UK leadership probably agreed with them but saw it as an absolute necessity to commit to an assembly if the SNP tide was to be stemmed.

The bitterness between the unionist and devolution wings broke out at the Scottish party conference held in March 1974 in Ayr. A devolution motion was defeated among boos, shouts, personal attacks and pretty poor speeches, my own included. Tam Dalyell had been at the rostrum before me, suggesting that Scottish people were more interested in beer, bingo and football than the issues which would engage a Scottish assembly. I lost my temper at the insult to working-class people and made the worst speech of my life. The one good speech was given by the MP, John Robertson, who stated the democratic case for Scots handling their own affairs.

At the civic reception that night tempers had not cooled. Willie Ross went out of his way to be woundingly insulting to John and we devolutionists left in despair before there were any more ugly scenes. We stuck to the task, however, and a key man in our efforts was Alex

Neil, then Labour's Scottish research officer. We also had Bob Brown, a well-respected senior journalist, who was acting as Labour's unpaid press officer, and Jimmy Frame, another journalist, from the *Edinburgh Evening News*. Chris Baur, *The Scotsman*'s political editor, was also very helpful in private, while maintaining his journalistic integrity in his fair reporting of all sides.

Alex Neil kept us up to date on all that Ross and others were doing to prevent a devolution commitment in the coming election manifesto. Bob Brown undertook to write a number of pro-devolution articles for the Scottish papers under the name of James Alexander. So, in Alex, we had an ally in the National Executive Committee (NEC) in London, more on the grounds of expediency, rather than principle. With Wilson agreeing, the National Executive issued a policy statement committing the Labour government to creating an assembly and the Scottish Executive was expected to endorse it.

On 22 June, the Scottish Executive met but only eleven attended. The rest were at home or in the pub watching Scotland play Yugoslavia in the World Cup. The vote to reject devolution and defy the UK leadership was 6–5 – crisis. The only way that vote could be reversed was with a special conference. To get a pro-devolution result, the trade unions' bloc votes had to be mobilised and this was done by Alex Kitson. The conference met in Dalintober Street Co-operative Hall, Glasgow, on 16 September. Alex Kitson's fix carried the day by a 4–1 majority. I would say that a majority of the membership did not believe in devolution and felt they had been steamrollered into it. Dalintober Street was to play a part, later, when the 1979 referendum on an assembly failed.

From his inside position, Alex Neil was able to tell us that, in spite of the Dalintober vote, Willie Ross and his Minister of State, Bruce Millan, in charge of the campaign, were determined that the most prominent advocates of the assembly policy, John Mackintosh and me, would be excluded from press conferences, radio and television programmes and party political broadcasts.

John Mackintosh, Professor of Politics at Edinburgh University, who was to win back his Berwick and East Lothian seat in October, was a long-time supporter of devolution, as were Donald Dewar, who at the time was without a seat in Parliament, and Bob Maclennan, Labour (and later Liberal Democrat) MP for Caithness and Sutherland. North Lanarkshire MP and later Labour Party leader, John Smith's name is closely attached to devolution but, like me, he was very much a late convert to the importance of the constitutional question.

As support for the SNP continued to surge, my fellow Scottish Labour MPs felt the pressure. John Geddes in Irvine, who printed all my election material, told me that a number of Labour MPs had come down to his print works, asked to see my election leaflets and had copied the material into their own election addresses. I remember John telling me, 'They hate your guts but like your stuff.'

Then as now, London rules in the Labour Party in Scotland when it wants to. London HQ entered and overruled Ross's edict banishing us from any official role in the campaign. John Mackintosh, George Foulkes, who was standing for Edinburgh Pentland in October 1974 but would lose to Malcolm Rifkind, the economic journalist Helen Liddell and I were all committed to devolution and, in the last week of the campaign, we were picked to take part in a prime-time Scottish party-political broadcast. There was no script. We were told to make a strong case for a Scottish assembly as set out in the UK National Executive's policy. That had been issued, in both London and Glasgow, on 5 September 1974, and, on page 9, it stated:

> The Scottish and Welsh Assemblies will therefore participate in the decisions of how best to promote their development, for instance by drawing up their own economic plans along the lines set out in 'Labour's Programme 1973'. *Substantial executive powers in the trade and industry fields* will be transferred from central government to enable the Assemblies to make decisions in the light of their own needs in the promotion of employment and industrial regeneration. (emphasis added)

John Mackintosh was the anchor man and the chap from the London HQ who was in charge thought it was 'brilliant' but said it would have to be cleared by London before it could be released for broadcast, as it set out definite policy positions for the assembly. It was approved and broadcast. In a survey of the public, done during the election, the broadcast was seen as highly influential in how people finally voted. Here are some key passages:

> JOHN MACKINTOSH: In effect, we are advocating a directly elected group of directly elected Members of Parliament sitting in Edinburgh, who will control Scottish health, housing, education, roads, agriculture and fisheries: all the matters that are particular and special to Scotland will be under their direct control. And I think it is important too that they will have

certain powers of taxation and revenue allocated to them so they can choose what is most important to spend our money on.

HELEN LIDDELL: Yes, and it's also very important that they'll have control of the Scottish Development Agency, which the Labour Party have said they will set up. The Scottish Development Agency will be a very powerful economic weapon, designed at bringing jobs to Scotland and it will be primed by North Sea oil so that the benefits of oil go to the ordinary working people of Scotland and build a new economy.

JIM SILLARS: Well, I think trade and industry are very important elements of the argument for devolution and I think the Scottish Parliament could more easily adapt, and better adapt, United Kingdom policies to suit Scottish circumstances.

The broadsheet election newspaper produced by the party promised a 'Powerhouse Scotland,' so our broadcast was dead in line with the new party policy.

When the first White Paper, empty of economic content, was published in 1975, I and several others felt we had no choice but to leave the Labour Party. Alex Neil, Bob Brown, the journalist and writer Neal Ascherson, journalist Jimmy Frame, Professor Joe Farrell, the educationalist Professor Lindsay Paterson, Colin Boyd, then a law student at the University of Edinburgh and now Lord Boyd, a senator of the College of Justice, and Charlie Gordon, a Strathclyde and Glasgow City councillor who later became a Labour MSP. Perhaps those who read the transcript and statement now will understand the sense of betrayal that led to our departure.

The election was held on 10 October. At the UK level, the numbers of seats won were:

Labour 319
Tory 277
Liberal 13

When the other parties were taken into account, Labour had an overall majority of only three. The results in seats and percentage of vote in Scotland were:

Labour 41 – 36.3%
Tory 18 – 24.7%
SNP 11 – 30.4%
Liberal 3 – 8.3%

The results in numbers of votes cast in South Ayrshire were:

Labour 22,329
SNP 7,851
Tory 7,402

The SNP's Roger Mullin, who became a good friend and was MP for Kirkcaldy and Cowdenbeath from 2015 to 2017, polled almost the same number of votes as Sam Purdie had at the by-election four years before.

Labour lost no seats to the SNP but the Nationalists' total went up to eleven (five from the Tories) and their share of the votes soared. The Labour policy of promising an assembly with powers would now have to be delivered or, as everyone generally thought to be the case, the SNP would come for us.

Threatened as never before by that result, Scottish Labour MPs showed commendable zeal for early action on the assembly pledge. The Scottish Labour Group was called to a special meeting in Glasgow on 17 October. It was not so much a meeting as a stampede in the direction of devolution, with the group making clear, at a press conference, that there was to be no 'backsliding' and emphasising their commitment by saying the 'Scottish Parliament should be operating within two years'. Tam Dalyell (yes, Tam!), the group chairman, declared, 'Clearly, the government and the Labour Party would be brought into disrepute if such a body was created "with no teeth".'

But, when the panic subsided, my Scottish MP comrades backslid in quick order. The rank and file reasserted themselves and the unions were not willing to do another Dalintober Street bloc vote bulldozing at the Scottish party's conference in the spring of 1975. There, a resolution demanding economic powers for the assembly was defeated. During the debate, I was attacked several times as the turncoat co-author of 'Don't Butcher Scotland's Future'. My riposte was that yes, I would have to live with that, but the party would have to live with the commitments it had made in October 1974.

By then, I had done my year as chairman of the Tribune Group and, in that capacity, had been required to have dealings with Harold Wilson.

My joyous view of him the night he was elected leader had long since given way to an understanding that he was an unprincipled, slippery customer who was not to be trusted.

I knew, given my prominence in the October campaign, that I would be offered a job. I was certain it would not be one intended to advance my position within the party but to bury me and stop my involvement in devolution. I was both too Left wing and too vocal in my demands for real power to be allocated to the assembly. I was right. I thought Wilson would offer me something at the bottom ministerial level at environment or social security, where I could be safely sent around the country opening waterworks or giving speeches to the third sector.

My friend Harry Ewing, MP for Stirling, Falkirk and Grangemouth and a key member of the devolution group, phoned the day after the October election to say he had been offered and accepted the post as junior minister at the Scottish Office. I was happy about that because he was deeply committed to the policy of an assembly with powers. I then waited for the Downing Street phone call, which came through at about 6 p.m. I was offered a job at social security. I said it wasn't my cup of tea and declined. Wilson asked me if that meant I would not work with him. I replied that I was honoured by the offer and sorry that I could not accept it and, of course, I would work with the government but I wanted to concentrate on getting the assembly.

It was well known that I had been offered a job by Wilson but, in the 1979 general election, Labour said I was a liar – that no job was ever offered – and produced a statement from Bob Mellish, Labour chief whip, to confirm that. The question of whether I was a liar or not was cleared up later in the 1988 Govan by-election.

The October election produced a Labour majority of only three but, if the Liberals were included, due to their long-standing support of devolution, there was sufficient majority to see an assembly established. I shared digs in London with Alex Eadie and Harry Ewing at Alex's son's house in Dulwich. I decided early on not to ask Harry to show me Cabinet committee or background papers on the assembly or to tell me off the record what key decisions were being made. In retrospect, this was a stupid thing for me to have done but governments leak and I wanted to make sure that nothing I might say could be traced back to Harry. My confidence in Harry was absolute – so much so that, in a TV debate with Margo, she in Glasgow, me in London, I refuted her forecast that a Labour assembly would be without real powers, by declaring my trust in him.

As well as devolution, there was, again, the issue of the EEC. Wilson, in opposition, had given in to pressure from the Left led by Tony Benn and committed a Labour government to a referendum on staying in or leaving. It took place in June 1975. The question set was 'Yes' for staying in or 'No' for coming out. Barbara Castle, Tony Benn and Michael Foot were the leading Cabinet ministers arguing for 'No', as were more minor figures like Neil Kinnock, Dennis Skinner and I. We hadn't a hope. The entire establishment – political parties, TUC, CBI, Institute of Directors, think tanks and the media – lined up for 'Yes' and its formal campaign was lavishly funded. In *Yes to Europe!*, published in 2018, the author, Robert Saunders, notes that the 'No' side raised only £8,000 while 'Yes' raised £2 million. That cash fuelled a powerful organisation and the first Project Fear – leave the EEC and the UK will enter a world of unmitigated disaster. The 'No' side had no nationwide organisation and carried an air of defeat from the start. When Barbara and Tony lost in a televised debate at the Oxford University Union, any hope we had was gone.

In addition to the imbalanced campaign funds, there was also the intervention of the European Commission. I was surprised one Friday morning, on picking up my copy of *The Cumnock Chronicle*, to find its front page and several on the inside had been given over to comparing the cost of living in Norway, outside the EEC, with our own, within it. The price of beer being higher in Norway was the leading piece, with other calamities listed if the people were daft enough to leave the EEC. I asked the editor why he was suddenly involving the paper in national affairs – he and lots of other local newspaper editors had been taken on a 'fact finding' visit to Norway, as guests of the European Commission.

In a debate in the Ayrshire mining village of Mauchline, I lost to my Tory next-door neighbour, George Younger. After I had stated my case for out, George turned on the fear – if they voted my way on Thursday, by the Friday, no more coal or steel could be sold into EEC countries. It was a breathtaking lie but, no matter what I said in reply about the contracts that had been signed guaranteeing continuity of exports, I could see I was speaking to a terrified audience who had stopped listening to me.

George Younger's lie was mild compared to others. Robert Saunders' *Yes to Europe!* records Sir Nicholas Fairbairn, Tory MP for Kinross and Western Perthshire, warning that a vote to leave the EEC would mean 'the closing of schools and hospitals and the stopping of roads, railways and mines'; Ted Heath claimed there would be food shortages; and *The Glasgow Herald* stated that coming out of the EEC 'would be tantamount to national suicide' (p. 361). Over four decades later, nothing much has changed. In 2016, a leaked report, alleged to be a government one, forecast the same shortages of food and medicines and much else besides the day UK left the EU.

By early 1975, the doubts and hesitations, as outlined in my personal memo and in the 1972 speech, were giving way to a more definite, concrete position. In a Commons debate on devolution on 4 February 1975, when the thought of leaving the Labour Party would have seemed impossible, I said this:

> If we are locked inside the EEC I would not argue that Scotland should come out. This, perhaps, is some comfort to my hon. Friend the Member for West Lothian [Tam Dalyell]. I believe that we should retain our close links with the other people inside the British Isles but I would certainly argue that it would then be in the interests of the Scottish people to have direct nation-State membership of the Community. If we were foolish enough to continue inside the EEC it might be time to write a new verse to an auld sang. [Hansard had it 'old song'.]

Knowing that my side was heading for defeat in the EEC vote, sure that, once the result was in, the SNP would leap upon the logic of Scotland becoming an independent state within the EEC, I wanted to forestall them and have a Labour source, not a purely nationalist one, for what I thought would now become obvious to everyone. With the help of Bob Brown, in the two weeks before the vote, I drafted a paper setting out the logic of Scotland in Europe as a member state. A few days after the result, I had held a press conference, setting out this new idea. My assessment of the SNP was wrong. Nothing came from them. Worse, at the press conference I might as well have been talking in Swahili. The journalists couldn't get it. It was an idea well before its time. When I got down to the House of Commons that afternoon, it was no different. Fellow Scottish MPs who had never understood the speech I made back in 1972, shook their heads and wondered what I was going on about. Even my close friends Alex Eadie and Harry Ewing were puzzled by why I was making a fuss about something that seemed outside the boundary of practical politics. That was the reality – it was an idea in my head only and, if I tried to push it, I could lose the influence I had within the Scottish Parliamentary Labour Party on the immediate priority of getting a powerful assembly in place.

*

Before the EEC campaigning in March and April 1975, I had travelled to the USA with Neil Kinnock for what we termed 'the CIA tour'. Every major country has programmes, all expenses paid, for MPs from other states to visit, meet their politicians and learn more about the country and its people. The US had one for up-and-coming young MPs from the UK. A visit lasting a full month was on offer but we opted for three weeks. We could go anywhere we liked, with only one compulsory stipulation that, for the first five days, we had to be Washington DC for meetings with senators, Congress members and others in the political sphere. Before we left the UK, Neil had deliberately revealed to a national newspaper the names of CIA agents in the UK but the trip was not cancelled.

At the Washington dinner parties and meetings, the talk was still about Nixon's resignation and the Ford administration. Few were polite about President Ford, depicting him as thick. All were intrigued by the election of Margaret Thatcher as leader of the Tory Party. No one knew her. We had a bizarre meeting with the chairman of the Senate Foreign Relations Committee, an old Southerner. The USA was heading for a humiliating eviction from Vietnam but here was this old man taking us over to a huge map of South Vietnam, saying he was convinced that the South Vietnamese military, with US help with equipment, would still be able to hold the Mekong Delta. It was pure fantasy and we felt sorry for his staff.

For me, there was an interesting meeting in the State Department when I discovered that Billy Wolfe, leader of the SNP, had been there a couple of weeks before. According to the US officials, he told them that, on the day Scotland won its independence, the Americans and the British would immediately be told to get out of the nuclear submarine base at Faslane. To my surprise, the US officials seemed to take this seriously. I was opposed to the base there too but this was a delicate subject in the days of the Cold War and not a sensible hostage to fortune to throw in front of a US government that would not hesitate to employ the CIA against the SNP. I was right. During the key period before the 1979 referendum on the assembly, the US Consul General in Edinburgh was a retired CIA officer, who departed as soon as the referendum was over and was replaced by a career diplomat.

Neil and I represented mining constituencies so it was from Washington to West Virginia that we went to meet miners and their national union president, who carried a gun. He needed to. The former union president was in jail for corruption. In the election to fill his place, the anti-corruption candidate was assassinated. The man now president had been his aide, stepping in as last man standing.

We attended a local branch meeting which was being held to discuss the latest pay deal the new president had negotiated. It was obviously a bad one. That was when I discovered Neil's romanticism – a facet of his personality that helped make him the loquacious speaker he became but one that was also a weakness. He could get carried away and that is precisely what happened at the now infamous Sheffield rally in 1992, widely reckoned to have been one of the reasons he lost the election. Neil got carried away by the union president's bravery, talking of him as a 'saint'. As a former trade union official, unlike Neil, I could admire the man's personal courage but, as that branch meeting demonstrated, he was a poor leader.

Later, this romantic side of Neil came out again when we took part in a US government-sponsored seminar at Harvard with a group of trade unionists from what were then known as 'Third World countries'. Neil expressed his views on how trade unions were going to develop in their poor countries, with workers heroically building solidarity so that they would be able to take on the employers. It was brilliant emotional rhetoric but nonsense. My contribution caused the discussion to develop into a fierce debate. I poured cold water on Neil's words. For me, no Third World country was going to mirror how the Industrial Revolution had created Britain's working class – that was how the basis of our solidarity was born, how it grew and how it led, in turn, to trade union organisation. In many developing countries, child labour was built into the economy, with tribal, caste and other religious divisions also at play – all were deep rooted and all posed obstacles to the kind of worker solidarity that Neil was so sure was coming.

13

Leaving the Labour Party

I came back from America to Scotland to take part in the EEC referendum and, once that was over, I was looking forward to the publication of the devolution White Paper that would set out the assembly's powers and then be translated into a Bill. I was relaxed because of the faith I had in Harry Ewing. Although he was a junior minister, I believed his experience with nationalism in Scotland and the reputation he had earned as a committed devolutionist would make him the equal in political weight to the more senior Cabinet members who, along with him, were on the committee drafting the White Paper. I should have known better. That was my second big mistake – the first having been my failure to ask Harry for inside information.

I made another mistake in the run-up to the White Paper. The SNP group in Parliament had put down a motion for debate that called upon the government to commit placing the Scottish Development Agency (SDA) under control of the assembly. There was consternation in the Scottish Labour group about how to vote. It was decided to vote against on the grounds that it was premature to make such a decision. I was in a quandary because control of the SDA was, in my view, central to the powers of the assembly and it was one specific power that the party political broadcast had identified as coming the assembly's way. It was not politically possible for me to vote with the SNP but I should have abstained. I didn't and the local SNP Cumnock branch secretary, John Ferguson, justifiably made a telling attack on me in *The Cumnock Chronicle*. I was in no position to answer. Had I abstained and argued with some others to do the same, the government would have been alerted to a real problem if they did not include the SDA in the assembly's powers. My failure to do what was required sent out the wrong signal.

Harry had promised to let me see the White Paper on the day before its publication so that I could be ready to weigh in with support because, on the evening of its launch, we were both going to appear on a special television programme on the BBC. Before I went over to pick a copy up from his office, I received a phone call from Stewart Maclachlan at the *Daily Record*. He asked if I had read it – the press all had an embargoed copy by this time. I said I was on my way to get it. There was a loud groaning from Stewart who said, 'It's terrible.' I replied that it couldn't be that bad.

I went over to Harry's office in the Commons and took the White Paper, 'Our Changing Democracy: Devolution to Scotland and Wales', back to my office, where I sat down to read what I was certain was going to be something to shout about. It was the opposite. This was no powerhouse assembly, free to tackle Scotland's problems and armed with sufficient economic power to do so. Its whole tone was of deep distrust of that very idea and it was more concerned with constraining and restraining than letting Scottish ideas run free in a Scottish context.

It made the secretary of state into the equivalent of a powerful governor general who was able to 'intervene' when Westminster thought the assembly policy 'would be seriously harmful'. There was only to be 'influence' in respect of the SDA, through its ability to appoint half of its board, while the secretary of state appointed its chairman. The Highlands and Islands Development Board was not free to decide on funding for 'industry, fishing and agriculture' and Westminster would 'lay down a system of guidelines and cash limits on individual projects', while decisions on major industrial projects were to be decided by the secretary of state. It stated that 'powers over land must be qualified'. There was to be no transfer of any power from UK departments on industry and commerce, only consultation. The assembly was to have a budget of just over £2 billion for roads, housing, schools and hospitals but, being totally devoid of any economic power, it lacked any ability to produce policies on jobs.

John Robertson, MP for Paisley, who became a founder member of the Scottish Labour Party (SLP), brilliantly described the White Paper as making the 'Assembly more closely caged than a lion at the zoo'. I was shattered. My trust in Harry had been foolish. I had expected too much of him as a junior minister. He had obviously been brushed aside by Cabinet heavyweights who knew they had to produce something but were determined that the 'something' was as empty of content as they could get away with.

I took the White Paper back over to Harry and told him that I would denounce it. Our friendship did not break but I never put my trust in him again on devolution. From his office, I went down towards the

Members' Lobby, where I met David Lambie, MP for Central Ayrshire. He looked at me and said 'Is it that bad?' I said worse than bad. That night on television I refused to support the White Paper.

I found out that Stewart Maclachlan and I were not alone. The reaction in Scotland was the same as mine but multiplied many times – anger and the feeling that Labour had diddled the Scots at the election and made cynical false promises. I felt a special responsibility because of that party political broadcast. Had I sold the people a pup? I thought of people like my father, who had always put his absolute trust in the Labour Party, and how that trust had been abused.

The final straw came on 2 and 3 December, when the Scottish Labour group met to discuss the White Paper, to be followed the next day by the whole UK Parliamentary Labour Party. On the evening meeting on the second, John Robertson and I were given a verbal going-over by the whole group with one exception, Jimmy Dempsey, MP for Coatbridge, who surprised them all by saying that I was right about the commitments we had made in the manifesto, in the party's statement on 5 September and on the broadcast that John Mackintosh had anchored. Unfortunately, John was not present that night. The group backed the White Paper.

It was how they backed it that was outrageous. Hugh Brown, MP for Glasgow Provan, said he was not going to be bound by 'these wee bits of paper' (the election promises) and Norman Buchan claimed that the party had given no commitments on economic power. Next day, the PLP was very happy with the Scottish group decision. My despair and anger grew. The press was full of speculation about me leaving the party. As the PLP meeting went on, I was coming quickly to the conclusion that I could not remain a member. Dick Mabon, MP for Greenock, urged me not to leave, saying, if I did so, it would damage the chances of getting a Bill through. He was correct because, by taking myself outside the party, I was doing three things: firstly, I was eliminating any role and influence I had within the party and destroying the pull I had within the trade union movement; secondly, a number of my colleagues would be glad to be rid of me; and, thirdly, any potential I had to lead demands for change in the coming legislation would be destroyed.

Alex Neil, as research officer in Scotland, had a great deal to do with the pro-devolution statements issued by the UK party and in drawing up the manifesto. He was well liked, had made his mark not only in Scotland but also at the UK level where, along with Cabinet ministers, he was part of UK policy meetings. Everyone knew he would go far. But his politics were anchored in principle. More than anyone else, he knew just how deeply the Labour Party had committed itself to a powerful assembly and how much of a betrayal the White Paper was. He resigned and was not the only one to do so.

I take nothing away from our adherence to principle but Alex, John Robertson, Bob Brown, Jimmy Frame and I were guilty of being swamped by emotion and suffering a rush of blood to the head. This is said in hindsight. The sensible thing would have been to sit down, objectively analyse our position and weigh up our strength inside the Labour movement in Scotland. The government had been rocked by the adverse reaction. Looking back, through much more experienced eyes, it is probable that, had we remained in the Labour Party and fought for amendments to get at least some more powers, we would probably have got the people to pass the 40 per cent rule and bring an assembly into being. I did have a powerbase within the party, especially with the unions, and I could have used it to put pressure on the government to yield here and there. And, from inside the Labour machine, Alex Neil, with the excellent relations he had built up with Cabinet ministers, especially with the deputy leader Ted Short, would also have been in a position to exert influence. But, by causing a split with Labour, not only did I destroy that powerbase, I also allowed the scene to be set for the disunity and bitterness that did so much damage to the Yes side in the 1979 referendum.

But boiling anger reigned within us and out of the Labour Party we went.

It is pure speculation of course but, if we had remained in and helped achieve an elected assembly in 1979, independence might have been seen, in the terrible times ahead, as the only way to free Scotland from Mrs Thatcher's policies. It is one of the ifs of history.

Whatever fault may be laid at our door on quitting the party, none of us, as far as I know, ever regretted setting up the Scottish Labour Party (SLP). Indeed now, I regularly meet people who tell me we were, sadly, years ahead of our time and that a Labour Party in Scotland, fully independent of the UK one, is what is needed because the present one is still seen as, and is, no more than a branch of the UK national party.

Leaving the South Ayrshire Labour Party put me in a dreadful emotional state and, on 10 December, I wrote a long letter of explanation to our full-time agent, Jim Tanner, prior to the constituency party meeting on 20 December:

> There is need to explain further to you my reasons for this step. I am sick at heart and in the depth of despair because of

the twisting and turning and cynicism shown by my Labour colleagues with regard to the matter of our pledge to the people on the powers and status of the Assembly.

You know from your own experience that our election material was lifted in both the February and October elections by a number of Labour candidates who are now MPs.

You know the demands that were made for me to be used as a speaker and instrument for devolutionary enforcement for various candidates during both elections, especially the October one.

What sickens me is that the twisting and turning betrays a fact: we in the Labour Party were insincere in the promises we made. The experience I went through on Tuesday night, 2 December, when Labour MPs were dismissing our documents and statements as 'wee bits of paper', shows that the worst feature of our performance is that we believe the people are stupid enough to believe anything, and so we can say anything and get out of it later.

I value idealism and integrity in politics. I know that idealism must be tempered by what is practicable when we come to formulate policies prior to elections but once made the integrity of an election pledge must be inviolate. That is patently not the case with the Assembly, a matter I regard as of the utmost importance.

The letter went on to explain:

I have tried not to get the Assembly out of perspective. There are other things of importance. But I believe this issue transcends all else in its importance to the people we claim to represent. If their needs are to be met, especially in the industrial and job sector of activity, we must have substantial power vested in the Assembly. I believe now that what might have been acceptable two years ago is no longer on, and will need to be vastly improved upon. How that is to be achieved is something I am struggling with now.

On 16 December John Robertson issued this short statement:

If the Labour Party in Scotland accepts what is being done then I will be faced with what will be for me very grave decisions.

The loyalties and hopes of a lifetime are not to be discarded easily or lightly, indeed that piece of surgery is likely to have fatal results.

I am not yet without hope but time is running out. What gesture I can make to political honesty will not disturb the still waters of the Scottish Labour Party, yet however modest my contribution may be I have to make peace with myself and I find the need for decision very pressing.

When I finally told the South Ayrshire constituency party that I was leaving and would not stand for Labour again, my local reputation was quickly transformed from that of being a good MP, to one whose uselessness had been covered up. That was only the start of the character assassination. At a subsequent Labour conference, without naming me, Willie Ross put the knife in when he said there was a 'special hell' for traitors. I found that the party of brotherly love could be vicious not only to 'traitors' like me but could target family as well. I was said to be suffering from a nervous breakdown due to my son being 'maladjusted' but he was just a normal young boy.

In January 1976, Alex Neil, Bob Brown, John Robertson, Joe Farrell and I, along with others, like Neal Ascherson, Charlie Gordon, Isobel Hilton, Bob and Isobel Tait and Bill and Isabel McCrorie, were key to forming the SLP with a view to fighting for a better form of devolution. Labour accused us of having intended doing this all along. That was untrue. We were totally unprepared and that fault led to us being wide open to infiltration by the ultra-Left, the International Marxist Group (IMG), who saw the chance to have two MPs to manipulate and control. These were not proletarians but well-funded middle-class people mostly up from London.

I can never prove it but I always suspected that members of groups like the IMG, while genuine in their views, were useful idiots for MI5 and Special Branch. Numerous such groups have demonstrated time and again that they will ultimately damage or destroy any organisation to which they attach themselves. One characteristic of these ultra-Left groups is their deep distrust of anyone in a leadership position, who they always see as a potential betrayer of the cause. The result is splitting – and splitting is their way of life – as one faction claims to be 'purer' than the other.

These ultra-Left groups may not be the pawns of MI5 or the CIA as some of us believe but they do play a destructive role in the socialist movement and could not be more 'useful idiots' if they were. The ones who attached themselves to the SLP were well funded, claiming to be financially supported by an anonymous millionaire. I never believed it. After the SLP collapsed, I was invited to the US embassy to a discussion on how it happened, with the ambassador present. They were very interested in the IMG. The effect they had on the SLP was to exhaust us, and finally to be instrumental in blowing us to smithereens at our first conference in Stirling. Those of us who were left limped on as best we could to the 1979 election in the hope that I could hold South Ayrshire, and thus have the basis of a second go.

But the effect of the IMG was not the reason the SLP failed. Labour, with its solid backing from the trade unions, was structurally strong and, once the initial angry reaction in Scotland to the White Paper wound down, there was no space for the SLP to develop and grow to a point where we had a strong enough national organisation that could seriously challenge it. The SLP did have branches and we won council seats in South Ayrshire but we were thin on the ground.

Our first electoral test was in the Darnley Glasgow council by-election in 1976 with Joe Farrell as candidate. We got 15 per cent of the vote and something similar in a regional by-election in Irvine. But they proved a high-water mark. The death blow to our hopes came in the 1978 Garscadden by-election, which saw Labour's Donald Dewar returned to Parliament and the SLP's Sheena Waldron getting only 1.6 per cent of the vote.

When I departed from Labour in 1976, I anticipated demands for a by-election and went to see Bob Mellish, the chief whip. By-election dates were, by convention, in the hands of the party holding the seat. There was no time limit. When Dick Taverne resigned his seat in Lincoln over his opposition to the party's position on the EEC (he was for staying in), Labour kept it empty for six months, intending him to carry the blame for non-representation. It didn't work. I, unlike Taverne, had no money and would not be able to sustain the family over six months without an income. No one would employ me if they thought in six months I was going to fight an election.

I told Bob I would resign and make way for a by-election, provided I received, in writing, a guarantee that Labour would move the writ to no later than three months after my resignation – three months being the longest time I could have held out financially. Behave yourself was his reply. But it was important to put my willingness on public record. I was reported in *The Scotsman* on 9 February 1976 as saying: 'The Cabinet just need to request me to have a by-election.'

*

Much later, when Labour thought it had the measure of the SLP, I came under constant pressure to resign. At every surgery in Cumnock, I was visited by a delegation from the NUM demanding my resignation. One delegation came to London and cornered me in my office for about two hours over that one demand. I finally put a stop to it when, pointing to the one Communist among them, I asked if they would be taking the same line if I had left Labour to join the Communist Party. Silence.

Those years, from 1976 to 1979, saw me in a dreadful state psychologically and medically. I was steeped in the Labour Party and the trade-union movement. There was a special place for traitors in the party's song 'The Red Flag' and the hostility directed at John Robertson and me was very unpleasant. It was lucky for me that there were only newspaper reports of critical speeches and remarks and letters to the editor and not Twitter in those days. But what was dished out to me had an effect. When I spoke in the House of Commons, several former colleagues would bait me. It was so bad one night that when I went up to the Hansard offices to have my speech checked, the shorthand reporter told me he had found it very exciting to watch. I told him it wasn't exciting to be the bear in the bear pit.

I was under extreme pressure. Along with Alex Neil and Joe Farrell, I had to try to rebuild the SLP, keep up our campaign touring the country talking at public meetings, take part in the devolution debates in Parliament and hold my usual constituency surgeries. Very few in the constituency party had left with me but two who did, Bill and Isabel McCrorie, were rocks. They not only set up an SLP office in the constituency but started fundraising and generally bolstered me when I was feeling very depressed. Bill became my election agent and Isobel did a power of work helping him. I owe both a debt that can never be repaid. Janet Ferguson was another great help with organisation in the constituency.

But the agony of having left the party I was politically born into never left me. My marriage was falling apart, my health was suffering and I developed ulcers. But there could be no let-up and no sign of political or personal weakness. One consequence, and benefit, of that terrible experience is that, after some time of being a target for abuse, I developed one of the thickest skins in politics, to the point where I did not, and still do not, care what is said about me, no matter how vile. Not arrogance. I know who I am as my own most severe critic.

*

As well as being a disaster for me, the White Paper and the Bill were disastrous for the government too. Its mistake was having Scotland and Wales together in a single Bill, making it one of many clauses, thereby giving lots of opportunity for amendments. As a constitutional measure, the Bill was taken with the whole House constituting a committee. This opened the way for filibuster – not just from the Tories but from Labour MPs as well. An assembly may have been an election promise but that did not matter at all. They did not want it and they would kill the Bill if they could.

Today, Bills in the House of Commons are timetabled to the needs of a family-friendly Parliament. This now gives the government tight control over the legislative agenda. That was not the case in the 1970s. If governments found the opposition was being too successful in holding up a Bill, a guillotine motion was tabled and voted on. This set out a strict timetable for discussion on each clause. The guillotine was always controversial. Governments were loath to use it, knowing the opposition would kick up a huge fuss and accuse them of gagging Parliament and a full day had to be devoted to a debating it. That was bad enough for normal Bills but, when the guillotine had to be applied to a major constitutional one, which might transcend party lines, the government was open to outrage and attacks from more than one side of the House. This was one such Bill.

When the Labour government tabled the guillotine motion, on paper it had a majority. It could count on the votes of those who had supported the Bill at second reading – Labour, Liberals, SNP, Plaid Cymru and SLP. If it had the support of Labour MPs, the Liberals, the SNP group, and Plaid Cymru, John Robertson and me – all declared supporters of devolution – the government would have enough votes to win a guillotine vote. Lose it and the Bill was dead.

The potential line-up of votes was:

For	Against
Labour 319	Tory 277
Liberal 13	Ulster MPs 9
SNP 11	
Plaid Cymru 2	
SLP 2	

Although their policy was federalism, the Liberals did favour devolution and had voted for the Bill at its second reading. But their leader, David Steel, had other priorities. He wanted his party to come in from the fringes where its small numbers placed it and to be seen as being close to the centre of government and having influence on it. That would enhance Liberal standing and improve their chances at the next election – a vote for them would no longer be a 'wasted' vote. The Liberals wanted a government crisis and the way to get it was through a No vote on the guillotine. Steel had no way of knowing whether Labour MPs threatening to revolt would actually do it but, for him, it was a chance worth taking. In the guillotine vote on 22 February 1977, there were 283 votes in favour of the guillotine and 312 against. The Liberals, Tories and Ulster Unionists were joined by 22 Labour MPs, while 23 others abstained.

As Labour faced its crisis, in stepped Steel to offer a Lib–Lab pact – not a coalition but a pact under which the Liberals would be consulted by the government on a day-to-day basis – thus showing the public, as Steel intended, that they counted in the power structure of the country. The irony was that little could be seen of its usefulness. After Steel had been in to negotiate with the prime minister, the buzz in Labour ranks was that the PM, Jim Callaghan, never expected it to be so easy. But that didn't matter. What was important for the Liberals was the appearance not the substance.

This is a chapter of Liberal history that is little known about – how they took a cold calculated decision to sink devolution for the sake of party interest. But they alone were not responsible for the defeat of the government guillotine. The Bill had gone but Labour's nationalist problem remained. So we got a new Bill – one just for Scotland, with fewer clauses and, therefore, less open to filibuster. But Labour MPs still had a shot in their locker – a new clause for a referendum with a rule that 40 per cent of the total electorate had to vote Yes. If not, the Act would compel the government to table an order to repeal it, in total, with a vote for or against the Order in the House of Commons.

John Mackintosh, Margo MacDonald and I had formed a Yes group. We had arranged a press conference in Edinburgh the morning after the 40 per cent vote. We made a bad mistake. Thinking it would be good, on this occasion, for us not to be at the front, we brought in three non-politicians as a way of showing how wide the support for the assembly was. These three people had never taken a press conference before. It did not go well and they got a rough handling from the journalists. As the three of us sat at the back of the room, we began to realise that neither the case for the assembly nor case against the 40 per cent rule was getting over. That mistake lost us the opportunity to underline what an underhand measure that 40 per cent rule was. The referendum would be held using an old electoral register that had been compiled almost six months before. The names of those who had since died and those who had moved house without reregistering, which was often the case, were still on it. Although they could not vote, those whose names were on the register remained part of the total count of electors against which the 40 per cent would be judged. In that total, of course, were also those who would abstain. By not fronting the press conference ourselves, we had missed the opportunity to drive home to the public the stratagem being used against the policy of the Labour government by its own MPs. We couldn't admit we were worried by the 40 per cent barrier but we were.

My stepmother put her finger on it when she said to me, 'Jim, with that move, they don't intend it ever to happen.' That sense of defeat which she picked up was to stay with the Yes side throughout the campaign.

14

The 1979 Referendum

The referendum campaign was fought in late 1978 and early 1979, in the worst possible circumstances. Labour was split, with MPs like Robin Cook and Tam Dalyell and the influential figure, Brian Wilson, openly campaigning for a No vote, whilst others simply sat on their hands. Norman Buchan MP was an example. When a daily newspaper asked every Scottish MP how they were voting, he declared that, because it was a secret ballot, he wasn't saying. Sitting on the hands was the tactic of Labour activists, getting revenge for the Dalintober Street conference. There were instances of SNP members giving out Labour Yes leaflets because the local Labour branch refused to do so.

We were faced with the prospect of campaigning for a weak assembly, far from the 1974 October promise – the very thing that drove me to leave the party – but it was the only one on offer. The choice was stark – vote against it, with those who were totally opposed to the whole idea of devolution, and it would be rendered stone dead. By then, the rush of blood I had at the time of the White Paper had long gone and I was more able to view things objectively. The assembly on the ballot paper was the only one available so I campaigned Yes.

I was not unaware of the irony in doing so especially when one major figure, with great influence, advised a No vote because the assembly lacked sufficient powers and that, by rejecting it, we would get a better one. That was Sir Alec Douglas-Home, a former Tory PM. I do not recall, after the vote, him ever demanding that more powerful assembly.

There was no single Yes campaign group. I was toxic to many across the political spectrum, including Labour people who were pro-Yes. My involvement in the group put together with John Mackintosh and Margo MacDonald meant that such people would not join. I offered to resign and step away but that was refused because there were so few people with a national reputation willing to spend the energy to campaign. It was a shambles but John Mackintosh's two young Tory students, Ian Hoy and Paul Martin, who were our only organisers, could not blamed for it. The problem was that we had no money. I had to pay for the printing of the first leaflet, and expenses involved in campaigning came out of our own pockets. Our group was broke and only survived the final days when Donald Bain, who had been the SNP research officer but was now working in Italy, flew over and donated £1,000.

A cruel blow was the premature death of John Mackintosh. As Professor of Politics at Edinburgh University and a high-profile Labour politician, he was able to reach across and influence a wide range of people but he was gone. Then there was the weather and the winter of discontent, when trade union anger at the Labour government's wages policy finally boiled over – strikes everywhere. I left one meeting in Lanark, got to the car and, with my ulcer playing up, vomited blood all down my shirt. I lived alone at the time in one of a row of cottages in the village of Annbank in south Ayrshire and, when I got home at about 11 p.m., my neighbour knocked on the door to tell me that we had no water. A pipe had burst and, with the men on strike, there would be no repairs. I had one clean shirt left. The next night I debated with George Younger in Ayr Town Hall and a young woman reporter subsequently had a piece about it in the *Ayr Advertiser*. She was not impressed by me, writing that I had deplorable taste in shirts.

The campaign took place during very bad weather with heavy snow and ice. There was no gritting because of the strike so it took more than two hours to travel from Glasgow to Edinburgh. Driving to Dumfries and back to attend meetings through very heavy snow when no snow-ploughs had been out was a nightmare.

Tam Dalyell suggested that he and I do a debating tour of Scotland and I accepted. We travelled together, stayed in the same hotels and ate together. We were friends, respected each other and remained friends for the rest of his life. The audiences, which were big, except in Dundee, welcomed the chance to hear genuine debate in which rancour was absent. We did eighteen debates. Today, I suppose, on social media, Tam would be flayed by Cybernats but, back then, there was an acceptance that people could have different opinions on the constitutional question and discuss and debate the issue in a civilised way, with the benefit being a better informed public.

Tam had been a consistent opponent of devolution, except for his moment of 'panic' after the October 1974 election. I did not bring that up in debate because it was a forgivable aberration in his record. Not once did he bring up my previous record as the 'hammer of the Nats', thus acknowledging that it is perfectly legitimate to change one's mind. Never, during the campaign or afterwards during my candidacy against him in 1987 or right up until his death, did I alter my view that he was a man of extraordinary integrity.

The 1979 referendum was the second time Project Fear was used. Although what was on offer was a weak assembly, it was painted by the No side (contrary to Sir Alec Douglas-Home) as though it was almost the same as independence. The Scottish economy would collapse, we would not be able to pay pensions and we would be, as Tam put it in our debates, on a 'one-way street' to independence. The No campaign had people on the King's Cross–Edinburgh train putting on uniforms, then going round the train after Berwick asking passengers for their passports. A great stunt but nothing to do with the assembly we were voting on.

Project Fear and Home's 'Vow' (like the one from former PM Gordon Brown in 2014) had effect. In New Cumnock, amidst the snow, I was standing outside the polling station when a women came up and told me she didn't know how to vote. Her son was a customs officer at a Scottish port and she was worried he would lose his job if there was an assembly. I told her customs was not within the remit of the assembly but could not convince her and in she went to vote No.

The referendum question Scots had to answer on 1 March 1979 was 'Do you want the Provisions of the Scotland Act 1978 to be put into effect?'. The result was a narrow win for Yes:

Yes 1,230,937 – 51.6%
No 1,153,502 – 48.4%

Turnout 63.72%

But getting a majority could never be enough for the Yes side. The 'dead' on the electoral register and abstentions (shown by the turnout) effectively counted against us. No didn't need to win a majority to scupper devolution – they could lose the vote but win with their second weapon, the 40 per cent rule. It was a clever piece of gerrymandering.

*

I am now about to explain just how comprehensively the Labour Party betrayed its 1974 pledge and how, simultaneously, the SNP committed political suicide. Those who do not read Acts of Parliament – that is most of us, including MPs and MSPs – may want to read what is written below twice as it may be difficult to understand, at first, how the Labour government could be compelled by law to do something but then be free to defeat what it had been compelled to do.

When the Yes vote failed to pass the 40 per cent barrier, under the terms of the Act, the government was now compelled by law to bring forward an Order to the House of Commons repealing the Act in its entirety – not to amend it but to repeal it. Three things are important here: there was no timetable for when the Order had to be tabled and voted on; nothing in the Act said the government had to vote for the Order it was required to table; and, if the Order for repeal was defeated, the Act would stand and the government would be able to set up the assembly. That 'repeal' part of the Act had been forced upon the government by rebel Labour MPs. The Order repealing the Act was not government policy. It was merely required to act like a postman delivering an Order to the House of Commons. There was nothing to stop the government inviting the House of Commons to vote it down. That was the only way the Labour government could honour its election promise to the Scots who, after all, had voted Yes by a majority of 4%.

The Labour government could have put down a three-line party whip instructing its MPs to vote down the Order, knowing it had the additional votes of the SNP, SLP and, most probably on this, the Liberals under the new Lib–Lab pact. However, many Labour MPs made it crystal clear to the whips that they would defy a three-line whip and vote, along with the Tories, for the Order and thus kill the assembly. When I privately suggested to Walter Harrison, deputy chief whip, making a vote against the Order a vote of confidence for Labour MPs, he told me that, so determined were many to put an end to devolution, the government couldn't take the chance with them, even on that kind of vote.

Jim Callaghan's government, faced with that level of defiance, was paralysed. He dare not table the Order because, when it was approved by Labour MPs, ether going into the Tory lobby or abstaining in large numbers, with the assembly no more, Labour would face the SNP in Scotland saying, 'We told you Labour would betray you.' So, nothing was done. Tabling the Order and holding a vote to repeal the Act were two of the first actions taken by Margaret Thatcher's new government.

Labour has been lucky in the telling of that period in history. It was Labour MPs who killed devolution in 1979. *They* voted against the guillotine. *They* thought up the 40 per cent ploy. And *they* refused to vote against the Order. But Labour has hidden its complicity under the cover of the SNP's incredible mistake. In Parliament and among the membership, the Scottish Nationalist Party was enraged by the conduct of Labour MPs and the failure of the government, who it had supported throughout the devolution debates, to deliver on the Scots' majority. It was another rush of blood to what should have been a cool head. Their tactics were maladroit. By not tabling the Order, the Act granting the assembly was not repealed – just suspended. There was time to see if, through negotiations that could buy the government more time, there was some way out of impasse – slim as that chance was. But Andrew Welsh, the SNP's chief whip, and Margaret Ewing, the party's deputy whip, went to meet Michael Foot and handed him their motion of no confidence in the government. They claimed he went pale. If that made them feel good, it didn't last long.

The SNP no confidence motion was the trigger for the real one from the official Tory opposition. Margaret Thatcher knew that, with SNP support withdrawn, the government could be defeated. This vote would not be about the assembly but the government's general policy, its conduct of economic affairs and whether a general election would follow it. The Lib–Lab pact did not include support on confidence, so the Tories could expect the Liberals in their lobby too.

A general election didn't worry the SNP. As they read it, in Scotland, Labour's failure to deliver guaranteed them victory, with more seats. It was a plausible theory but it failed to take into account the political fact that class mattered and that working-class people could replace something that had previously dominated, as a priority – which the assembly question had done for almost five years – with another matter.

Despite Labour's known faults and despite having openly betrayed the people on the assembly issue, a Labour government, for the Scottish working class, was infinitely preferable to a hard-Right Tory one led by Margaret Thatcher. The prospect of a confidence vote bringing on an election, after which a Thatcher government was a real possibility, meant devolution was relegated from top spot – keeping her out had become the new imperative.

There was evidence of that change in priority at the ballot box. But the SNP could not see it. On 28 March 1979, in the House of Commons, Western Isles MP Donald Stewart led the no confidence motion for the SNP, spelling out the erroneous thinking:

> I say to the Government and to the Conservatives that Scottish desire for self-government is alive and thriving. Resentment is growing at the apparent wish of the majority here to frustrate that desire and to make divisions in Scotland . . . It is a pity that more Labour MPs do not back their own party policy and legislation, and the Government may have to pay the price.

The 1979 Referendum

Norman Buchan, Labour MP for West Renfrewshire, rose and, pointing to the clear ballot box evidence I mentioned above, said:

> I have news for him [Donald Stewart]. There was a [local government] by-election last night in East Kilbride. I shall give him the figures.
>
> In 1977, only two years ago, the SNP gained 65 per cent of the vote in that area. It polled 1,155 votes against Labour's 618. It beat us by nearly two to one. Last night Labour topped the poll with 45.8 per cent. The SNP had slumped to 39 per cent – which is a turnover of about 30 per cent – between 1977 and 1979.

Labour lost the no confidence vote 311–310. Had the SNP not produced that no confidence motion and put themselves on the spot, they could have abstained, Labour would not have lost and they would not have become the objects of derision, earning the damaging nickname 'the Tartan Tories', who brought down Labour and let Thatcher in. It wasn't just that by-election result in East Kilbride but the private polling Labour was doing that enabled Jim Callaghan to describe the SNP MPs as 'turkeys voting for Christmas'. I attacked them for being so incompetent, saying that, if they had been in charge at Flodden, we would have lost even if the English had been on our side.

We then went into the 1979 general election. Those of us in the SLP in South Ayrshire, with Bill and Isabel McCrorie in charge, had a happy campaign, until the last week when the NUM intervened against me, in the northern part where it was a powerful influence. The pits were plastered with Labour posters, with NUM officials calling on miners to vote Labour and punish me for leaving the party. On the Tuesday before the poll, the Scottish national union took out a full-page advertisement in *The Daily Record*, attacking me and calling for my defeat. After the election, a QC advised that the advert was defamatory but I had neither the money nor the heart to test that in court. The results in South Ayrshire were:

Labour 14,271
SLP 12,750
Tory 10,287
SNP 3,233
Labour majority 1,521

The general election results in Scotland saw Labour take 41.5 per cent of the votes and the number of Labour seats went up to 44, a gain of three. The SNP had 17.3 per cent of the votes and won two seats, a loss of nine.

*

In the nine years I was MP for South Ayrshire, I can claim only two personal legislative victories. The first was in 1972, when Strathclyde Regional Council and the District Councils, as second-tier authorities, were being set up. The Bill to do so was a Tory government one but, when you mess with local government, party politics can go out of the window. Local heritage is what counts. The Bill proposed that territory from Girvan southwards would leave Ayrshire and join Galloway. I am an Ayrshire man and the planned division of my county with all its common history – Bruce was born at Turnberry and then there is Burns – was not on. Although that part of Ayrshire was, like its proposed partner Galloway, Tory-voting territory, 'my' Tories did not want Ayrshire split up either, given their affinity to the county and its heritage.

But the Labour Party liked the proposal. Getting rid of Tory South Ayrshire guaranteed them control of the lower district, when it was formed. Willie Ross, who supported my amendment to ensure all of Ayrshire stayed as one authority, was called along with me to a private Labour meeting in the County Buildings. There, Charlie O'Halloran, leader of the Labour group in Ayr, threatened us with expulsion if we did not obey their instruction to allow Galloway to swallow part of Tory Ayrshire. If I am a nationalist of any kind, it is an Ayrshire one and I was determined that my county would not be truncated. My amendment to the Bill, in the standing committee, was successful. We were not expelled.

The other victory came, with UK-wide implications, when, after Labour won the February 1974 election, Heath's industrial relations act was being replaced by a Labour one. An amendment I tabled, moved and voted on – against the front bench of Michael Foot, then Secretary of State for Employment – stated a worker could only be unfairly dismissed in a probation period of six months, instead of the one year wanted by the government. I won the vote and that remained the law until Margaret Thatcher's government made it a two-year rule.

During my time as MP for South Ayrshire, I made sure that the Tory voting areas of farmers and fishermen got the same service and consideration as the people in the mining north, where the Labour majority lay. That, of course, was as it should be but there was also a political benefit. In a sense, this policy 'neutralised' the Tories. They were never going to vote for me but I never gave them a reason to mobilise fully in order to defeat me. That is not cynicism – it's just sensible politics and also the service people are entitled to get from an MP.

My education as a socialist also benefitted from that. Listening to farmers talking about how important it was to care for their land, cattle, crops and the farms' place in nature, I came to realise why the Stalin and Mao communist regimes' agricultural policies were such spectacular failures. There is a unique link between the farmer and the land. He and he alone decides how to farm and break that, as they did with collective farms owned by the state, and you court disaster.

I was a member of the 1971–72 Select Committee on Scottish Affairs which looked at land use. John Smith, Gavin Strang and Bob Hughes were also Labour members. It too was educational. Land was always, and remains today, a contentious subject in Scotland. There were clear examples in the 1970s of big landowners frustrating legitimate public needs, such as housing development, but the Tory majority on the committee was not prepared to recommend any significant changes to land use policy. So, I wrote a minority report, as did Gavin Strang.

Mine centred on the need for public ownership of the great estates, breaking the power they exercised over rural communities, with an innovative system of compensation for previous owners based on a life-only pension, rather than current use or development value. I justified this by pointing out that, in many cases, the value of land had been enhanced by public investment through agricultural payments and the adjacent supporting infrastructure for their farm labour of housing, roads, schools, hospitals, electricity etc. I did not set out a case for a Stalinist type of a public-owned agricultural industry on the acquired land. I sought the expansion of owner-occupied farms and a great increase in the number of tenant farmers both of which I saw, and still do, as the best model for our nation's agricultural policy. In the report, I also took the opportunity to dig up Labour history on the land issue. In 1972, due to copyright law, Tom Johnston's book, *Our Scots Noble Families* (first published 1909), challenging the legality and legitimacy of claims made by the landowning class, was not available. It is now.

When Johnston became Secretary of State for Scotland in Churchill's Second World War coalition, he set about trying to buy up and destroy every copy. The only one I could get my hands on was in the House of Commons Library. In my report, I incorporated the foreword written by Ramsay MacDonald, who was then in his Socialist prime. He was embraced by the establishment much earlier than Johnston.

Show the people that our Old Nobility is not noble, that its land are stolen lands – stolen either by force or fraud; show people that the title-deeds are rapine, murder, massacre, cheating, or Court harlotry; dissolve the halo of divinity that surrounds the hereditary title; let the people clearly understand that our present House of Lords is composed largely of descendants of successful pirates and rougues; do these things and you shatter the Romance that keeps the nation numb and spellbound while privilege picks its pockets.

The scathing attack by Johnston and MacDonald on the large land-owning class was founded on detailed research, including how extensive public lands, in the likes of Ayrshire, Aberdeenshire and elsewhere, were filched by sections of the aristocracy abusing their power. The theft of land came long before the Clearances. I quoted it then and here to illustrate how the British establishment can take raging socialist radicals and, bit by bit, tame them and take them into their fold.

15

New Paths

When I was defeated in South Ayrshire in 1979, I was around £8,000 in debt and unemployed for a time. I finally got a job in Edinburgh as director of the Scottish Federation of Housing Associations, a mix of community-based and private housing associations. The community-based associations were engaged in rehabilitating tenement property in Glasgow and setting up local self-management. The physical rehabilitation was important but of even greater significance was placing power in the hands of local people in dealing with the professionals employed by them and the sense of community responsibility that was built up. The community-housing association movement was in its early stages of development in Scotland compared to England.

My job was to deal with the Scottish Office as the source of funding and its policy. During the short time I was in this job, the most important thing I did was to prevent the housing associations being drawn into Mrs Thatcher's council house sales policy. Logically, there was no reason why it did not extend to housing association stock as it too was publicly funded. But, if the Glasgow housing association stock had been sold into the private sector, it would have been a social disaster, splitting the communities and so eliminating 'community' as a factor and halting the human development that was taking place.

Malcolm Rifkind was the minister responsible. When we had a meeting about whether the association housing should be included in Scottish right-to-buy legislation, using my trade union experience, I asked for what I knew was possible rather than trying to achieve the impossible. I didn't argue that housing associations should be excluded per se, given the principal thrust of Thatcher's policy was home ownership and that Malcolm, a junior minister, was expected to apply it. I would not have won that argument. Instead, I concentrated on the need for time to be given to the community movement to develop, build and learn from membership of the federation, in partnership with older private-based ones, and argued that this partnership was in too early a stage of its evolution to be dismantled through selling off. I pointed out that this would present a damaging situation in the Glasgow associations – people who had already been rehoused in rehabilitated tenement property would reap considerable benefit, high prices, from being able to sell. But those with substandard flats, still not renovated, would not get the same price as the 'lucky' ones. The housing associations would disintegrate in bitterness and the communities would be split.

Rifkind was not a Right-wing zealot. His Edinburgh constituency included Wester Hailes where he knew the importance of community. As Scotland would have separate right-to-buy legislation, we had presented him with a case that was easy to accept and so housing associations were not included. Some tenants in the older well-established private housing associations in Edinburgh were not happy but the majority, based in Glasgow, were.

*

In 1981, the SNP was at a very low ebb but the student nationalists at Stirling University were full of beans and asked me to stand in the election for student president – the equivalent of rector at Edinburgh and Glasgow although not quite so prestigious. It involved representing students on the University Court. The principal was Professor Ken Alexander, whom I had met at the STUC. The post was only for a year. I didn't think there was any chance of winning but didn't want to let the young people down. There was a hustings and Margo came with me, warning that this generation of students was going to be a new experience for me and to watch what I said. At my turn to speak, I started with 'Mr Chairman'. The first question was from a female who wanted to know why I had addressed the 'Chair' as 'Chairman' – to which I replied, 'Because he's a man, hen.' Margo told me I was a disaster. But I was elected.

Jack McConnell was the leader of the Students' Union and sat on the court too. He was a bit suspicious of me at first, given that I had left the Labour Party and was now in the SNP, having joined in 1980 after the failure of the SLP, but we worked well together when the Thatcher government, with Sir Keith Joseph leading the education and science department, was imposing real cuts and real changes in the way universities operated. It was obvious to me, even then, that Jack was heading for a political career. He became general secretary of the Labour Party in Scotland, First Minister and is now Lord McConnell. We have been friends since those days.

There is no better time to serve and observe the leaders of an institution than when it is facing a crisis – which was the case with all universities then, as they sought to adjust to the Thatcher regime with its financial cuts and changes. Seeing how little opposition the academics put up against the government's proposed reforms and the infighting between departments to survive was an eye-opener.

I did not find the housing association job challenging and left after a while to take up a position in late 1980 with a small Scottish company which hoped to find contracts for consultancy work in the developing world. One of the partners was Donald Gorrie, then a Liberal councillor and later a Lib Dem MP. He was among the most decent men I have met in public life. The founding partner was David Thomson, a fisheries expert with years of experience in Third World development. There were no five-star hotels for him – he lived with the local people he worked with. He was a credit to the Christian Church to which he belonged. David asked me to join them because of my organisational skills and also because, sometimes, there was a political factor in government contracts.

Thanks to David, we landed a small but good contract as fisheries and organisation consultants in the Philippines. Our segment of work was within a $76-million World Bank-funded project. The funds were to be used to create a new marine university in Manila, which would work in partnership with associated colleges in different parts of that geographically widespread country. We made the same error as many small start-ups do – under-capitalised, we were working on a business plan that was too optimistic. That was a lesson we had still to learn. The project was run by Filipinos and, although its leader, Lito Alinea, was capable and his young staff, all university graduates, were bright and able, none of them had any organisational or administrative experience. When I got to Manila, I found a shambles. There was no agenda for meetings during which decisions were made on equipment procurement and building contracts and no minutes were taken. No one seemed to be responsible for implementing decisions taken at a meeting and subsequent meetings often went over old ground. My job was to bring organised order to the chaos.

I was also tasked with persuading two very reluctant college principals, one in Zamboanga, on Mindanao, and one in a rural fishing area in Cebu, to take part in the project. I failed. Not because of any fault on my part but because both were wary, rightly so as I discovered, about what was being proposed. As well as building the new university, the existing college buildings would be demolished and replaced by state-of-the art new ones. So why the reluctance? I was to find out when I went to see Vic, the principal in Zamboanga, with whom I had become friends. Talking to him in his office, I noticed, on looking out of the window, a group of students doing what looked like Tai Chi. Were they? No, no, he explained, they were tying up a ship but, as the college had no ropes, they had to practise without one. What an opening that gave me. Why turn down the offer of a new college with everything he required? He explained the reality – if he signed up to the project, his college would be demolished but a new one would never be built so it was better to keep what he had and do what he could with it.

From him, I then got the tale of the previous World Bank loan of $65 million for a new agricultural university in Manila. There had been five wooden teaching blocks originally. Four were demolished, leaving only one until the new university building was completed. It never was. Vic refused point blank to have anything to do with the project, saying the same would happen to his college. It was the same with the Cebu College principal. He was resentful of me coming to persuade him to take part so, when I and the young female staff member accompanying me arrived at night, instead of receiving us with the usual Filipino hospitality, he told us to sleep on the desks in one of his classrooms. Our meeting next day did not last long.

Back in Manila I visited the previous project Vic had told me about and it was as he had claimed. There was a skeleton concrete structure and that was all. The $65 million had all been siphoned off by the corrupt Marcos regime. The World Bank was aware the money had disappeared yet here it was with another multimillion-dollar loan which was likely to go the same way. The young Filipinos I worked with deserved better. They were all intelligent and committed yet were at the mercy of a kleptocratic regime. Often they were not paid for months. It was no wonder that their greatest ambition was to get into the USA. Shortly after my contract ended, I learnt that two of them had, in fact, gone to America, preferring illegal immigration over living in a society corrupt from the top downwards which, for all its copying of the American political system and its appearance of democracy, was run by a small group of enormously rich families.

When the World Bank representative came to discuss the project, I expected a detailed examination of what had been done and what was proposed. No such thing happened. We saw him once in the office. His main interest was being fixed up in a brothel. As long as he was 'well looked after' by the senior project officials, there would be no adverse report. I am sure it is different now. Once the organisational structure

132

had been put in place, my contract ended. After that experience and others that were to follow, I developed a considerable scepticism about the claims made for the value international aid organisations bring to developing countries. The one group I did admire was Voluntary Service Overseas, a charity which places young British people with particular skills in poor communities. They were excellent. No five-star hotels for them either – they lived in the communities they served.

We went searching for consultancy work in Malaysia and got a contract. Unfortunately, in the final stages of negotiations the government introduced a requirement for us to post a performance bond beyond our financial resources. Again this was a lesson in under-capitalisation. But the experience of spending months there in negotiations was not without gain for me as I learned a lot about the world outside the UK and Europe. I learned a lesson on how decisions taken by an imperial powers can have unimagined and unintended consequences and leave a legacy of difficulties – and how fairly large ethnic minorities make compromises in delicate situations for the sake of stability and security. During British imperial days, Chinese and Indian people were taken to Malaysia as cheap labour. As a result, Malaysia now has three distinct ethnic groups – the majority indigenous Malays, Chinese (around 30 per cent) and Indian (around 10 per cent). The Chinese had grown both in numbers and economic power and that was the cause of massive riots by Malays in 1969, after which a policy of positive discrimination in Malays' favour in the economic sphere was introduced.

At the political level, there is always to be a Muslim Malay prime minister. An Indian doctor explained to me that his group occupied posts in professions, such as medicine and accountancy, which did not threaten any other group economically. Young Chinese businessmen explained that they often had a Malay fronting up their companies to disguise their economic control. In the government department I dealt with, the director and deputy were Malay and the number three was Chinese. He explained that he could not become head of the department and accepted this as the price of social stability.

I had private talks with Malaysian civil servants about corruption in the country, which was endemic. They told me that Western politicians like me made the mistake of applying a British template to their system, whereas the points of reference for their people were quite different. In Britain, it was a virtue for an MP to be modest and not to flaunt wealth whereas, in Malaysia, the people's view was that, if their MP could not enrich himself and his family, there was precious little chance of him doing anything for them.

A Difference of Opinion

The company sent me to Zimbabwe soon after its independence. I met a number of politicians, including ministers, and was impressed by them. In discussion with the education minister, who had taught at Trinity College, Dublin, for ten years while in exile, I raised the issue of corruption, pointing out that it was widespread in Africa. He assured me that the Mugabe government knew the pitfalls and would be clean. About a year after that visit, I read a small piece in *The Times* – the first person to be done for corruption was that very same education minister, who had got involved in a fiddle importing second-hand cars.

While there, I talked to David Smith, who had been Ian Smith's finance minister in the white Rhodesian rebel government. He was kept on for some time by Robert Mugabe. Smith was a Scot from Argyll and he too was impressed by Mugabe and optimistic for Zimbabwe's future. He told me of a meeting he attended with Mugabe along with leaders of Mozambique, Angola, Zambia and Malawi, the other frontline states. Samora Machel, the first president of Mozambique, had advised the new Zimbabwean leader not to make the same catastrophic decisions he and the others had made in getting rid of the white skilled workers and turning the country upside down. Smith believed the message had got through to Mugabe and he, along with most in the international community at that time, was impressed by the way Zimbabwe was being handled by the Zanu-PF government. We were all wrong.

I also learnt from a meeting with a minister that the amount 'pledged' by several countries to aid Zimbabwe's recovery from the civil war was not the same as that delivered. In fact, out of billions of dollars, only the contribution from Kuwait had been delivered in full. Ever since, I have always treated the 'pledges' at donor conferences with a question mark.

Our small company folded but I managed to get a personal contract in Saudi Arabia, in 1983, through an Arab friend, Fakhri Shehab. He had been an economic adviser to the Kuwaiti government, had taught economics at Oxford and Glasgow and was well connected in the Gulf. He had a large property in Bridge of Weir and I met up with him in Scotland.

The Saudi Arabia of the 1980s was nothing like it is today. The oil boom had seen money spent on infrastructure but the Saudi population was still largely untrained so the drafting of commercial laws and the planning and management of much of the economy was done by expatriate workers from America and Europe, with the hard physical work of construction, in the intense heat, falling to thousands of workers from the poorer developing countries. There was a world of difference between how the two groups were paid and treated. Payment was by nationality – Americans and Europeans were well paid while Filipinos, Thais and Indians were all paid differently but all at the bottom level. Saudi employers kept the passports of the Third World workers so, even if they found the situation worse than what had been promised, they couldn't escape and go back home until their contracts were up. The employment laws in Saudi were based on Western standards and drafted by Westerners but how could a poor tea boy from Kerala, earning only 700 rials a month, take his Saudi employer to a court headed by a Saudi judge?

My friend Fakhri Shehab had been asked by his friend Jamal Alamdar if he could find someone to help a Saudi friend and business partner, whose company was in trouble. They asked me to go out and have an initial look, which I did, for a week. I came back and said it looked in bad shape but I would try. So back I went as managing director of Saudi Construction and Supply, office in Al Khobar in the eastern province, with the truck fleet located 40 kilometres out in the desert.

The Saudi was Prince Turki bin Jalawi. His tribe had allied themselves to Abdul Aziz al Saud when he set about conquering and creating Saudi Arabia. The reward was to give the bin Jalawis royal status. Being that kind of 'royalty' didn't take the bin Jalawis into the inner core of decision-making, as that was always reserved for the al Saud family. A governorship of a province might come the way of one of them but rarely. But one advantage for the bin Jalawi royals was, like all the Al Saud princes and princesses, they did not need to pay for their water, electricity, telephone and other expenses and, in addition, received an annual stipend from the government. Prince Turki took pleasure in demonstrating this to me by tearing up his electricity and telephone accounts, with no danger of being cut off. It was not a formula for prudence.

The company had no construction side but had trucks and trailers. These transported materials from the Saudi port of Dammam to Iraq during the Iraq–Iran war of 1980–88. I had never run a transport business but again the fact that I was an organiser helped. I recruited from Scotland an experienced transport manager, Jim McKay, and Dave Reynolds, an experienced works foreman, and we established ourselves there.

Mess is not the accurate word for the state of Prince Turki's company. Like many other Saudis in that first flush of oil wealth, as the oil price rose and Saudi took control of ARAMCO, the national oil company, he thought it was easy to make money. He had no business background. Barclays Bank, which had provided the capital to set up the company, had to reschedule debt repayments several times, whilst the manager of the Saudi–French Bank, hosting the company account, told me Prince Turki did not understand the difference between cash flow and profit – when money landed in the bank, he simply took it out. The first thing I did was to insist on keeping the chequebook.

The other problem, which was a big one, was that he did not understand that, if you borrow cash from a bank for your business, you have to pay back all that you borrow. To help me get a grip on what assets there were, Barclays gave me the chassis numbers of 48 Mercedes trucks they had funded but I could only find 24. The other trucks were from the USA and there was no record of which bank loan bought them or how many there were supposed to be in the fleet.

When I reported the 'missing' Mercedes trucks to Prince Turki, he told me none were missing as he had only bought 24. Yes, he had borrowed the cash for 48 but only bought 24, using the other half to take the family to America, England and Europe. When I explained that the 24 would have to generate enough business and profit to pay Barclays back for the 48, he declared this as unfair. I was never able to persuade him differently. Then there was the question of insurance. He refused to have any for the fleet. If things happened, that was Allah's will and he saw insurance as betting against that will. As it turned out, we only had one write-off. That was sustainable but any more would not have been.

There were human problems too. With the exception of two Saudis, members of his entourage on 5,000 rials a month, who did no work and who I sacked, the drivers were all from Thailand. They lived in huts in the desert where the fleet of trucks were parked. They were paid 900 rials a month but not regularly. This was because the works foreman, a Sudanese bus driver, had wangled it so that his nephew, a cook from Sudan, got the job of finance manager. There were no records of payment to drivers so there was no way of knowing what was owed to them. They all claimed that their pay was in arrears, with some saying they'd had nothing for three months. Nine of the Thais had completed their contract but there was no money to send them back home. They lived by fishing. There were no garage or workshops. We found spare parts buried in the sand. There were no real jobs now for the Sudanese foreman and his nephew but we did not sack them as they had no place else to go.

Our management team created order out of chaos and built a garage and workshop with the money I collected from our local debtors. But it was like pushing water up a hill. Once the Thai drivers left Dammam port, we had no control over them and they sold stuff off their lorries as they made their way up to Iraq. We only knew about the deficit on delivery when Iraqi government officials came to claim money back for stuff not delivered. I could not blame the drivers because, before we arrived, they had often not been paid and selling from the back of the lorry was guaranteed cash. Juggling between getting money in, paying the Thai men back pay, getting some home and paying a few but not most of our creditors, my team was getting new lessons in management, human relations and cultural differences in a non-Western setting.

The Thai drivers were remarkable and admirable men. They spoke no Arabic or English yet took their trucks and trailers to Dammam, loaded up and went through Kuwait to deliver to clients in towns and cities in Iraq, many of which had no street names. When I asked our Thai foreman, Viwat, who did speak English, how they managed to do it, he shrugged and said they passed information to each other as they learned different routes

The early 1980s were Saudi's first experience of a recession after the initial construction boom. Companies in my area were cash short and I had to start learning rudimentary Arabic in order to deal with debtors and creditors. I am not naturally good at languages but necessity is a great teacher.

It was also a time when Saudi Arabia had only started to develop. People who had been desert dwellers were now finding themselves in towns and cities and having to confront a whole new way of life they knew nothing about. They were not familiar with the laws of supply and demand, nor did they have any experience of modern management. Saudi is very different now with a powerful, university-educated, techni-cally competent, growing middle class who are well versed in managing huge industries and companies on an international scale. But, back then, it was at the very bottom of the learning curve. Here is one exam-ple, but not a rare one, that illustrates this. Ali Al-Naimi, born in 1935, was literally a barefoot Bedouin boy, part of an extended family who travelled around the eastern desert seeking water and a place to graze their livestock. Later, when oil began to flow, he got a job, in 1947, at the age of 12, as a typist, with ARAMCO, the giant oil company. Step by step, as the Saudis got to learn the business, he progressed within the company until, in 1984, he became the first Saudi to be president and, in 1988, the first Saudi to become chief executive. From 1995 to 2016, he was Minister for Petroleum and Mineral Resources. He was no placeman. Contemporaries in the global oil world knew him as a formidable negotiator who knew the industry inside out.

In Saudi, I came up against a culture very different from mine. Islam and tribal and family connections were fundamental to how society operated. It was easy to think that women did not count. They were covered from head to foot. The men had strict control over them in public and they could not travel without a senior male's consent. Yet, as I discovered, it wasn't quite like that. I had a young Saudi called Majed, who spoke good English, as my personal assistant. His father had deserted the family and he was the oldest male. But his mother ruled the roost inside the house. I answered the phone on several occasions when 'Where Majed?' was loudly demanded. Majed explained to me that outside the house, in the public arena, he was in complete charge of his mother. But inside the house it was the reverse. He told me of an occasion when his brother was put in a local jail for drinking alcohol. His mother insisted that the family turn off the house air conditioning for a full day and night, so every member would experience what her other son was going through.

Prince Turki's friend Jamal thought he could help the company out of its commercial troubles by initiating activity on the construction side. A group of men came from Sweden, with four containers holding everything they needed to build a portable factory to make a type of light breeze block. This had superb insulation properties that would cut down on the cost of air conditioning. The idea was that they would get contracts to build several hundred houses and then move on to another site with another contract.

Two model show houses were constructed next to our workshop. It could not happen now in modern Saudi Arabia but, back then, it was different. One of my Saudi colleagues took a breeze block home, threw it against a wall and it broke. That was that. His opinion that it was ridiculous to think you could build a proper house with such poor material did the rounds locally. Eventually, after six months with no contracts, I had to explain to an incredulous Swedish engineer that he had failed the wall test and had better go home.

To sort out the financial records, I recruited Ahmed, an Egyptian university-trained accountant, but the extent of the company's debt only became apparent bit by bit, visit by visit from creditors, when they came along after hearing there was now a European management team in place. As our understanding of the debt mountain grew, I told the prince he would need ten million rials to clear the debt and more to put the company on a road to recovery. He had gone to school with the king and told me he felt sure he would get the money from him. He never did. The rest of the country was in the same boat and there must have been a long queue of similar supplicants at the king's *Majilis*.

New Paths

The debt was a bigger problem than I first appreciated. Saudi law decreed that, if a company or individual owed money and did not pay, the creditor could obtain an official document from the police demanding immediate payment upon presentation to the debtor. If the debt was still not paid, the manager in charge of the company or the individual went to jail until it was settled. I managed to stave off our creditors but, one morning, two of the smaller creditors whose combined debt was only 250,000 rials came to the office. As I was using whatever money I got in to keep the trucks rolling and the Thai men paid, I could not pay and waved away their police document. Ahmed told me that next day the police would come back with them and I would be arrested. I immediately contacted a lawyer who told me that, although I had never incurred any of the debts, I was 'the man in the chair' and was, therefore, responsible for them. He advised me to stay in my villa within the prince's compound because the police would not enter any property owned by a prince.

However, I decided to go into the office the next day because, by then, I had a reasonably good understanding of the local police – untrained, inefficient and not used to argument, they just expected to be obeyed. So I prepared. Sandals were out. Highly polished shoes, a crisp, clean short-sleeved white shirt and pressed trousers that would have passed a military parade. I chose the prince's office for the expected visit. Never once did he use it. His desk was on a raised platform and the furniture was plush. I anticipated, correctly, that the police and creditors would be uncomfortable in these surroundings, which exuded authority.

I started brusquely, with Ahmed as translator, asking why the police were here. When they mentioned the debts, I said that was Prince Turki's problem, not mine, as I had never incurred them. That caused confusion. Then I asked under which Act of Saudi law they were here. More confusion. Then I asked under what part of the Koran did it say I had to pay the prince's debts. The policeman was getting angrier and the sweat was pouring down Ahmed's face. Then I asked if putting me in jail would force Prince Turki to pay the debts. The man was transformed. At last, this idiot had understood. Then I said I had a better idea – he should arrest Prince Turki's uncle, the governor of the eastern province, a proper bastard if tales were to be believed. That did it. '*Kelas* [Finished]!' he shouted and then, '*Calaboose, calaboose* [Prison, prison]!' and he waved for me to go with him. I replied, '*La, la, la* [No, no, no]!' and waved him away. I told Ahmed to tell him to get them out of my office as I wanted to hear no more of his nonsense. To Ahmed's astonishment, the policeman and the creditors left.

A Difference of Opinion

Ahmed was in a state. He said they would be back because no one could refuse to be arrested in Saudi Arabia. I said I knew that but, this being Saudi, they would go back to the police station, have a fag and a coffee and say, 'This cannot be – we're going back to get that guy.' But, as I explained further, they would wait until tomorrow to come back, by which time Ahmed, our management team and I would be safely in my villa in the prince's compound. Next day, a number of police did turn up at the office with handcuffs at the ready. Instead of us, however, they found the Sudanese cook, a supernumerary on the payroll, who happened to be sitting at a desk with his feet up reading a newspaper. By their logic, anyone at a desk, feet up and reading a newspaper must be management so they took him. The prince had gone off to Riyadh. I finally managed to get hold of him and, next day, we had 250,000 rials and the Sudanese was out of jail.

Margo and I had married by this time and I phoned home to tell her about the problem I might face. She panicked and phoned Malcolm Rifkind, who was then a foreign office minister, demanding that, if I landed in jail, the foreign office had to get me released and fly me home. Margo never understood Saudi Arabia and, when I sought to explain some of its apparent contradictions and the reasons for them in its culture, she was inclined to denounce me for excusing hypocrisy.

It eventually became evident that the prince was as skint as a prince can be in Saudi – that is, despite his government-granted income, he had no capital to put into his company. That didn't stop him showing me his plans to convert a Land Rover to have a mobile platform so that he and his father could go shooting game in Sudan – at a cost of $30,000. With him as the owner, the company could not be saved. The transport manager and I left. The works foreman, Dave Reynolds stayed as his wife had joined him and had a job as a schoolteacher. The day Mrs Reynolds and another single female teacher arrived was when I acquired a 'second' wife. They were both detained at Dammam airport because they were women travelling alone. Mrs Reynolds was allowed to phone Dave and I went with him to 'claim' the other woman as my wife. That claim was enough – no papers were needed.

Those early years in Saudi were an adventure as well as learning experience which I built on over the next twenty to thirty years whilst working with the Arab–British Chamber of Commerce. During those years, it was fascinating to watch this unique country's development. When I was first there, there was only one functioning factory on the Dammam industrial estate. Now, it and others are full.

Saudi Arabia is deeply conservative. Wahhabi Islam's influence runs deep and that fact has meant that, although the Al Saud family has wielded enormous power, they have never been dictators – perhaps up until now. Their ability to rule has been based on an alliance with the religious scholars and leaders. The latter's resistance to change by anything that could not be found in the Koran or Hadith explains why reform moved at a glacial pace no matter how many of the young were educated in the USA and Europe or that its businessmen were involved internationally. Whatever hedonistic activities rich Saudi royals and others got up to in their visits to London, Paris and elsewhere, when their feet hit the sand back home, they complied in public to the strict rules of Wahhabi Islam.

Of course, no states and societies engaged in significant trade and economic relations with others can be hermetically sealed. Among the rich royals and business tycoons, there are double -standards and outward appearances bear no relation to what happens indoors. When I worked in Saudi, once a month the Dammam docks were closed to all vehicles except trucks which had no company identification. They were there, as was well known, to meet the 'whisky ship'. Years after my first experience of Saudi, I attended receptions in rich men's villas where we were greeted at the door by a butler with a tray of cocktails.

Not only the very rich can pretend one thing and do another. There is a causeway linking the eastern province of Saudi to Bahrain, where there is a relaxed attitude to alcohol and entertainment. Every Thursday afternoon it is packed with Saudi cars. A friend in Bahrain took Abdul Karim, secretary general of the Arab–British Chamber of Commerce, and me to an entertainment in the ballroom of a hotel. 'These are the Russian ladies,' he explained. In we went to find six Russian blondes with short skirts dancing on a stage, being ogled by a group of sozzled Saudis. I said to Abdul Karim as we left quickly, 'Lenin never meant it to end like this.'

There is a story, I am sure apocryphal but instructive, about the arrival of television in Saudi Arabia. The mullahs were not happy and, during a meeting with King Faisal, lectured him about there being no mention of television in the Koran. Faisal acknowledged this and said he would now have to seriously consider the matter. The mullahs left happy, until they got outside the palace, where they found camels instead of the cars they had arrived in. When they asked where the cars were, they were told that King Faisal wanted to remind them that there was no mention of cars in the Koran. Television did arrive in the kingdom but its content was dire. Watching wet paint dry would have been more exciting. In the 1990s, to please the mullahs, there was a royal decree banning satellite dishes but they were everywhere and no instructions were ever issued to the police to ensure they were taken down.

The entrance of the present de facto ruler, Crown Prince Mohammed bin Salman (MBS), was initially seen in the West as melting the glacier. He showed a remarkable attitude to reform – women were allowed to drive and no longer needed male approval to board an aircraft on their own, the opening of cinemas and the building golf courses where women can play if they're suitably dressed. I, along with others with experience of the kingdom, have been more cautious. Of course, the changes he made are welcome but we see it as a mistake to think that the strong undercurrents of Islamic conservatism no longer exist. No ruler, by whim or decree, can change ingrained attitudes at a stroke and, in seeking to do so in an arbitrary manner, MBS will have made enemies, not least among the most religious, which includes the Shia in the Eastern Province. They hate the Al Sauds and are always a ticking time bomb.

It is also the case that no ruling dynasty which has named the country after itself will shed power easily, as those human rights activists arrested in May and June 2018 can attest. One Arab friend of mine from the Gulf saw the MBS 'reform' as using 'bread and circuses' for the general population while he strengthened his grip on society by intimidating others in the royal family and the business class. He looks cursed with hubris – the kind of hubris that would demand the murder of journalist Jamal Khashoggi at the Saudi consulate in Istanbul in 2018 in such a blatant manner. Not one Arab I know, along with the CIA, believes that it would be possible for the assassins to act unless under his orders. The trial of the actual murderers and the death sentences given to some of them, if carried out, did not bode well for MBS. I could not see the kind of Saudis I know doing nothing if their relatives were to be executed by the man who sent them to carry out his orders. It came as no surprise, therefore, that no executions were carried out. Khashoggi's son, who was not allowed to leave Saudi Arabia, became a tool in the hands of MBS's PR stunt when he was photographed with King Salman as, surprise, surprise, his father's killers were pardoned and given prison sentences instead of being executed. Nor will it come as a surprise if, in due course, it is made known that all the killers are free.

Then there is the family. The political strength and continuity of the Al Saud family, who have not been free from attacks in the past, has been due to family solidarity through consensus on who to choose to govern and how he is to do it. Who the kings in Saudi are has always been a careful balance between the various groups within what is now a very large family. Following the death of King Khalid, his eldest son was ruled out as his successor because he was an alcoholic. Another son from the same mother, Fahd, was a playboy who had lost $3 million in one night in a casino. However, it was felt he could change and Fahd was chosen. But the Crown Prince was Abdullah, who had a different mother and so came from another strand of the family. It would appear that MBS has sought to destroy that consensus and balance and it remains to be seen whether he can succeed or whether the family, who may believe he poses serious threats to them individually and has placed their collective long-term interest in jeopardy, will be able to reel him in or out.

MBS gets most of the publicity but the real mastermind of the new authoritarian and foreign policies of the Gulf States is Mohammed bin Zayed (MBZ) of Abu Dhabi. His grip on that emirate is total – security forces use facial recognition technology that is said to be nearly as 'good' as China's and in his jails are people with independent minds, intellectuals and past local leaders. Abu Dhabi is part of the UAE, a small country but MBZ has made sure the UAE punches well above its weight and exercises influence not only in the Gulf but also in other regions of the Arab world. It was his policy, along with that of Saudi Arabia, that wrecked the solidarity of the Gulf Cooperation Council (GCC) by isolating Qatar, although this policy was finally rescinded at a GCC summit in January 2021. He is complicit in the war in Yemen and has drawn Egypt, Saudi Arabia and Bahrain into his authoritarian net. He showed MBS how to muscle in on power.

When his father Sheikh Zayed was alive, MBZ was only number three in the pecking order but, to everyone's amazement, when the new hierarchy was announced after the Sheik's death, he emerged as the Crown Prince due, it was said, to his mother's influence. She had form having shunted out Sheikh Zayed's other wives. No doubt, as well as his mother, he had the advantage of being in control of the armed forces. The nominal ruler of Abu Dhabi, Sheikh Khalid, is a mere figurehead.

MBS and President Sisi of Egypt are regular visitors to Abu Dhabi. Although there are specialists on the Gulf states, the public in the UK rarely gets any in-depth analysis of what our 'allies' are up to. Only occasionally, when a UK citizen is arrested, is there any negative reporting on them.

16

Into the SNP

I joined the SNP in 1980 after they had been hammered in the local elections. If they had done well, I would not have joined but their heavy defeat meant nobody could accuse me of jumping on a bandwagon. A chap in the Labour Party in Glasgow said to me, 'You have an unerring eye for leaping on to a sinking ship.' But the decisive reason was the setting up of the 79 Group within the party, which was pushing for socialist policies. I was not universally welcome but I was fairly quickly elected to the National Executive.

When a party has been thrashed by the electorate and is, as a consequence in some turmoil when trying to find a way back, it makes mistakes. At the 1981 conference, I took part in a debate supporting civil disobedience and the SNP leader, Gordon Wilson – a man who was wiser than me and who did not approve of the idea – gave me the 'poisoned chalice' of running the campaign. A small group of us thought of something big – breaking into and occupying the assembly building in Edinburgh – to underline how the Scots had been diddled by the 40 per cent rule in the 1979 referendum.

Our planning was good. We broke into the assembly, were arrested and charged under a Scottish vandalism law, passed by the Westminster Parliament. That gave us an opening on the constitution. Had we been charged under common law, we would have no case. Despite not passing the 40 per cent rule, there had been a majority for an assembly and we prepared to assert in court the supremacy of the referendum majority and so challenge the claim of sovereignty over Scotland made by the UK Parliament. Our court case took two days. There were five of us, with Dougie Robertson (now a Professor at Stirling University) setting out a flow chart to aid how we saw the debate developing. I was spokesman. My main assistant in preparing our legal material was Chris McLean, a law student and later the SNP's media official. On the first day, I argued with the sheriff that the 1979 Order repealing the Assembly Act was

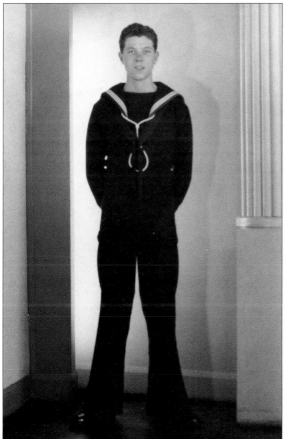

Above. Matthew Sillars and Agnes Sproat on their wedding day, 23 October 1931. Jock Sillars, best man, Alice Sproat (far left) and Nellie Sproat (far right), bridesmaids.

Left. In my first Royal Navy uniform, 1955.

Royal Guard, HMS *Mercury*. I am third from the right, front row.

With my brother, Robert (left), who was in the RAF. This photograph was taken during his National Service, 1955.

In Hong Kong, where I proved to be an adept five-a-side hockey player.

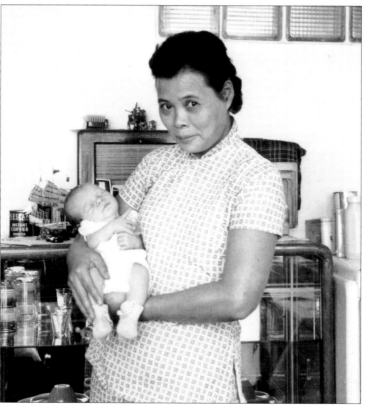

Mui Ying, our Chinese amah in Hong Kong, with my son, Matthew.

Talking to a Primary 7 class at Coylton Primary School during the South Ayrshire by-election of 1970. The class was having its own mock election.

With Neil Kinnock in Boston at the end of our 1975 tour of the United States.

Above. With Alex Neil during a Scottish Labour Party press conference, 1976.

Left. A cartoon showing what was expected of the SNP during the 1978 regional council elections. The result turned out to be not so good.

PARLIAMENTARY ELECTION
SOUTH AYRSHIRE
Thursday, 3rd May, 1979

Jim Sillars

the Scottish Labour candidate for South Ayrshire

What Sillars said last time

"Jim Sillars pledges to vote for setting up a Scottish Parliament with full powers over Scottish affairs, plus economic powers."

and

"There is need to restore respect and trust in our Parliamentary system of government. The principal responsibility rests with politicians who must be honest with the people, and never promise that which they know they cannot fulfil."

Election Address 1974

Dear Elector,

At the last Election I made certain pledges. Pledges based on no superficial appraisal but on serious analysis designed to produce lasting solutions to the problems facing Scotland and the UK. The Labour Government progressively reneged on fundamental issues — unemployment, wages policy, devolution. I was forced to choose. Either I had to abandon socialism and my election pledges in favour of a hypocritical Parliamentary career with the Labour Party. Or I had to reject the Labour Party in favour of socialism and political honesty.

I chose socialism and honesty. Twice at that time I formally offered Labour's Chief Whip a by-election in South Ayrshire. Twice Bob Mellish said "No." I believe subsequent events have proved me right on crucial issues. But especially over the disgraceful treatment meted out to Scotland on devolution.

My experience drove me to conclude that we need a Scottish Labour Party not thirled to any London organisation, speaking freely and boldly for the Scottish people but working in partnership with the rest of the UK.

Jim Sillars

Above. A Scottish Labour Party leaflet produced for the South Ayrshire general election, 1979.

Right. The famous Turnbull cartoon summing up the mood of the Scottish nation in the 1979 referendum.

A poster advertising debates between Jim Sillars and Tam Dalyell during the 1979 devolution referendum.

With Lito Alenia, having a day off work in Manila, Philippines 1981. This was the period when I did consultancy work in the developing world for a small Scottish company.

Margo and me on our wedding day, 1981.

Margo outside BBC Broadcasting House, London, in 1985, when she anchored a consumer programme on BBC1.

A publicity photograph of Margo used to promote her *Face the Facts* investigative programme on BBC Radio 4, 1986.

Margo and me at home in Woodburn Terrace, Edinburgh, 1989.

With Margo MacDonald after winning the Govan by-election for the SNP in 1988. (Trinity Mirror/ MirrorPix / Alamy Stock Photo)

Margo and me with the Penilee Gala Queen, Govan constituency, 1991.

At a trade conference, London, while working for the Arab–British Chamber of Commerce, 1993.

Above. At a reception in Bahrain, 1995 (third from the left).

Above. Speaking on behalf of the Arab–British Chamber of Commerce at a trade conference in the Gulf, 1999.

Above. With Abdul Karim Al-Mudaris, Mrs Mudaris, Miss Mudaris, Brian Wilson Minister of Trade and Jim Prior at the Arab–British Chamber Annual Dinner, 1998.

Left. With Margo and daughter Julie and four of our grandchildren – Stephen, Matthew, Beth and Adam – outside our villa in Portugal, 2003.

The Boyle cartoon on my re-entry into politics to campaign in the 2014 referendum.

The Margo Mobile campaigning in Clydebank during the 2014 referendum.

invalid because the Scots had voted in a majority for the assembly, that the 40 per cent rule was against the principles of democracy in which a majority was what counted, that, ipso facto, the UK government's legislation had no legal validity in Scots law and that, therefore, the charges against us were also invalid. I later learned that the procurator fiscal, knowing that, in the past, every nationalist who went to court cited the Act of Union, had prepared for that eventuality. He was a bit miffed to find that we had taken a very different constitutional argument.

The sheriff seemed to enjoy the debate between me, the procurator fiscal and himself. The whole day was taken up with this constitutional case. On the second day, the verdicts were delivered. The case against the party official, Iain More, who, under my instruction as a party official, had taken us and our break-in gear in a lorry to the railings outside the assembly building and then departed, was found not proven. The rest of us were found guilty. I was fined £100, the others £50. I appealed. This required an appearance and a stated case before the Court of Appeal and I found myself about to face Tam Dalyell's father-in-law, John Wheatley, the Lord Justice Clerk, and two other judges. Going into court that morning with Chris McLean who was lending his legal knowledge, a couple of advocates told me the word was that Wheatley was going to fillet me.

Before then, Margo MacDonald and I had married on 10 April 1981 and set up home in a flat in Balcarres Court, in Edinburgh's Morningside. Margo wasn't upset by my arrest and thoroughly approved of the idea at the heart of the challenge we were mounting, at both the Sheriff and Appeal Courts. Although there were nationalist advocates and QCs in the legal system, none wanted to represent us at the Appeal Court. A couple did come to our flat, said what a splendid thing we were doing and, as Margo noted, drank our whisky before leaving, without pointing to a single piece of legal principle that might guide us.

I don't know if the rumour about John Wheatley taking me apart was based on the assumption that I would use the opportunity to try to make a grand political statement but Chris and I had no such intention. Our case was framed entirely within a legal and constitutional context. We were challenging the supremacy of the UK Parliament by asserting the supremacy of the Scottish people, with that right anchored in law, as expressed in cases and by legal scholars.

Any possible tension between us and the judges disappeared when it became clear that we were not engaged in political theatre but were arguing a well-prepared case backed by impeccable references. We cited

Lord Cooper in *MacCormick v Lord Advocate* in the 1953 Queen's title case, where he said:

> The principle of the unlimited sovereignty of Parliament is a distinctively English principle which has no counterpart in Scottish constitutional law. It derives its origin from Coke and Blackstone, and was widely popularised during the nineteenth century by Bagehot and Dicey, the latter having stated the doctrine in its classic form in his *Law of Constitution*. Considering that the Union legislation extinguished the Parliaments of Scotland and England and replaced them by a new Parliament, I have difficulty in seeing why it should have been supposed that the new Parliament of Great Britain must inherit all the peculiar characteristics of the English Parliament but none of the Scottish Parliament, as if all that happened in 1707 was that Scottish representatives were admitted to the Parliament of England. That was not what was done.

Of course, that is exactly what was done and one suspects that, in choosing to set out his view in the way he did, Lord Cooper was telling us that, whatever the Treaty of Union may say, the political facts leading to the English rules were just that – Scots joining a continuing English Parliament.

We quoted great Scottish legal scholars such as James Dalrymple, Viscount of Stair, and George Buchanan, the latter from 1579, to prove that the idea of the King being sovereign was not held to be so in Scotland, where legal history showed it to rest with the people and, therefore, this English theory of parliamentary sovereignty having been transferred from the King could not be applied to Scotland.

We quoted Buchanan:

> The Scottish Nation, which from the beginning has always been free, has created Kings upon the condition that the government entrusted to them by the people's suffrage may also if necessary be removed by the same suffrage.

Buchanan is an echo from the 1320 Declaration of Arbroath which, for that time, offered the novel and revolutionary idea that a people could remove an anointed monarch – much more radical than Magna Carta.

Chris, who was identified as a law student, and I were treated with the utmost respect by Wheatley and the others. They listened carefully, asked questions and conducted the appeal in a pleasant atmosphere. The judges did not rule immediately but took it to avizandum, meaning they were going to give consideration to the legal and constitutional submissions we made and would rule later. We didn't expect to win the appeal but no immediate dismissal was, I believe, a compliment to the case we had argued. A man sitting at the back of the court came up to me and Chris, as we packed up, to say it was the finest party litigant appeal he had heard. Some weeks later the appeal was dismissed and a long written judgement set out the judge's legal answers to what we set out. Their decision was that Parliament was sovereign and no Act passed by it could be challenged. When I was subsequently a law student at Edinburgh University, I found it amusing to hear the lecturer refer to *Sillars v Smith* (1982) SLT 539 in the constitutional law classes.

Our challenge to the sovereignty of Parliament, once the appeal was heard, stimulated a discussion within academic and legal circles, with articles appearing in a number of legal journals and I was invited contribute to some of them.

Our research had answered the question rarely asked in Scotland – how, if Lord Cooper was right, as he was, in pointing to the sovereignty of Parliament as originating in the writing of English legal scholars only, did it end up in Scottish constitutional law when Scottish scholars had long opposed the idea's legitimacy? We found it did not enter Scots law as a result of any considered, serious debate in our law journals or by an Act of the UK Parliament. Indeed, Scottish judges up to 1842 thought differently from the English scholars. In a civil case *The Edinburgh and Dalkeith Railway Company v Wauchope*, the legitimacy of an Act of Parliament was the relevant question. In answering it, the Court of Session held, in effect, that no Act of Parliament was sacrosanct. But, in a short statement, on a final appeal of the case in the House of Lords, Lord Campbell changed Scots constitutional law, as our law lords and legal scholars, had understood it for centuries, with these words:

> All that a court of justice can do is look to the parliamentary roll; they see that an act has passed both Houses of Parliament, and that it has received the royal assent, and no court of justice can enquire into the manner in which it was introduced into parliament. I therefore trust that no such enquiry will hereafter be entered into in Scotland, and that due effect will be given to every act of Parliament . . .

That there might have been a different legal view in Scotland was given short shrift. Thus did the purely English view of the constitution come into our law.

Nothing came of our civil disobedience. There was no real appetite for it among the party membership and certainly none among the public. It was a mistaken policy and I take full responsibility for it. But later, when I was looking for employment in Scotland, I was to pay a price for it.

*

In 1985, Stephen Maxwell, a key member of the 79 Group and one of Scotland's top intellectuals, came up with idea of me collaborating with him in the writing of a book charting our individual political developments. We were very different people from very different backgrounds – his was as an academic and a life-long nationalist and mine was as a former unionist Labour supporter. We decided we would also include a series of essays on current major issues to the dual narrative format. Polygon agreed to publish it but, unfortunately, Stephen could not engage in the project for personal reasons so it was left to me.

These were not good times in Scotland. Mrs Thatcher's policies were having devastating effects and the miners had been defeated. But I thought our nation could escape from this gloomy decline and arrive at better political times. So I set about writing *SCOTLAND: The Case for Optimism* which was published in 1986. In it, I sought to analyse what had gone wrong in the 1970s with the broad self-government movement and the SNP. The assessment made was that errors by the SNP and others came from being catapulted into the top level of British politics without having the necessary experience. The defeat in the 1979 referendum was not due to some inherent defect in the Scots and, if we learned the lessons from that period, the SNP and the broader movement would be better equipped in continuing the fight for independence. I made an effort to address the Scottish Left's attitude to the 'national question', something that continues to be a thorny problem for many in the Labour Party today. Of particular importance was the class issue that the SNP had dodged or denied and I did not forget to look at our relationship with England and the framework for independence that membership of the EEC offered.

The book was warmly received. I suppose, looking back, it shone a light of hope, even if a small one, in those dark years. Even today, people still tell me of its influence on them and their view of independence. The book was also the subject of a debate – well, more of a discussion really – I had with Donald Dewar one night in Old College, Edinburgh

University, chaired by Alex Salmond. Donald deserves all the credit given to him for the setting up of the Scottish Parliament but, on that night, he was the pessimistic one. Devastated by the result of the 1979 independence referendum, he found it difficult to share my optimism for the future. It was my analysis of the reasons for our lost that led me to believe a win was possible next time but Donald took a different view.

*

I was unemployed after coming back from Saudi Arabia and, being regarded as too controversial a figure, I was finding it impossible to get a job in Scotland. The break-in at the assembly didn't help in that respect. At one job interview, the employer asked what I thought people would think of his company if they employed me. Then came an opportunity. A London charity advertised a job in Scotland. They were looking for someone who knew Scottish local government, the health service and Scottish politics. The salary was very low but I needed a job. I had been a councillor and trade union official, had served on a hospital board and had been an MP for nine years and I still contributed articles on public policy so I thought I was in with a chance. The chairman of the interview panel was the Labour MP Frank Judd. It seemed to go well. But the job went to a person who had never been to Scotland before and who knew nothing in the areas specified in the job application. The message from every job application I made was clear – I was not employable up here.

With only Margo earning – she was a freelance journalist with a variable income – we were very hard up. At one particular Christmas, we managed to buy presents for the children but the best Margo could afford to get me was a hired video of a Western which, on viewing, we discovered was a copy of a copy. My friend David Thomson and his wife Margo sent us a food parcel.

Our close friends Charlie and Anne Stoddart kept urging me to study law with a view to earning my living as a solicitor. Charlie taught law at Edinburgh University, was the author of legal textbooks and became a solicitor and later a sheriff principal. He thought I had the mind for it and put me in touch with Alexander McCall Smith, who was the dean of the Faculty of Law at the university, and he invited me for an interview. He explained that, although I had no Highers, he thought that, given my public service, I deserved a chance to enter the university via a special exam that I would have to sit, as there could be no privileged open door. I sat the exam, which included a long interview, more an interrogation, from an academic brought in for the purpose. I passed.

So, in September 1985, I became a first-year law student and loved it. All was going well into my second year and I earned a pass in criminal law and merits in every other subject. But I had been adopted as the parliamentary candidate in Linlithgow, facing my old friend Tam Dalyell, at the next general election which turned out to be in June 1987. I knew I could not beat Tam. My aim was to raise the SNP total. In the campaign, I didn't actually face Tam. He never appeared on any hustings and a substitute took his place while he was out and about through the rest of the UK attacking Mrs Thatcher on the sinking of the *Belgrano*, during the 1982 Falklands War.

I had to make a choice – attend university lectures and tutorials or give proper time to the campaign which was starting in late spring. I chose the campaign. The reason was that, whatever my private view of the likely result, SNP members thought we could win. Their enthusiasm and commitment was total and they deserved a candidate giving a full-time effort to the campaign. The result was a disappointment to the members. The votes cast in Linlithgow were:

> Labour 21,869
> SNP 11,496
> Tory 6,828
> SDP 5,840
> Communist 154

The 1987 national result in Scotland for seats won was:

> Labour 50
> Tory 10
> Lib 9
> SNP 3

Nationally, the party's percentage of the vote went up from 11.7 per cent in 1983, to 14 per cent in 1987, with Alex Salmond gaining Banff and Buchan. Although the local activists were in the dumps about West Lothian, our vote went up 6.5 per cent and set the basis for a big SNP advance in the next local elections.

No sooner was the election over than my old Arab friend Fakhri Shehab phoned to offer me a job heading up the public relations department at the Arab–British Chamber of Commerce (ABCC) in Belgrave Square, London, where he had become the economic adviser. The money was equal to an MP's salary and a car came along with it. So, a choice to be made – two more years to finish my LLB degree, followed by a diploma year and then, hopefully but not certainly, a trainee year before finally qualifying as a solicitor or taking a well-paid interesting job. I chose the job and lived in Ealing, along the road from Neil Kinnock who I met again.

There was to be another attraction to living in London. In 1987, Margo had broken through into all-UK broadcasting, fronting high-profile BBC radio and television programmes in London. So we were able to be together part of the week and, once a month, I went back home to Edinburgh for the weekend to see the rest of the family.

Public relations turned out to be a misnomer for the department at ABCC. Basically, we organised the big annual dinner, which was Arab London's business night of the year, and seminars in various parts of the UK, mostly in England, for British business about trade opportunities in the Arab markets.

The British press were not interested in a chamber of commerce, even an Arab one. The PR was all crafted towards the Arab press, which I didn't handle, just observed. London, with no censorship, was a big centre for the Arab press. The British press has its shady parts but I had never met a really corrupt press before joining the chamber. People paid to get things in – and things out – of the Arab newspapers. One Arab journalist made an excellent living by gathering the dirt on the Saudi royals when they were in London and Europe and then going along to the Saudi embassy where he threatened to publish what he'd compiled. He was paid off every time. Luckily for him MBS was not around then.

When we were visited by a delegation from Jordan, it struck me that it would make an ideal partner for our Scottish Development Agency (SDA) and relations were quickly established. As the Arab–British Chamber of Commerce staff member, I was responsible for organising visits from the SDA to Jordan. This led to an unexpected offer from the SDA for me to take up the chief executive's post in a new company called Scottish International, whose business was to promote and seek contracts for Scottish companies bidding for international architectural contracts. I left the ABCC in early 1988 but remained in touch with the Arab friends I had made there, especially the secretary-general, Abdul Karim Al Mudaris, who later became an important influence on my life and work.

In the newly created SDA company, my job was to build up international contacts with governments and governmental organisations, using Scottish university alumni to get information and introductions where appropriate. I visited Singapore, Malaysia, Hong Kong and China as a start, with the next step being to compile projects where we might have an opportunity to tender. Before I joined, the company had come close to success in the competition for the Hong Kong University tender. We had a small staff and everyone knew it would take time to get to grips on an area of international business where Scottish companies were not well known. Then, out of the blue, came the Govan by-election.

In late 1988, Bruce Millan, former Labour Secretary of State for Scotland, resigned his Govan seat to become a European Commissioner. A number of us met and decided that, given the strength of the Labour vote there, Kenny MacAskill should be the candidate we would push inside the SNP as he was a well-known Left-winger who would help bring the Labour majority down a bit. Then there were second thoughts in our group and it was decided that I would have a better chance of a bigger reduction in the Labour majority, if I could get three weeks off work. I asked the company board and, to my surprise, they said yes because, in the words of one, 'Labour needs a kick up the pants.' A look at the 1987 election result shows that neither the board nor I, at that time, thought I had a chance, other than to give Labour that kick in the pants.

The 1987 general election result for votes cast in Govan had been:

> Labour 24,071
> Alliance 4,562
> Tory 4,411
> SNP 3,851
> Communist 237
> Labour majority 19,509

The Right wing in the SNP did not want me as candidate and were pushing for Iain Lawson. Iain had come from the Tory Party but, despite our different political backgrounds, we became not only political but also personal friends who could talk openly with one another. Iain knew that he was not the candidate to make a mark in Govan but the Right insisted he should be on the short list. His speech to the selection meeting was a most unusual one. To the amazement and anger of the Right-wing delegates, some of whom walked out, he said I was the best candidate for Govan and they should vote for me. I was duly selected.

A big issue, probably the biggest, in the by-election campaign was going to be the poll tax. Scheduled to start being levied in 1989 in

Scotland before being rolled out in England and Wales, the legislation had been passed by Westminster in early 1988. Tommy Sheridan, a member of Labour's Militant, had already mobilised a non-payment movement and the SNP had had to decide whether to join it. Kenny MacAskill produced a paper for the National Executive in which he identified the basic weakness of the Tory legislation – non-payment would not be a criminal act as it would fall to civic law to implement it and, if non-payment reached a mass level, there was no way the system could operate. The SNP joined in, helping to boost the numbers Tommy was aiming for.

By backing non-payment, the SNP had put me as candidate in a powerful position. My main opponent, Bob Gillespie was saddled with the 1988 October annual conference decision of his party to oppose non-payment, obeying its leader Neil Kinnock's dictum: 'Law makers must not be law breakers.' That was not the position he took as an MP when trade unionists deliberately broke the Tory industrial relations law and defied and destroyed the Industrial Relations Court. But Neil had moved on from his radical past.

Two aspects riled the Scots – that we were chosen as guinea pigs for the poll tax and that, as a method of raising money, it was fundamentally unfair if poor families were required to pay the same as very rich ones. I don't think we were guinea pigs. It was a fatal accident of timing but few believed it. The fact that it was a product of Thatcher's government added another toxic layer. Knowing they were courting trouble by opposing non-payment, Labour decided to have a short, sharp election campaign of no more than three weeks, believing they would be able to stave off a build-up of resentment against their poll tax position. That was a mistake in my favour.

Another serious Labour difficulty was those 50 seats, out of 72, won in the 1987 general election. Labour was a giant but, being unable to protect us from a despised Tory government laying waste to our industrial base, an impotent one. Alex Salmond, tellingly, summed them up as 'the feeble fifty' – a truth that was widely recognised. I could ask the people of Govan what difference another vote for Labour would make against the poll tax and the Tory wrecking would make. The answer would be none. Nevertheless, it looked impossible for the SNP to win. Hammer Labour on its weak spot, reduce its majority and get into second place – that was as much as we could hope for. However, I intended to fight the election to win. A candidate leads a campaign but cannot meet every elector. The prime task is to enthuse the activists with what I call the 'percussion style' of leadership. The candidate at the top hits the party activists with the conviction that he or she is of the right calibre, with the right policy and the will to win. The activists then hit the electorate, conveying their belief in the merits of the candidate. Those voters who have been hit by the enthusiasm and conviction of the activists, then hit others with a similar enthusiasm. The percussion model produces political impact.

By the time of the Govan by-election in 1988, Alex Neil had also joined the SNP. One cold damp night, before the campaign properly got under way and before I had been publicly announced as a candidate, he and I went into Govan and knocked on a number of doors. We asked people if they had voted Labour before and most said they had. We then asked if they would consider shifting to the SNP in the by-election. A good number said yes to the second question, with most explaining their reason for this was their disappointment with Labour. When we met to compare notes, we came to the conclusion that the by-election was winnable.

A couple of days later, during an interview with Fiona Ross for STV, she asked if I believed I could win, to which I replied yes. Afterwards, off screen, she said I obviously had to say that on camera but was I serious? I told her yes – I was going to win. That is what I had set out to do.

Polling day was 10 November 1988. I had a superb election agent in Allison Hunter so I was totally free of any organisational worries and able to concentrate on the politics. The reason a three-week campaign was an advantage was because I was physically capable of going hell for leather over that short period, to make an impact. It also meant Labour did not have much time to try to find answers to the criticism I was going to make.

I needed ideas and help on how to make an impact. They came principally from Iain Lawson, Gil Paterson, who would later serve as SNP MSP for Central Scotland, then West of Scotland and later Clydebank and Milngavie, Alex Neil and Alex Salmond, who had won the seat of Banff and Buchan for the SNP in the 1987 general election which he would continue to hold for the next two decades. Their advice on the political strategy and the method of campaigning was invaluable. I was also lucky in having Alex Salmond arrange for James Mitchell, then a lecturer at Strathclyde University and now Professor of Public Policy at Edinburgh University, to be my permanent aide. His help, advice and support were important in keeping my spirits up and this was sometimes necessary in private. He had a great sense of humour. Lots of laughter in a campaign is a great asset. Margo's campaigns were always marked by laughter and fun.

It was Iain and Gil who came up with the idea of the Snappy Bus, a small Toyota flat-top van that Gil made into a very visible covered mobile speaking platform, equipped with a very loud loudspeaker. It was a piece of campaign genius. Pat Kane of the band Hue and Cry came along for a day with Craig and Charlie Reid of the Proclaimers and they all helped to generate huge interest.

With the Snappy Bus easy to handle in traffic and to park, I was able to make myself and my views known quickly in every street in the constituency. We would go out and attack 'the feeble fifty' one day, then go on about destroying the poll tax the next day, changing the message as the campaign developed. And, as it developed, I found it easier to talk to people about the state Scotland was in, the need to change the constitution, and why I supported independence. I made about twelve to fifteen speeches a day from it and could get off it easily to meet and talk to people in the street.

New and different, the Snappy Bus was a source of pride and a morale booster for the activists, who followed us in other vehicles to knock on doors, give out leaflets and get people to put up posters while I made a speech. We were increasing our support day by day and becoming serious contenders. The fact that I had been a left-wing Labour MP who had never deserted my socialism – a socialism I preached through-out the campaign – also helped. I kept getting messages from Gordon Wilson, SNP leader, in a good-natured way, telling me that I may have been straying from party policy now and again. Essentially, as John Pollock realised, I was fighting an SLP campaign but under a different flag. In openly declaring myself a socialist, I was also emphasising that I was no party hack but had a mind of my own.

The party hack issue mattered in Govan. On top of Labour's weak points mentioned above, there was another one in the shape of the Labour candidate, Bob Gillespie, a trade union official who could not be himself in the campaign. Bob was as Left wing as I was, probably in favour of non-payment of the poll tax and a long-time opponent of the nuclear weapons which Neil Kinnock had now embraced, reversing a lifetime's position on the issue. Bob was kept under tight control, with one of the London HQ minions always present at the hustings to make sure he kept to the party line. There was one disastrous, embarrassing meeting when he read out a speech written for him. I was able to exploit this control. With him in the orthodox Labour cage, I could set out the Left-wing arguments in favour of mass non-payment of the poll tax and attack the Tory government's position on nuclear weapons –especially given the proximity of the base at Faslane – so that Bob was left looking and sounding like a stale party functionary incapable of an opinion of his own.

Although we were behind, the canvass returns said we were gaining. Allison Hunter had a team recording them every night, charting where our strength was growing and where we still had to make an impact and what issues we should emphasise from the Snappy Bus. Using a loudspeaker outdoors is an art that takes a particular voice and speaking style to be successful. Few can achieve it but Iain Lawson, Alex Neil and I all had that gift. The combination of Allison's daily intelligence briefing, the Snappy Bus speeches and Gil Paterson's organisation of workers at street level were all vital if we were to win.

My press campaign was conducted with the aid of Bob Brown. Our experience in the SLP had cemented a deep friendship which also included his wife Margaret. He became a wonderful shoulder to lean on when, at times, I felt a bit despondent. One particular interview is worth recounting and it put paid to the Labour claim that I was a liar about being offered a job by Harold Wilson after the October 1974 election. The journalist conducting the interview was Joe Haines, who had been Harold Wilson's close aide and was now working for the *Daily Mirror*. Haines confirmed, with Bob Brown as witness, that I had been telling the truth because he had been listening on an extension to the exchange between me and Wilson.-

Another important figure, both during the by-election and afterwards, was Andy Collier of the *Scottish Sun*. Like most Left-wingers, I was hostile to that newspaper and, on agreeing to an interview, I expected questions designed to trap me. Instead, I found myself talking to a professional journalist whose questions and subsequent follow-ups revealed someone who was genuinely interested in my position on a variety of issues and who reported fairly as well as critically. I was impressed.

Social Democrat candidate Bernard Ponsonby was impressive too. He was a natural in politics with an immediate command of issue and a wonderful sense of humour but he had no chance of winning as the campaign had quickly become a two-horse race between SNP and Labour. Bernard went into a career in journalism and became political editor of STV. In that role, he made a valuable contribution to Scottish political life but he would have been even more valuable as an elected representative.

The first television debate was on the BBC. The main issues that emerged were the poll tax and the scourge of drugs within the community. On the latter, there was sharp criticism of the police in their failure to tackle the level of criminality associated with the drug trade. We were all asked at the end of the programme what we would do about the drugs problem. Bob Gillespie said he would call a summit, a proposal that left the audience cold. I said that, if elected on the Thursday night, I would pick up the phone to the chief constable at 9 a.m. on the Friday morning and demand a meeting. My answer was the most practical one and the one I found was most favoured when talking to people the next day. I did phone the chief constable at 9 a.m. on the Friday morning and got the meeting I needed. After I was elected, I established a close working relationship with the police. I got them to be more visible in tackling drug crime and, as the community's confidence in them grew, I became a channel of information through which information about the local drug trade was passed on to them. I was known among the drug dealers as 'that fucking drug buster'.

According to the opinion polls, we had made headway but were expected to finish well behind Labour. At the start of the campaign, the polls on 28 October were Labour 58 per cent, SNP 24 per cent. But we did not panic. Our canvassers were happy, coming back with an increasing number of don't knows. Certainly, Bob Gillespie believed the polls. My voice was hoarse from all the outdoor speaking and he would pour me a drink of IRN-BRU during the hustings – most solicitous of the man who would finish well behind me. Bob was complacency itself while the ground was beginning to shift from under him.

The STV debate format featured each candidate questioning the others. My concentration would be on Bob Gillespie. I knew Bob reasonably well before the campaign. I was aware of his deep hostility to the EU and I doubted if he would have bothered very much about the nitty-gritty of the issues emerging at that time. I saw the EU as Bob's weakness.

It came to me while in the shower on the morning of the debate – I would ask him his views on additionality. Briefly, the issue was whether, when the EU put a pound into a project in the UK, the UK government would contribute another pound. I was going to gamble on Bob's ignorance. If he did know about additionality and could expound on it, I was sunk. But, if he didn't, I was going to make him look out of his depth in front of what was bound to be a big audience.

It turned out better than I had hoped. When I asked his views on 'additionality', Bob hadn't a clue that it was an EU issue and started to talk about workers' wages. As he stumbled for words, with hands going all over the place, he knocked over the floor mike. Everything had to stop until it was put back up. It was a disaster for him.

Next day, when talking to people in the street, it was obvious that 'additionality' had been the final campaign changer. Our canvassers found the don't knows plumping for the SNP. Iain Lawson and I intensified the Snappy Bus impact at street level and Gil Paterson and Alex Neil took teams of activists to extend the number of posters that were showing support. Our team's tails were up and you could feel it flowing our way.

The media knew Bob had made a mess of the STV debate but, guided by the poll on 7 November, three days before the vote – Labour 53 per cent, SNP 33 per cent – were sceptical that it could make the kind of difference required for a win. They were also sceptical of our claim of a surge of support suggested by the number of window posters going up. Window posters did not vote, we were told. But those putting them up did.

Gordon Wilson came to campaign alongside me in the last week and told me to pack my bags for Westminster. We won. We would probably have won even if Labour had let Bob Gillespie be himself but it would have been much closer. The results for the main parties were:

SNP 14,677
Labour 11,123
Tory 2,207
Social Democrat 1,246
SNP majority 3,554

That campaign put to rest the gibe about Tartan Tories and the blame for letting in Thatcher began to fade. It had taken almost a decade.

One asset and one problem during the by-election was Margo. The asset was that everyone in Govan knew who she was and many claimed to have voted for her in 1974. At meetings I was often introduced as 'Margo's man', which was a mark of approval. The problem arose from the fact that she could not be seen in the campaign because she was then head interviewer – interrogator would be more apt – for STV's political programmes. The producer for these programmes was John Brown, Gordon Brown's brother. Scotland is a small place.

One night, as we were all packing up at the end of a long day, with everyone saying how tired they were and looking forward to a good night's sleep, I told them how lucky they were – I was going home to a public meeting of one, called Margo.

17

Westminster Second Time Round

As is usual, after a surprising by-election result, I was interviewed by all the UK mainstream news and current affairs programmes. It seemed to come as a shock to their English listeners and viewers when I described Margaret Thatcher as a 'bigoted English Tory' who had no democratic right to rule over Scotland.

I have always attracted letters of a vile nature, most, but not all, anonymous. My friend and fellow MP Eric Heffer, from Liverpool, was the same. He used to explode. I told him to follow my practice – I write back to those with an address saying I keep a file of the most abusive letters received but was sorry to say his (they were all from men) did not qualify.

I was not particularly welcomed when I took my seat. Westminster, the heart of the UK establishment, didn't take kindly to someone who had caused a major disruption with possible serious political and con-stitutional consequences. Labour was in angry shock especially as their defeat had been inflicted by a 'traitor'. However, that was not quite universal. My old pals Eric Heffer, Stan Orme and Dennis Skinner were fine, as was Tam Dalyell. John Smith, who was a near neighbour in Edinburgh, was his usual friendly self.

When I took the oath to the Queen, I again deliberately missed out 'the second' in her title and watched as the clerk hesitated, as his prede-cessor had done in 1970, and then decided it was better just to ignore what I had not done.

The Labour whips did the office allocation for the opposition parties and I was given an office in one of the Norman Shaw North Buildings, located above Westminster tube station. It had been the office of John Taylor, the Ulster Unionist, but was never occupied as it was deemed unsafe for him. The staff used it as a storeroom, so it was not in a good condition.

At the end of my first week back, I spent the weekend speaking at public meetings in the Highlands. Returning to the Westminster offices on the following Monday morning, I asked for my office key, only to be told by the clerk that I couldn't have it as I was to be what he termed 'evicted'. I didn't make a fuss. I just said I had to get my stuff out and would give him back the key as I left. It was obvious to me that the powers-that-be were intent on making life difficult. This tactic was tried successfully on Ken Livingstone, who the Labour establishment hated. He didn't know the rules and made a great public fuss about having no office and, in a speech of complaint at the door of the Commons, said he was going home – just what his Labour enemies wanted. By then I was out and was not available to advise him what to do.

Once in, I phoned the Serjeant at Arms' office. A very snooty woman answered and she obviously took delight in confirming that the office was no longer mine and I had to leave, with no alternative available. But those who had decided to evict me had forgotten or did not know that I was no rookie and I knew the rules. So I told her not to worry because I would move my stuff to the government front bench and do all my constituency work and other correspondence in the seats normally used, but only by convention, by the prime minister and min-isters. An MP can reserve any seat in the Commons with a prayer card before the House assembles, which guarantees the seat for as long as he or she wishes. That, I said, is what I would do very early each morning so that I could go through my mail and answer letters. I told her the prime minister and other ministers could still do their duties from the dispatch box but not from my seat. She rang off. A few minutes later the Serjeant at Arms himself called back, telling me 'not to panic' and that he was coming over to see me. The word had got out because next I got a phone call from Andrew Welsh, our whip, also telling me not to panic. I was the only one not in a panic because I knew I had them. The Serjeant at Arms explained there had been a mistake and, of course, this was my office. Both of us knew there had been no mistake. But now, not only was I to stay but the office would also be painted, carpeted and brought up to standard. This small incident might seem trivial but it was important. I had to show the House authorities and Labour that they were not going to put salt on my tail and would just have to accept that I was there. The fact that I had beaten them at their own game meant I was acknowledged as being there on my terms.

There were only four SNP MPs – Margaret Ewing, Andrew Welsh, Alex Salmond and me – with Jim Eadie and Flora McLean doing research. Later, we were joined by Dick Douglas, originally the Labour MP for Dunfermline. He was the man I had been election organiser for way back in Pollok in 1967. Dick had served on the Defence Select Committee and, like Alex Salmond, was an economist. Thus, we may have been small in number but there was nothing wrong with the quality.

The parliamentary agenda and timetable are run by the government and official opposition for their own convenience. The Liberal Democrats got a nod of acknowledgement but we and those from Northern Ireland and Plaid Cymru were regarded as minnows with few rights, such as being able to command significant debating time on subjects of our choosing. We were occasionally given half a day for a debate.

Any SNP group, small or large, has a different role to that of the unionist parties. Of course, we were similar to them in that we served and represented individual constituents and constituency interests and it was vital for us to make ourselves known for the weight we might carry as politicians, through the quality of our contributions to debates and questions in the House chamber. In my experience, civil servants and ministers are wary of political heavyweight MPs, who can command attention and make trouble for them, both in Parliament and the media. We had to do this from minnow-group status and, if we were to have any impact, it had to come from respect for our abilities in specialist areas. Margaret Ewing did this in social affairs, Andrew Welsh in housing and local government, Alex Salmond in economics and I made my mark in foreign affairs. In Dick Douglas we had a specialist in defence.

But that difference between the SNP and others is that our intention was and is to change the British state by taking Scotland out of it. We had a function to perform in London but independence is not to be won there but in Scotland, by energising our activists and seeking to win over more people to independence. This demanded a lot of time spent campaigning back up north. We also had to keep up the morale of our activists, a remarkable group of people who held on tenaciously to the goal of independence at a time when the idea was derided (and I had done my share of it) with every advance followed by a giant setback. They wanted us to give two fingers to Westminster whenever we could. There were few opportunities for doing that but there was one event in the parliamentary calendar – the Budget – when the House is packed and the media are geared up to bring news and analysis. In 1988, Alex Salmond had interrupted the chancellor's speech, making the first news reports not about the chancellor's proposals but the SNP showing disrespect to a venerated occasion of state. The question was, when I got there, whether it could be done again and differently in 1989.

A Difference of Opinion

I delved into the Commons Bible, *Erskine May: Parliamentary Practice*, a compilation of rules and precedents built up over centuries by many speakers, for how I might subvert budget day. There was then a vacancy for Glasgow Central, following the death of its Labour MP. The party holding the seat when a death occurred would always move the writ for the by-election and set the date. But a by-election writ is a matter of privilege and any MP can move the writ, irrespective of party. In *Erskine May*, I discovered that a matter of privilege takes precedence over any other business before the House – even over the Budget statement.

The moving of a writ usually only takes a few minutes but there is no time limit. Explaining why a writ should be issued allows the MP moving it to cover a great deal of ground, if he or she wants to. This can include a physical description of the constituency, its history, demographics, the work its people do, social problems, the issues of housing, roads, social services, education, facilities and so on. I had file upon file on these aspects of Glasgow Central and intended using them to make a very long speech. My plan was to rise just before the chancellor on a point of privilege, move the writ and talk for over three hours. That would ensure every TV and radio station, not only in the UK but elsewhere, would carry the story of an SNP MP blocking the Budget. It seemed foolproof. And it was until I did a very foolish thing. Concerned for the officials who would have to advise the Speaker on the spot that I was within my rights, I told the chief clerk of the Commons what I was going to do. The man went white as a sheet and thanked me politely. I learnt afterwards that he went straight off to the Speaker.

As I made my way to the chamber, ready to give a very big two fingers to the Westminster establishment, little did I know that the constitutional brains of the House – the clerks, the Speaker, the Leader and Shadow Leader of the House – had worked out how to snooker me. All that was required was a new ruling by the Speaker that a Private Notice Question would come first. So, right at the start, as I rose to speak, Neil Kinnock, through prior arrangement with the Speaker, asked under a PNQ if the chancellor would make a statement. The Speaker then told me to sit down, which I refused to do and, after a few minutes, the Leader of the House moved that I be removed. After a vote, I was duly escorted off the premises and suspended for a week. My plan had not worked but I had created a situation that cheered our activists back home because, although not in the way I had planned, the Budget had been disrupted.

Shortly after I got back into the House, I took my revenge by frustrating another important piece of government business, without warning anyone this time. As the writ had still not been moved, I moved it and delivered a three-and-a-half-hour speech, thus messing up the government business and timetable. There was hostility again but I spoke mostly to an empty House as all knew nothing could be done to stop me unless the Speaker hauled me down on being out of order. I never was.

In case anyone thinks what Alex and I did in disrupting the Budget was easy, that was far from being the case. We had to act and hold our ground defiantly in a small packed chamber where the hostility and rage came at us in waves.

*

Iraq never existed until the British made it a state, when they got their hands on Mesopotamia with the break-up of the Ottoman Empire in 1918. Prince Faisal, who led the Arab revolt against the Ottomans, along with Lawrence of Arabia, had been made king of Syria by the Arabs but was violently ejected by the French. The British then made him king of the new Iraq but made sure they effectively controlled the country.

Kuwait had been a British protectorate from 1899 until it achieved independent state status in 1961. Iraq then sought to incorporate Kuwait and threatened an invasion. Britain took up a military posture in defence of Kuwait and no invasion took place. Iraq did not accept Kuwait's independence until 1963 and thereafter maintained a lingering claim.

At the end of the eight-year Iran–Iraq war in 1988, which ended without a winner, Iraq had racked up huge debts, most them to fellow Arab states in the Gulf, who had been happy to lend. As one Gulf diplomat told me, as long as Iraq and Iran were weakening each other, neither could emerge as the regional power none of the others wanted to exist.

Saddam Hussein charged Kuwait with deliberately increasing oil production to lower the price, so making it impossible for Iraq to make the money needed to tackle the debt payments from its oil production. Meetings between the two at the Arab League were vicious verbal brawls. Arabic lends itself to the most superb insults. All efforts to find a peaceful solution failed. Saddam saw taking over Kuwait, with its sovereign wealth fund, and massive oil reserves, as the easy way out of his debt problem. Iraq invaded on 2 August 1990. Western powers feared that he would not stop at Kuwait but would go on to take the oil areas of Saudi Arabia and so control the main source of their supply.

A Difference of Opinion

The Arab League was in a state of disbelief that one Arab state should attack another. Yasser Arafat, the Palestinian leader, sided with Saddam, which proved to be a disastrous decision for the hundreds of thousands of Palestinians in Kuwait who held down good jobs. They were all expelled when the Kuwait government returned after that first Gulf war. King Hussein of Jordan was between a rock and a hard place as most of his oil and much financial support came from Iraq. But he was also a recipient of Western aid.

In such a complex situation, it took some time for the USA to stitch together a coalition that would enable a large military force to evict the Iraqis from Kuwait. That coalition had to include Arab states to provide the necessary legitimacy for Western action. Before the Iraqi invasion, I was in contact with a number of Arab friends from Iraq and other parts of the Gulf and I formed the clear belief that Saddam was not bluffing about invading Kuwait. His armed forces were poised on the Kuwait border in significant strength. Convinced he was going to invade, eight days before he did, I wrote to Douglas Hurd, the Foreign Secretary:

Dear Douglas

I appreciate that you and other EC governments may be awaiting the outcome of the inter-Arab efforts to settle the dispute, but given the difficulties that other Arab states face in dealing with Iraq, now arguably the most powerful and certainly the most free-moving of all in the Arab League, I believe that other pressures must be brought to bear. As a permanent member of the Security Council and because of Britain's historic ties with the region, a special responsibility would seem to rest with us. May I urge you, therefore, to place the issue of Iraq's conduct before the full Security Council with a view to that body providing Kuwait, a small nation with considerable elements of democracy built into its system (unlike Iraq), with international assurances about its security in the light of aggression from Iraq.

I am of course aware that you and your department will not have been idle on the issue, and that considering taking the issue to the Security Council is a matter of fine judgment. However, and again I emphasise Hussein's record, when faced with Iraq seeming to mobilise for conflict, I believe it is right to call upon the UN to act decisively to preserve the peace and protect the rights of small nations.

164

I believed that, had Iraq been faced with a Security Council resolution warning that, if it did invade Kuwait, it would face UN sanctioned military action to expel it, Saddam would have been forced to pull back his army from the Kuwait border.

I never received a reply and the UK did not take the matter to the Security Council before the invasion. At the time, I suspected that the Foreign Office thought it not worth considering the assertion by the SNP group that Saddam was about to invade. After all, what did we know about foreign policy, when it was assumed at Westminster that our minds never lifted above the level of dustbin collections in Scotland? That establishment attitude towards we SNP MPs was confirmed when I was interviewed early one morning on the *Today* programme after we had chosen to use our rarely allocated half-day debate to discuss the war which was then underway. It went something like this: 'The Iraq war, the SNP?' the interviewer asked with a voice laden with sarcasm. To which I replied, 'That's your problem, not mine.' When I got back to the Commons, I met a Tory MP who congratulated me on putting 'that arrogant bastard's nose out of joint'.

On that first Gulf war, I found myself in a difficult position within the party. In those days, unlike now, the power centre was the National Executive. Parliament was due to debate military action but members of the NEC were hostile to a war and unhappy about our parliamentary group voting to endorse it. I was for military action to expel Iraq from Kuwait. After a long discussion at the NEC, during which I made clear that I believed military action was inevitable, a compromise was reached – on the government motion we would abstain, while I would have some latitude in my speech and be able to develop our policy if war did happen. Striking a balance between our parliamentary group's views, and those of the NEC was not easy.

When I spoke in the debate, as a member of the realist school of international affairs, I made my views clear:

> International affairs have nothing to do with morality; they are founded on state interest and the practical limits of power that can be applied in a given situation . . . If Kuwait were noted for its wheat and not its oil there would be no crisis and no army. Is it really in the best interests of the West to have war before every aspect of diplomacy has been exhausted?

Tony Benn and other Labour MPs had tabled an amendment to the government motion, arguing that, in no circumstances, should military action be used to force Iraq from Kuwait. George Galloway had noted I was not calling for an early attack on the Iraqi forces and questioned whether the SNP would back the Benn amendment. I said no, we would abstain on it and do the same on the government's motion. I was, thereby, able to meet the anxieties expressed at the NEC, without fatally compromising the position I wanted to take – and did take – when the war started.

George Galloway is an interesting personality, who I regard as tragic. He has an acute political mind and he is a magnificent orator. As a debater, he can cut to the core of complex issues – as US Senators found out when he took them apart in a senatorial hearing in which they, not he, were supposed to emerge as victors. Tragic? Yes because of one flaw – an inability to work with others and build a broad basis of support for the causes in which he has been involved. That flaw has taken him out of frontline politics time and again, when his ability was needed. He is now regarded as a maverick but he has all the ability to be much more than that.

*

Legend has it that the SNP, because they were an obdurate lot, refused to take part in the constitutional convention set up in 1989 after the Govan by-election and were, therefore, unhelpful in pushing for change that would benefit Scotland. Like many a legend, that is a distortion of the truth.

As a direct result of the SNP victory in Govan and the party's predicted share of the votes rising to 28 per cent in the polls, there was panic in the Labour Party. That, in turn, created a window of opportunity for the growing number of pro-devolution groups, non-party on paper, to demand the creation of a constitutional convention to draw up an agreed plan for a Scottish parliament. A meeting to take this idea forward was called with the SNP invited to attend. The atmosphere was not good. Labour was still smarting from its defeat and had to sit in a room with me, the traitor. Most people attending from the ostensibly non-political organisations were actually Labour.

The proposition that faced the SNP at the conclusion of this meeting was that a convention of 100 delegates, drawn from political parties and pro-devolution non-party organisations, was to be formed. The SNP would be offered three seats on condition that we signed up in advance to accepting whatever the majority agreed to. Independence would not be on the agenda. Given the exclusion of independence and the fact that Labour and its allies would have a massive majority, there was no way the SNP could sign up under those conditions. At the end of the meeting, Gordon Wilson went with the other leaders into a press conference. He did not put enough emphasis on how humiliating the terms the SNP had been offered were and the media was left with the expectation that the SNP would attend the next meeting of the newly formed Scottish Constitutional Convention (SCC).

We in the leadership then made a tactical error. The National Council, a larger group than the NEC, was due to meet the following weekend. It would have been prudent to place the facts before them and ask for our refusal to take part in the convention to be approved. That would have meant the terms becoming known and the decision being taken after consideration by a wider group within the party. But, in the middle of the week, we decided to announce that we would not take part. We did not prepare the media and it was like a little bombshell – and those bombed reacted badly. The SNP had, and still has, a number of people who would settle for less than independence and they were furious at the decision not to participate, believing that we had ruined a golden opportunity to advance the cause of self-government. They also had a point in that we should have reported our view to National Council and awaited its decision. At the end of a robust debate, marked by a fierce verbal clash between Alex Salmond and Isobel Lindsay, a leading party member and former parliamentary candidate, the leadership won, using the argument that no independence party could accept the terms offered. Now, many years later, on reflection, I think the leadership was correct.

*

On 24 July 1997, following a triumphant Labour general election victory, Donald Dewar, the Secretary of State for Scotland, introduced his White Paper 'Scotland's Parliament'. It was a far better proposal than the one put forward in 1975 but 22 years had passed. Scotland had endured large-scale deindustrialisation and needed full economic powers. On that test, I could not vote for his proposals. Nor could I support his proportional representation 'additional-member' closed-list system for electing MSPs. It was openly admitted in Labour circles that this was designed to prevent the SNP ever getting a majority (proved wrong in 2011). Another disturbing consequence of the list method was that it placed too much power in the hands of party leaders, which meant they could influence and even control who got on the lists. Moreover, the parliament's money would come from a block grant from Westminster and there were statutory demands on such a budget for things like the health, education, police, fire, roads, ferries and other services. There would, therefore, not be a big discretionary amount left for anything new and innovatory. Some people in the financial field told me that they estimated almost 90 per cent of the budget of the new parliament would be used up under predetermined expenditure.

The White Paper was followed by a pre-legislative referendum, in which the SNP was enrolled and participated with enthusiasm. Margo MacDonald campaigned for the double yes – yes to the parliament and yes to it having some tax powers. I told Margo the offer was the minimum, giving Westminster the ability, which it would use, to spin out devolution for twenty years, by giving a little more and then a little more. Moreover, I feared it would settle us into devolution and provincialise us. I abstained. I do not regret that decision. I believe my doubts have been proved correct. Schedule 5 of the 1998 Act, the reserved subjects, was where real power continued to reside with Westminster, and still does.

*

Not long after the Govan by-election, Jack Irvine, editor of *The Scottish Sun*, invited me to lunch in London and offered me a weekly column. There I was, a Left-winger being invited to contribute to *The Scottish Sun*, a newspaper detested by the socialist movement, and get paid for it. Jack told me I could write whatever I liked.

Knowing the political attacks that would come my way for taking the *Sun*'s shilling, I talked to Chris McLean, the SNP press officer, but Chris argued that this had to be set aside against the fact that it was a major newspaper with a large working-class readership. It would have been daft not to take the platform offered. I signed on to the *Sun* and I was duly attacked by Labour MPs and MEPs, with the latter producing some good cartoons of me with a *Sun* hat on. I wish I had kept them.

I had a great relationship with Jack Irvine as editor and not once did he try to guide what I was writing. The column continued even after I lost Govan in 1992. In all, I wrote for thirteen years, under three editors. Jack Irvine was followed by Steve Sampson whose heroes were contrasting – Mother Teresa and Kelvin MacKenzie, the notorious editor of the UK *Sun* – and finally Bob Bird. I had the same excellent relationship with them as I had with Jack, with a free hand to write what I wanted.

*

As we approached the 1992 election, there was evidence of growing support for the SNP. This was also the view of the paper's political editor, Andy Collier so I asked Bob Bird if he would accept a memo from me about the commercial benefits to the paper if it were to come out in favour of independence. In the memo, I argued that the *Sun*'s Scottish readership tended to be younger working class and that the failure of the Labour group in Westminster had also loosened ties they may have had with their parents' party. Therefore, if the paper was seen to be supporting independence, it would boost the circulation. Bob took his time but then, agreeing, he went to a meeting with Rupert Murdoch to present the case. I don't believe for a moment that Murdoch was in favour of independence or anything like it but he was a newspaperman and saw the commercial benefit of agreeing, as he did.

When Bob launched the independence edition on 22 January 1992, it was a sensation – the first and only paper with a large circulation to come out in support of the SNP's position. There was a huge boost to party morale and, with a major paper on a rising circulation punting the idea of independence, the SNP was in a better position in the public eye than ever before.

The money I earned from the *Sun* I used to provide additional funds for my office in Govan and the costs of campaigning nationally. There were few places available for an office in Govan and we ended up renting above the Rangers shop. The rent was high. The administration expenses from the House of Commons came nowhere near the cost of rental and staff so the *Sun* money was a financial lifeline. Taking an office with Rangers as my landlord might seem a big risk. But Steve Butler, the office manager, was Catholic and lived in Govan. Steve told me it would not create problems. He was right. I was to discover that all community organisations in Govan were strict in their refusal to harbour any religious sectarianism. The sectarian problems came from outside the constituency.

Steve Butler came to the SNP from the Labour movement and had been the SNP trade union organiser. He, his wife Angie and son Kevin were very close friends of ours. It was a perfect partnership – I could rely on him one hundred per cent. My secretary was Lindsay MacCallum, who came with me from my previous job. She was Royal Navy trained and had been a senior secretary to a captain in NATO. Again, I had someone who was top flight I could rely on. There were also part-time members. I paid top people top wages.

In 1991, I became the party's deputy leader and, as such, I was campaigning all over the country, which was expensive. Every member of the NEC paid out of their own pockets for the travel costs involved in campaigning and attending meetings. None of the *Sun* money, on which I paid tax, was used for personal purposes. It helped to cover the costs of my parliamentary office in Govan and to meet my party campaigning costs, which were heavy.

*

There is one aspect of the story of Scotland and North Sea oil that has been ignored. How was it that, with the new North Sea oil industry consuming vast amounts of steel, Scotland's steel industry was whittled away from being one of the largest in Western Europe to closure? Another one for future historians to look at the facts and scratch their heads and wonder how a nation, one of the best educated, at that time, in the world, could allow itself to be so misused.

Ravenscraig steel plant in Lanarkshire went from employing 13,000 workers to only 700 directly by the late 1980s but with around 10,000 other jobs tied to its continuation. If no steel was made in Scotland, what was left of our manufacturing industry would suffer. It was under continuous threat from its owners, British Steel. The main steel shop steward was Tommy Brennan.

The SNP's campaign to save Scottish steel was led by Iain Lawson, a member of the NEC. I was out of Parliament and not heavily involved at that time. The key to ultimately saving the Ravenscraig works was the Gartcosh finishing plant, which added value to the Ravenscraig output on the spot. If it went, Ravenscraig would be next, rendered uneconomic. When the Gartcosh closure appeared imminent in 1985, two meetings took place in the plant's social club – one in the main hall with the workers and one in a smaller hall with the Labour MPs. Iain Lawson, who was leading the SNP steel campaign, was present in the politicians' meeting. Donald Dewar had prepared a statement of surrender and it was being passed round to be signed. Before it got far round the table, Tommy Brennan came in and delightedly announced, 'Great news – the men have voted to fight on!' Dewar had to tear his statement up. Iain said nothing in public at the time about the prepared but now torn-up statement – he was there to aid the workers, not exploit the situation the beleaguered Labour politicians were in. But it showed that Labour had no fight in them and were now merely concerned with political management of steel closures.

After that decision to fight on, Tommy Brennan led a steelmen's march to London and Iain Lawson went along with them. They were promised by the UK Labour leadership that a debate in the House of

Commons on the Scottish steel industry would be arranged to coincide with their arrival in London in January 1986. But, when the marchers got there, there was to be no steel debate. Labour chose instead to mount an attack on the Tory government over Westland Helicopters. On the face of it, this was not a big issue but it was to become one when a bitter Cabinet fight developed between the defence secretary, Michael Heseltine, and the prime minister, over whether Westland was to be rescued by a European consortium (Heseltine) or the US company Sikorsky (Thatcher). Fuel was added to the fire when a letter from the Attorney General to the prime minister, the contents of which were hostile to the Heseltine position, was deliberately leaked to the press. This was a major breach of protocol as the Attorney's legal advice is, traditionally, kept secret.

The Westland affair was a genuine crisis for the Thatcher government, with Michael Heseltine stamping out of the Cabinet and announcing his resignation in the middle of Downing Street. Margaret Thatcher was implicated in the leak and the trade secretary Leon Brittan was forced to resign because of it. But Labour could have chosen another day for the Westland debate. It was not a one-day, blown-up crisis but a running sore on the Tory body politic. They could have kept their pledge to the steelwork marchers. The irony was that Neil Kinnock blew it with his opening speech which was so long winded and torturous that Margaret Thatcher was reputed to have said in the middle of it, 'Well, that's me off the hook.'

*

Until I worked politically with Iain Lawson I thought the best campaigner I had ever met was Winnie Ewing but Iain was in a class of his own. He had prodigious energy, was inventive, aggressive and able to dig up information that no one else could find. When I got back into Parliament I was able to join him on the steel campaign and, although not an MP himself, he remained the leader. We did everything we could to rally public support to the side of the steelworkers. This included the two of us undertaking a seven-day fast outside the Scottish Office, St Andrews House, taking no food, just water, in the hope that the publicity would make it difficult for the government and the Labour Party to manage the closure of Gartcosh as quietly as they'd wanted to.

Iain next came up with the idea of a few of us in the SNP buying 100 shares each in British Steel, giving us as shareholders the right to attend the AGM in London and directly challenge the chief executive and board on their decisions. Most shareholders were large investment groups with millions of shares but our hundred shares gave us equal right to attend and be heard. When it came time for questions, Iain was on his feet. He caught the chairman's eye and he was called to speak. The board then endured his expert destruction of their policy in respect of Gartcosh and Ravenscraig, followed by a string of pertinent questions which the chief executive was most unhappy to address. Eventually they silenced him.

I put my hand up and was called and, once again, they found they had another problematic person. I was not as able as Iain but had enough information to make them squirm a second time. After they finally dealt with me, thinking the rebels had finally finished, we demanded a vote of all the shareholders on their policy in Scotland. The vote was lost massively, of course, but we had signalled to the board that the fight was still on. However, with the SNP only having four MPs at that time and being unable to act for Scotland the way the Labour Party could have done, there was a limit to what we could achieve. The lesson was a simple one. If you want to exercise economic power, you must first have political power. We didn't have it. Labour had it but did not use it. Gartcosh closed in 1986 and Ravenscraig followed suit in 1992.

18

Party Leaders and Party Politics

Gordon Wilson was MP for Dundee East and leader of the SNP when I joined in 1980. The 1979 general election disaster had publicly brought underlying tensions to the surface. Those who had run the party in the belief that being a Scot was more important than class issues were being challenged by a younger group. This group included Alex Salmond, Kenny MacAskill, Chris Cunningham and Roseanna Cunningham and they were allied to those, like Margo MacDonald, Stephen Maxwell and Andy Currie, who thought that class did matter and that the 1979 result proved it. They formed the 79 Group.

Not being a member of the SNP then, I knew nothing of the 79 Group until the press reported its formation and the 'traditionalist' wing's opposition to it. But I was in the party and in the 79 Group when tensions between the two broke out at the Ayr conference in 1982. During one of the lunchtime fringe events, a dreadful verbal brawl took place between some from the 79 Group and traditionalists. The conference threatened to disintegrate.

Gordon Wilson stepped in first thing in the afternoon and demanded that the 79 Group disband or else. That caused a walk-out by them. The next day, the conference backed Gordon and the 79 Group executive was instructed to disband it. Having not done so, the main players who set up the group were expelled. As that did not include me, I remained in one of the senior vice chair posts, having been re-elected by the conference.

I used that position over the next year, along with Gordon, to lower the temperature. Gordon Wilson, who had great integrity, was not a vengeful man and he knew that the party had lost a lot of ability with the expulsions. He and I had political differences but, at the personal level, we got on well. He understood that I was seeking a healing end to the matter, not a divisive one. Also, it finally dawned on the traditionalists that they had to listen to this younger group of very able

173

people and, ultimately, with an agreement that the group would not be re-formed, which I made plain at a National Council meeting, they all came back into membership. I was particularly pleased by that because I saw in both Alex Salmond and Kenny MacAskill outstanding leadership potential. Margo did not come back in as, by then, she was employed in television and radio broadcasting and her employers preferred her to remain out. They were anxious not to have a prominent current member of the SNP interviewing MPs and representatives from all political parties and thus preserve their reputation for neutrality. That was understandable. Margo was a professional journalist and there were no complaints about her.

Inside the SNP, the traditionalist versus Left struggles continued but they were conducted at a higher level of debate. The Left began to make progress at the expense of the traditional wing, with more of them becoming office bearers and members of the National Executive Committee as time went on.

Gordon Wilson was not cursed by an ego and, in the aftermath of that 79 Group episode, his personality enabled him to develop a collegiate style of leadership – meetings of the NEC were conducted in a fair way and we were able to debate without rancour. His work rate within the party remained phenomenal and it was entirely due to his efforts, which included funding his party work out of his own pocket, that it survived the darkest days. There are those in the SNP today who joined only after the 2014 referendum and they will have no idea what it was like for Gordon and others in the sixties, seventies and eighties to keep the cause alive during times when victories, such as that of Winnie Ewing in 1967 and those of the seven and then eleven MPs in 1974, were followed by heavy defeats and the party was constantly being dismissed as nothing but a flash-in-the-pan protest . Gordon did not have a voter-friendly personality but his honesty was widely admired and he won and held his seat in Dundee from 1974 to 1987. He gave the appearance of being a very rigid uptight person but underneath was a man of deep emotions that could boil over.

Alex Salmond

I have not been in the inner circle of the SNP since my defeat in Govan in 1992 but, from the outside, I have been highly critical of Alex Salmond's leadership and policies. Most commentators have thought this is due to my dislike of Alex but they are wrong. His political ability has always been obvious but he was not 'Super-Alex'. During his time at the helm,

I wrote in a pamphlet, 'Wise leaders are better leaders.' – a statement which stands in opposition to the 'strong leader fallacy' that gripped the party during his time and now. Alex acted as if he was master of all he surveyed within the party and his acolytes encouraged him in this belief. With none of them able to offer serious opposition, the strong leader fallacy grew over the years.

'Salmond tightens grip on power' was the headline of a report on the party's 1993 conference by Peter Jones and Joanne Robertson in which they wrote, 'A jubilant Alex Salmond stamped his personal authority on the Scottish National Party yesterday by publicly ordering party dissidents to shut up.' By the 1998 conference, the headline over Iain MacWhirter's report was 'Cult of Personality means that Salmond is the only show in town'.

I had first-hand experience of this desire to shut up dissents when the party compiled its list of candidates for the first Holyrood election in 1999. The leadership's attitude to two people, Stephen Maxwell and Margo MacDonald, was instructive. Three hurdles faced all would-be candidates. The first was getting the endorsement of a vetting committee to be placed on the list of approved candidates. The next was being selected by a constituency. Only then could a candidate be placed from one to twelve on the party list for any constituency. The higher the position on the party list, the greater chance a candidate had of entering the parliament. As far as the Lothian list was concerned, those in places one and two were almost certain to get in. It was very doubtful if anyone in place three would succeed and those below place three had no chance – they were there simply to make up the required number to twelve.

Stephen Maxwell, an acknowledged intellectual of the highest calibre, with a record of service to the party second to none, was refused entry to the candidates' list. He had given up a promising academic career to work full time for the party for low wages and he stayed the course through the most difficult years. Stephen, however, had an independent mind and could not give the assurance asked for that he would support every policy put forward in future. Being of sound mind, Stephen said he could not give that assurance as he did not know now what the future policies were going to be. That impeccable logic was, perhaps, too much for the vetting committee to accept.

During his academic career Stephen studied Moral Sciences at Cambridge and International Politics at the LSE. He was a research associate for the International Institute for Strategic Studies, a lecturer in International Affairs at the University of Sussex and a research fellow for Chatham House at Edinburgh University. He exuded the kind of intellectual talent and knowledge that would have contributed significantly to the discussions and debates in the new parliament of Scotland. The book *The Case For Left Wing Nationalism* was drawn from a series of Stephen's essays. Published in 2013, after his death in 2012, it showed that he would have been an adornment to the parliament. It was a sad reflection on the Salmond leadership that Stephen Maxwell was not considered fit to be an SNP candidate.

Margo MacDonald would have been rejected by the vetting committee too if, in the week before, Labour had not made a big PR blunder by rejecting Dennis Canavan, a Labour MP, as a candidate for the new parliament. That caused a public furore because everyone knew he was being bumped because he too was independent minded. At Margo's vetting, when it looked like she would be rejected, Mary Knox, a member of the committee, warned that, after Canavan, there would be an even greater furore if they rejected one of the best known and greatly admired politicians in the country. Margo got through 2–1. Dennis Canavan stood as an independent and won.

Defeated as a candidate for Livingston constituency, Margo was then invited to stand in Edinburgh South, a Labour seat. Alex Salmond went all out to stop her, supporting a former senior civil servant he thought would beat her. By support, I mean that he phoned round delegates to urge them not to vote for Margo. She won the selection meeting vote 25–0 and then it was 'stop Margo' from being number one or two on the Lothian list. It failed. Although she did not win in Edinburgh South, she took the SNP vote from 5,791 in 1997 to 9,445 in 1999. But, as number one on the SNP Lothian list, she was elected to the Holyrood parliament.

Thereafter, every effort was made by the party leadership to damn Margo and get her out of the Parliament next time. Alex had decided to go back to Westminster and John Swinney became leader but nothing had changed in respect of Margo, as I relate in Chapter 23.

*

I first met the young Alex Salmond in 1980. He was obviously quality. We worked closely together, along with Kenny MacAskill and others, building the Left-wing group within the party. That remained the case right up until after the Govan by-election and I became a member of the small parliamentary group.

Relations within the parliamentary group were good at first. Margaret Ewing, Andrew Welsh and Alex Salmond were all in the party when I was attacking it as a Labour unionist but none of them held that against me. Unfortunately, a rift began to develop between Alex and me. It grew from two matters – one small and one major.

The group needed a research assistant and Alex proposed a very nice young chap. During the interview, I asked him a test question – what did he think the Labour Party thought about our housing policy? He replied it wouldn't be his job to tell us what Labour thought – he would tell us about our policy. I told him no – we already knew our policy. I wanted to know what the other side believed its weaknesses were so that we would be better armed in debate. He just could not see that. When we came to discuss his application in private, I said he was not research material and Margaret and Andrew agreed. Alex was not happy and I suppose he had the task of telling the young man, who must have thought he had the job, that it was not his. I think Alex thought, given our close relationship, that I should have supported him and his candidate.

The second matter, far more significant, arose over him asking me whether I would support him in standing against Gordon Wilson as leader in 1989. He was upset when I told him I wouldn't because, at last, the dust had settled after the 79 Group affair and a challenge from him could open up old wounds. Alex was, by this time, deputy leader – a move I had supported as he was definitely a future leader. He argued that Gordon was too rigid in his style in public and would not inspire people to make the most of this new situation in which we had become a force in politics. I agreed with him about Gordon but made the point it was more important to preserve the party unity which had been so dearly bought. I am sure he felt I had let him down. I wasn't happy either because it seemed to me that Alex was willing to put his personal ambition over party unity. Gordon told me later that he was aware of Alex's view of his leadership and that, not once, as his deputy, did Alex ever contact him personally, only meeting him at National Executive, National Council and National Conference.

In early 1990, Margo and I got a call to go to Dundee to meet Gordon. Margaret Ewing was there. Gordon told us he was going to resign and make way for a new leader. He said in his opinion either Margaret or I should stand, as we would provide continuity with what had been established after the 79 Group problems. He knew Alex would stand too but thought he would not be right for the party at this time.

Margaret asked me for time to consider her position and I was happy to do so. Margo wanted me to stand. I found myself in a difficulty. Although I had won the Govan by-election, I knew that many party members, especially, but not exclusively, on the Right, did not trust me and had not forgiven my previous role as an independence basher. For some, I was also too Left wing. I was sure my candidacy would split the party and decided that, if Margaret wanted to stand, I would support her. My problem would be if she did not want to stand because I would be expected to do so by some on the Left who thought, as I did, that it was premature for Alex to take command – because 'command' it would be.

Fortunately, Margaret decided to stand so that was one problem out of the way. But there was another not revealed until now – I knew she could not beat Alex. Margaret was well liked, with a splendid party record, but Alex was in a different class – she promised continuity but he was going to take the party in a new direction. There was an excitement around Alex that was not there with Margaret. But, to those who knew him well, he was already showing signs of an ego and an authoritarian attitude – traits not then publicly obvious.

My view was that it would be good for the party to continue with a collegiate leadership for a transition period, which Margaret would have provided. A few more years of experience would be helpful for Alex, before taking over. But with him declared that could not be. A number of us, knowing he was going to win, were determined that Alex should know that winning did not mean absolute control.

The Glasgow Herald of 4 July 1990 reported on my position backing Margaret but that I'd 'hedged the bet with a masterpiece of fudge' as I had described Alex as having 'great qualities' and that his time as leader would come. I did genuinely think Alex, at 36, was too young to take the leadership because it would mean a very long time with him at the helm and that is not a good thing for any democratic political party. *The Herald* quoted me as warning that an Alex victory 'would block any future development of the leadership for the next 15–20 years'. I was, of course, also conscious that a fight for the leadership could reopen old wounds and the *Herald* piece noted that I had made it clear that I was campaigning *for* Margaret and not *against* Alex.

One of Alex's keen supporters was Jim Mitchell, a councillor from Paisley and a close friend of mine. At a meeting in Govan, when a group of us set out why we were not supporting Alex, including his tendency to resent opposing views, Jim stormed out. Six months later he told me we had been right.

Alex won easily – 486 to 186 – at the Perth party conference. The next day, I had an early indication of the new leadership muscles being flexed when a couple of journalists came up to tell me that I was no longer to be the party's European affairs spokesman, Alex having given the job to Rob Gibson, one of his strong supporters but not an MP. The journalists enjoyed seeing me embarrassed because I obviously knew nothing about it. However, I avoided getting drawn into commenting so there was no story of a split.

On the Monday following conference, I made sure I was in the party office when the new leader came to speak to the staff. I got Alex into a private room and let him know how angry I was to be placed in the position of speaking on European affairs in Parliament but not as the party's spokesman and told him that it was not on. I remained in the position but the breach between us widened. It had got bigger by the next annual conference in Inverness because I decided to be a strong counterbalance to him by standing for election as deputy leader against Alex's preferred candidate, the existing deputy leader, Alasdair Morgan. A very decent man and a supporter of Alex, Alasdair was not someone who could put a brake on the leader's growing authoritarianism. He later became an MP. In the constitution of the SNP at that time, the deputy leader had considerable powers – as, indeed, had all the other executive office bearers. That is not the case now. The counterbalance I aimed for disappeared with my defeat in 1992 and my need to find employment.

Whatever criticism I or anyone else can make about Alex Salmond, he has been the outstanding nationalist leader of any generation. His record in taking the SNP into government at Holyrood, achieving the right to hold an independence referendum and doing all that to beat an electoral system that was created to prevent him achieving those goals speaks for itself. But that authoritarian streak and a lack of empathy with and keen understanding of those who do not see Scotland's future as he does have kept him from being a great national leader. He could lift the party but never the nation.

As a party leader, Alex could wound opponents, much to the joy of the SNP membership, but could not bring others outside the party onboard when it mattered. In the closing stages of the 1992 election, Charles Fletcher, then Sky News Scotland correspondent, got the whole UK network to agree to cover his entire speech at a major rally. It was a breakthrough for the party. Charles expected a big speech, as did I. But, instead of talking to the nation, he talked only to the party audience before him, getting stuck into Labour, the Tories and Westminster. This was meat for the party activists but it lacked the 'bigness' of language and vision that might have attracted an audience outside the hall – the very people we needed to win over to the cause. He simply didn't have it. He could not bridge the gap. That same defect was evident in the

2014 referendum, when many people's dislike of Alex hit us on the doorsteps.

New leaders do not emerge naturally under an authoritarian system – promotion is not on merit but in the gift of the leader. Alex Salmond made and promoted Nicola Sturgeon. When she stood for the leadership on her own at Holyrood, with Alex in Westminster, she was heading for defeat at the hands of Roseanna Cunningham. So Alex stepped back in and took over, having previously declared that was something he would never do. He saved her for another day and she duly inherited the leadership from him.

There are important lessons for up-and-coming politicians to be learned from studying the consequences of the Alex Salmond years of leadership and the development of the cult of personality under him, which has been transferred to Nicola Sturgeon. First, it tends to invest in the leader all knowledge, judgement and wisdom required for the development of policies, which is actually a block on ideas and the discussion and debate that is so essential in getting policies right. Second, it sows the seeds of future disaster because there are no brakes on the ego of the leader. Ultimately it ends in tears.

I anticipate an ocean of tears when the full story emerges about how the civil and criminal cases involving Alex came about. There will be a price paid by the party for allowing itself to be in the grip of two personality cults for thirty years.

*

Alex Salmond started to be enveloped in serious sexual assault allegations when the Scottish government, in setting out a new anti-sexual harassment policy, decided to make it retrospective to include past minsters. That Alex was the target became clear when it was deliberately revealed to the *Daily Record*, for its edition on 24 August 2018, that the Scottish government was investigating his alleged sexual misconduct as First Minister. The *Record* followed up on 25 August with lurid details of the allegations, based on having received an 'exclusive' leak. Alex then made it public that he was seeking a judicial review of the way the Scottish government was conducting the investigation against him.

Seeking judicial review of a government action was bound to be expensive so Alex appealed for assistance by crowdfunding. Journalists who had always misunderstood my reasons for opposing Alex's style and practice of leadership assumed that I would condemn this, as many did. They were surprised but reported fairly that I backed his action. Like everyone else, my knowledge of the allegations came only from newspaper reports and Alex's surprising press conference where he declared himself 'no saint' but never to have engaged in criminality.

When he won the judicial review, with the government case collapsing, despite previously claiming to be a certain winner, I thought no more would be heard of the allegations. However, the permanent secretary declared that the Scottish government had not lost the 'war'. On 24 January 2019, Alex was charged with fourteen sexual assault offences (later reduced to thirteen), between 2008 and 2014, including attempted rape. I may have had a negative view of Alex's political actions but the Salmond I knew and knew well, for all those years from 1980 to 1992, was not a rapist. I phoned him to tell him so and asked to meet, which we did in a hotel in Edinburgh.

Alex showed me a great deal of the evidence that his lawyers had obtained from the Scottish government in the judicial review case, evidence of the trawl of people by the police in seeking to build a criminal case against him and his rebuttal of each of the allegations, which included breach of the peace twelve years ago. This latter one did not appear in the final indictment that went to trial. It would have been the strangest ever breach of the peace in legal history.

I later discovered, after his trial, that Alex's claim that there had been a 'trawl' by the police to find as many complainants as possible was no exaggeration. When discussing the case with a near neighbour, again after the trial, he told me about the experience of a female friend who was a senior civil servant. She had been astonished one night to answer the door to find a policeman there enquiring if she had any complaint of sexual harassment to make against Alex Salmond. She had none. Professor Joe Farrell told me about another episode in the trawl, relayed to him by a woman his family know. During a by-election in Glasgow, Shettleston, she had come up from her home in England to help and had gone canvassing with Alex Salmond. She received a telephone call from the police asking if she had been sexually harassed by him. The answer was no. How the police got her telephone number is an interesting question.

The clear impression I drew from the detail produced in my meeting with Alex was of him as the victim of a political conspiracy, conducted at high levels in the party, aimed at stopping him coming back into frontline SNP politics following his defeat in his Westminster seat in 2017. Two big political beasts in the SNP arena, one over-shadowing the other? That could not be permitted. On New Year's Eve, I sent Alex a text saying I hoped 2020 would be a better year for him than 2019.

Before the trial opened, Alex's defence team had sought to use what had been revealed to them in the judicial review case and by internal party sources, as admissible evidence of conspiracy. Two judges, in two separate hearings, refused. Journalists told me at the time this was a blow to Alex's defence. When the trial started, journalists, who had been in court, told me Alex was going down as the evidence built against him. But there was no way anyone like me, not attending court, could really know. Covid-19 had arrived so newspaper reports of the trial were not as extensive as they would have been. There was no doubt that the tawdry tales of him and the civil servants were extremely damaging to his reputation but nothing that was reported from the other accusers, whose charges Alex described in court as 'fabrications', dented my view of a conspiracy. The fourteen charges were reduced to thirteen during the trial and the general view among journalists who talked to me was that the prosecution was bound to get him on one at the very least. On 23 March 2020, Alex Salmond was acquitted of all charges. That I was pleased is an understatement.

On 29 March, newspapers carried a statement from the nine women accusers, still under the protection of anonymity, issued through Rape Crisis Scotland, stating that they were 'devastated' by the verdict. They claimed that:

> For too long, behaviour which should be condemned has been accepted and excused.

> For too long, perpetrators in positions of power have been shielded by their ability to influence and intimidate.

> For too long, women's complaints have been dismissed or swept under the carpet.

> For too long, women have been let down by organisational structures which should exist to protect them, not put them in situations which endanger their welfare.

A reasonable inference to be drawn from the 'devastated' and the assertions they made is that the jury's verdict was being brought into question.

Leaving aside the 'devastated', the statement was impeccable in its echo of the Me Too movement that began in the United States. That women the world over, from ancient times to modern times, have justification for those assertions is indisputable. Western women have

achieved significant changes in attitudes in what is not remotely acceptable behaviour by males but not even the first round in that battle has
been won by women in many societies in Asia and Africa.

There was in my mind and, as I found out, not in mine alone an
inkling that the 'devastated' part of the statement and where it was
issued from clearly implied that the verdict was wrong. It didn't seem
to strike anyone else but it did seem to me that it was a bit rich for
people who had the legal cover of anonymity to imply that the man they
accused was guilty no matter what the jury found. Perhaps they took
their cue from an article by Tom Gordon that was published in *The
Herald* on Saturday 28 March, the day before their statement appeared.
He pointed to the section of the Criminal Procedure (Scotland) Act
1995 that covers the possibility of a case being tried by thirteen jurors
where seven could be for conviction and six for acquittal but the verdict
would be not guilty because eight is the minimum required for a conviction. Intrigued by this journalist's detailed knowledge of the Act, I asked
a former judge if that might be the case with the Salmond jury. For the
Tom Gordon scenario to have played out in the Salmond trial, the jury
would have needed to inform the judge of the seven to six situation and
the judge, not the jury, would have declared him acquitted. But, in each
of the thirteen charges, the jury spokesperson was asked if it is was the
necessary majority – meaning at least eight – and the answer was yes so
the terms of the Act could not even be contemplated. Mind you, Tom
Gordon did write, 'I am not saying this happened in Mr Salmond's case.
But it is a reminder that juries can be curious beasts, and it is unwise
to second guess them.' Perhaps it is unwise, too, to speculate about
something that the Salmond jury never faced – a jury which, unlike Tom
Gordon, was most unlikely to know such a possibility even existed.

Alex Salmond's acquittal was a sensation but a guilty verdict, with
him in jail, ruined, would have been even more sensational. Lots of TV
documentaries had to be canned. One survived – the BBC's Kirsty Wark
one, which many interpreted as a retrial with a different verdict. I was a
contributor and, while deploring Alex Salmond's conduct as revealed in
the trial, I emphasised that, on thirteen counts, he had been acquitted.

Asked at the time by the *Scottish Sun* to comment on the verdict I
did so, pointing out that I was no fan of Alex, our friendship having
'evaporated in 1992', and listing what I saw of his faults – his expanded
ego, his authoritarian tendencies and his development of the cult of personality. But, citing the evidence I had seen in my private meeting with
him, I described the conspiracy of which he was victim as 'the dirtiest
blow I have ever witnessed in 60-years of public life, and delivered to

a man who, for all my criticism, has done more for independence than any other person alive or dead. He deserved better.'

In a longer follow-up article for the *Scottish Left Review* in May 2020, in which I declared that I was in neither the Salmond nor the Sturgeon camp, I emphasised:

> Alex Salmond was cleared . . . by a jury of eight women and five men. They saw and heard all the evidence against him, and watched and heard the accusers under cross-examination. In addition, they saw and heard him in the witness box, and similarly with his defence witnesses. Those salient facts should be borne in mind when, as has been attempted, doubts have been expressed about the verdict.

Unlike Alex's accusers who left after giving their evidence and so could not have heard the evidence of the others, that jury had been in court every minute of the trial, not just hearing but watching – something journalists could not do because the women gave their evidence and were cross-examined behind a screen. The jury also heard and watched Alex Salmond give evidence and be cross-examined, during which he described the most serious charges as 'fabrications'.

In the *SLR* article, I raised a point of importance: 'No one can say that the trial itself was other than fair. But was it the fairest trial that Alex Salmond could have had?' In the preliminary hearings, the judges ruled against Salmond's request to present Scottish government documents and WhatsApp messages between party officials as evidence of a conspiracy, citing such evidence as inadmissible. I pointed out that this was 'a major impediment in his defence'. This meant his defence QC, Gordon Jackson, was, as I contended, 'handicapped by those judicial decisions' and 'had to resort to euphemism in his final address to the jury, using "it stinks" to signal the conspiracy. It is a fair conclusion from the verdicts that the jury agreed.'

But, as I made clear, 'Alex Salmond did not emerge from the court proceedings unblemished, to say the least. His character and personality were turned inside out, with all the flaws exposed and the folly of the cult of personality laid bare. His conduct towards female civil servants was deplorable; and while his defence admitted "inappropriate" conduct with them, it did not give an inch to his SNP accusers – "fabrication" was the description of their evidence. Another euphemism.' I continued in that article to say, 'The criminal trial of Alex Salmond may be over, but the trial of the SNP both at party and parliamentary level is yet to begin. It is inevitable.' And had Covid-19 not intervened, I do believe that to be the case.

A couple of days later, I talked to Alex Salmond at length and I was made privy to a considerable amount of the new material that the judges had declared inadmissible. This new evidence that I listened to confirmed my belief that he had been the victim of a conspiracy. Alex Salmond is writing a book about this and, when it is published, this material will, at last, be available for the people to read. I believe it will have a volcanic effect on the SNP. But, even without Salmond's book in our hands, the parliamentary inquiry into the shambles the Scottish government made of the judicial review case, costing the taxpayer over £500,000, is proving a serious problem for the party leadership, not least for Nicola Sturgeon and her husband Peter Murrell, the chief executive. In one of his leaked WhatsApp messages, Murrell spoke about it being 'a good time to be pressurising them [the police]' and how it would be 'good to know Met looking at events in London'. In another leaked text, he wrote that 'the more fronts he [Salmond] is having to firefight on the better for all the complainers'. Both raise serious issues.

My view on this was laid out in the *Sunday Times* of 11 October 2020:

> To say the present position of the party's chef executive being the spouse of the party's leader, who is also the head of the Scottish government, in terms of party management is unhealthy is an understatement. But of greater importance is that the chief executive of a political party, who is bedside close to the first minister, has felt free to and able to seek to direct a prosecution against a citizen. This takes the present set-up from unhealthy to dangerous.

As I was bringing this book to an end in May, 2021, the thought struck me, as I am sure it does others, that it is always the cover-up that finally undoes the politicians who go well beyond the boundaries of decent conduct.

19

The 1992 General Election and Its Long-term Consequences

With Alex as leader and me as deputy, the SNP fought the 1992 general election on a clear platform for independence. It never did so again until the 2014 referendum. That will surprise many but, after 1992, the party dodged the issue by fighting elections on slogans like 'A strong voice for Scotland'. John Swinney, when leader, actually said that people did not need to support independence to vote for the SNP – a tactic which was repeated by Nicola Sturgeon and SNP candidates in the 2019 Westminster election.

We did not dodge it in 1992. That was unambiguously a call for Scots to vote for independence by voting SNP. Sean Connery was called in to do a radio broadcast and voice-over for both radio and television party political broadcasts. My role, like that of my colleagues, was to campaign nationally as well as locally to get the vote as high as possible. The party members were delighted. I got phone calls from all over from members saying how pleased they were, at last, to confront the electorate with a clear choice – independence or the union.

Steve Butler was in charge of local activists in Govan and, although I was committed nationally, I was also heavily involved in the constituency. The canvass returns were good and indicated a win. But I wondered. At one packed hustings in Penilee, near to polling day, candidates were asked about future economic prospects. I gave a mini lecture on the problems that confronted us because of the shift in world power from the Atlantic axis to the Asia Pacific and explained that a new epoch in world history was unfolding. I could tell that was not popular – it suggested too many difficulties to face. Ian Davidson, the Labour candidate, got up and scoffed at my stuff about the Asia–Pacific century and said, to applause, that all we needed was a Labour government – a magic political pill. I said to Steve as we left the meeting that I doubted we would win. He disagreed, citing the canvass returns.

186

My pessimistic view was confirmed with a Snappy Bus tour on the Saturday before the poll. Margo was with me. We said nothing to the activists but, once in the car on the way home, we reckoned I was beaten. I phoned Steve and asked him to do a double-check on the canvass over the Sunday and the Monday, which he did, reporting back that we were still winning. I was not convinced.

The SNP had been going up in the polls to around 30 per cent but, over the weekend, I saw lots of signs that our support was slipping. The Labour argument that they could win and that Scotland would be decisive in that was catching on. On polling day, I knew, by round about 10 a.m., that I had lost.

Those who head up party campaigns now put a great deal of emphasis on data and social media. As a former professional election organiser, I do not underestimate how valuable these are in shaping a campaign. But, however old-fashioned I may appear, there is nothing that can match meeting people – listening and talking to them and reading their body language. Hillary Clinton's presidential campaign manager, in 2016, put all his faith in data, which showed she was winning, whereas Bill Clinton, who could read the street, was concerned. His fears were dismissed.

The 1992 election produced a great result for the SNP, whose vote rose from 14 to 21 per cent but we lost Govan and that was what media attention focused on. The Govan result was:

> Labour 17,051
> SNP 12,926
> Tory 3,458
> Lib Dem 1,227
> Green 181
> Labour majority 4,125

Scots, especially in the Central Belt, had anticipated that Kinnock would win and had 'parked' any possible support for the SNP and independence to see him in Downing Street. He lost. And Scotland was funereal on the Friday morning. I was interviewed a few days afterwards and made what has become the famous, or infamous, statement that Scots were 'ninety-minute patriots'. That was my estimation of the nation as I had seen it move towards support for independence at thirty per cent, only to melt in the face of hope – false as it turned out – of a Labour government. Many see that statement as an insult to the electorate. But it was meant to tell them a truth about themselves – a people who would advance towards self-government and then hesitate, step back, hoping that English voters would help deliver the government they wanted. People say they want truth from politicians but one truth seldom mentioned is that the people often do not like the truth if, for them, it is an uncomfortable one.

The failure after 1992 to build a hard-core support for independence created the handicap faced by the movement in the 2014 referendum, with the polls showing only 29 per cent support at the start of the campaign in February. Just think how much higher Yes might have started from if, over those 22 years, the independence vote had been built up election after election. I and others were dubbed 'fundamentalists' when calling for a consistent campaign for independence at every election and by-election. Making the Scots make the choice every time was the only way to build layer upon layer of hard-core support. That was not done and, in two notable by-elections – Glasgow Shettleston (won) and Glenrothes (lost) – the SNP said it was 'parking' independence and placing it on 'the back burner' in those campaigns. Time and again, I sought to explain that you don't build up an independence vote by enabling the electorate to avoid it.

The division of SNP members into gradualists and fundamentalists is good shorthand for journalists reporting on the moment but it doesn't reflect the complexity of the constitutional issue over time. There are periods when the so-called fundamental approach is necessary. But there can be periods when living with the reality of a given situation and going for a lesser prize, such as devolution, can be the sensible course. It may be that Alex Salmond was right to adopt a gradualist approach and go wholeheartedly for devolution in the 1997 referendum and I was wrong to abstain.

Independence versus gradualism may now reappear in the nationalist movement because of Brexit and Covid-19. Both, in their different ways, will reshape British economic structures and politics in a manner that may materially change the issues that existed as central to the debate about independence and the Union, from 2014 to 2019. Covid-19 turned the world upside down. The normal was no more and it will take some time for the dynamics of the new world order to emerge and for us to find out if the changes, together with attitudes that developed during the crisis, assist the cause of independence or advance the strength of the Union vote.

On the face of it, the result of the 2021 Holyrood election, with the SNP gaining 48 per cent of the vote and 64 seats (one short of a majority) settles the question within the party in favour of a fundamentalist position. But is that really so? During the election campaign the SNP did not call upon people to use their vote as a declaration for independence but reverted to the pre-2014 position of 'parking' it. When Nicola Sturgeon was under pressure for dodging questions on the economics of independence, she replied, as widely reported in the Scottish papers on 26 April: 'If I was asking people a week on Thursday to vote on the question of whether or not Scotland should be independent, I am not.' And as the *Spectator* noted in on 14 May, on another occasion, when asked, 'What are they [people] meant to do if they want you but not independence?' Surgeon replied, 'They should vote for me safe in the knowledge that getting through the crisis is my priority.' Both these answers show that when seeking votes, Sturgeon, a fundamentalist rather than a gradualist, does not regard independence as an unbreakable principle.

But having sold that pass to gather non-independence votes, can the SNP membership find comfort from its manifesto claim for another referendum? Yes and no. Sturgeon, along with the Greens, can claim a mandate for a referendum, but she has pushed her proposed date for it into the second half of 2023. That is a hostage to fortune because in a democracy, politicians are not in complete charge. Unanticipated events and changes in public priorities, opinion and mood (think of the influence on our politics of the Covid-19 pandemic) make for unpredictability and volatility that can often make the victors of today the vanquished of tomorrow.

The one certain point that does emerge from the 2021 election is that the constitution matters above all else. A government went to the polls with a record of incompetence and tainted with political corruption in the form of gross abuse of power demonstrated by its conduct in blocking evidence to the parliamentary committee inquiry into the Salmond affair, from which emerged damaging findings that the First Minister had misled parliament on two occasions. It was those grounds of incompetence and abuse of power that kept me from voting SNP. I met many who agreed with me but who voted SNP all the same because the constitution was what mattered.

Anas Sarwar, the new Labour leader, began his campaign determined to concentrate on government incompetence and the need for post-pandemic economic reconstruction but was soon pulled into the constitutional arguments. For Tory leader Douglas Ross, it was about the constitution from start to finish, with every statement, article and leaflet obsessed with preventing a second referendum, and taking the remarkable position of urging Tories to vote Labour, which a number did.

A Difference of Opinion

The inescapable emphasis on the constitution means that powerful and influential unionist actors will take a more active part in the debate than hitherto – people such as Gordon Brown and, perhaps more importantly, the Westminster establishment, which means not just the Tory government but also the UK Labour party. The former have a say not only on the form of the constitutional debate but also on the timetable for it.

Take Nicola Sturgeon's preferred referendum date as the second half of 2023. It does not seem to have crossed her mind that that might be Boris Johnson's pick for the next Westminster general election once he repeals the Fixed Parliament Act, thereby giving him another reason for saying this is not the time for another Scottish referendum.

Also, in the meantime, among those with influence on the unionist side, there is a determination to ensure that if and when a referendum does take place, it will not be on the 2014 basis of independence versus the status quo but on independence versus devo-max dressed up in federalist clothes. The SNP would be in no position to reject such a choice, as that was the one Alex Salmond as First Minister and Nicola Sturgeon asked to be on the ballot in 2014, only for it to be rejected by David Cameron.

While the 2021 election appears to change nothing – a minority government and the referendum still postponed – the responses to it, both north and south of the border, are going to create new political dynamics, the consequences of which might, or might not, advance the cause of independence.

*

I did not join Alba, the new party set up by Alex Salmond, but supported and voted for it. Not one word did I take back of my strictures on Alex's period as leader of the SNP, but I believed that having gone through three years of hell, when he was turned inside out in public, lessons were learned.

Moreover, his argument was sound: that second votes for the SNP would be wasted and that if they went to Alba, a supermajority of MSPs for independence would strengthen Holyrood in its coming tussle with Westminster. In the event he was correct, with over 1 million SNP second votes producing only two list seats.

I wrote two policy papers for Alba: one on housing and the other on a written constitution, and I posted several articles on Iain Lawson's blog. Perhaps the most important was my analysis of the size of the potential Alba constituency, which was much smaller than political commentators seemed to grasp. The paper explained the obvious: there would be no votes from the unionist half of the voting population, and that in respect of the independence-inclined half, there was a substantial number who would do what Nicola Sturgeon asked and use their second vote too for the SNP. That Sturgeon component was bound to be a large one, so did not leave much room for Alba, which would also be fighting for votes with the Greens. That proved to be the case. As it turned out, once SNP voters decided to use their second votes as requested by Sturgeon, the arithmetical logic employed by Alba had no meaning and it failed to gain more than a small fraction of the list vote.

It was an unspoken understanding, but many who joined Alba or, like me, voted for it, were aware that Salmond was both an asset and a liability. His asset was his undoubted political ability; the liability was the mud sticking to him from what had been revealed of his conduct towards women civil servants during his trial. Whether he can again make a comeback is open to question, but if the leadership in the SNP believe that the result on 6 May delivered a personal coup de grâce to him, they could be mistaken.

20

Middle Eastern Journeys

Margo and I did not get back home from Govan until 6 p.m. the day after the 1992 election defeat. The phone was ringing. It was Abdul Karim Al Mudaris, secretary-general of the Arab–British Chamber of Commerce, who had been trying to contact me all day. He said he wanted to help me and asked if I would come down to see him in London on the Tuesday. Once there, he asked me to come back to work with the chamber as his assistant. His concern for me was that of a friend – a term which, in Arab culture, means much more than is understood in Western culture. However, I said no because I wanted to stay in Scotland to be near to the grandchildren. So, he offered me a consultancy – a one-day-a-week commitment at the office. That plus the *Sun* column gave me an income.

During 1992, Abdul Karim required major heart surgery and he kept urging me to go full time, saying he needed me to take some of the strain off him. Another person urging a full-time commitment was Dr Galal Ismail, economic adviser to the chamber. Abdul Karim and I were both close friends of Galal and, just before Christmas, he told me Abdul Karim needed my help urgently. We met in Abdul Karim's house in London where it was explained to me why my help was needed. His health was not the same after the surgery. I could take part of the burden of management off him, leaving him freer to deal with the Arab side of the chamber's life, especially the Arab governments and their ambassadors. If they were not happy with the chamber, it would not last. I knew how labyrinthine Arab politics could be and how much time he had to devote to handling the different countries, regimes and personalities. I could not turn him down. However, I explained I was not prepared to move home to London especially as the number of grandchildren was growing in Scotland. Margo's broadcasting career was flourishing there too so she was not so often in London. We agreed that I would come down early on a Monday and would go back on a

192

Thursday night, with a salary sufficient to allow me to do so. Friday was a 'dead' day in Arab London, with everyone at the mosque. On Mondays, I would arrive in the office by 10.20 a.m. and work late, so no time was lost by this arrangement.

So I started a new career – a most rewarding one too in that there were objectives to be achieved and the means of achieving them were available. I was not completely out of Scottish politics. I kept writing for *The Scottish Sun*, wrote articles and produced pamphlets. But my main effort was now in the Arab world of politics, diplomacy, trade and development. It was both a pleasure and a new level of political and cultural education. Abdul Karim and Galal Ismail both had an extensive range of contacts in the Arab world and, on the basis of friendship, were frank with me in their assessment of leading personalities, governments and factions within them.

My work at the Chamber did not prevent me keeping my membership of the Scottish Enterprise Board, to which I had been appointed, prior to the job, by Michael Forsyth, secretary of state, and I quite frequently took part in leading their trade delegations to the Arab Gulf states where, with my Arab Gulf contacts, I could help small and medium enterprise (SME) sector companies on these missions by opening doors that might otherwise be closed. Working with these trade missions and small companies gave me a revealing insight into the difficulties they face when they have no previous experience of export.

My job as assistant to the secretary-general at the chamber made me effectively number two to Abdul Karim. My main responsibility was to manage two departments – economics and business, which included a printing department, and public relations. The latter was a misnomer because its main function was to organise small trade exhibitions from the poorer Arab states and Palestine, held within the chamber. These did little to produce significant orders and were done more to please Arab ambassadors from the countries concerned, giving them publicity in the Arab press and TV. But remaining on good terms with the ambassadors in London was essential in maintaining the existence of the chamber. Our income came from the clearing of British export documentation we did on their behalf. It is complicated to explain but, basically, any Arab government could have withdrawn its arrangement with the chamber at any time and cut off the income stream. We employed 120 people.

Abdul Karim had been the Arab League ambassador to the UK when the League governments decided to set up joint chambers of commerce in a number of important political and trading countries, in which the secretary-general would always be Arab and the chairman always from the host nation. One half of the board was made up of members of Arab chambers and the host nation side was drawn from business directors with company interests in the Middle East. The Arab–British Chamber was the most successful and, therefore, the most important. You might think it would the USA one but Arabs found it hard going in Washington DC, where the Israeli lobby is king.

Chambers of commerce in the Gulf are more powerful and richer organisations than their counterparts in the UK or Europe. They are the single voice of the private sector and every business, however small, has to be a member of the Chamber of Commerce and Industry. A number carry out governmental responsibilities such as the registration of companies and, consequently, there is a close connection between governments and chambers. In Oman, the sultan appoints the head of the chamber and, until fairly recently, the secretary-general of the Dubai chamber was appointed ambassador to London.

The Arab–British Chamber had influence within the Arab world due to the diplomatic abilities of Abdul Karim. He was regarded as equal to the Arab ambassadors and had diplomatic status. Every six months, the whole board and senior staff visited an Arab state and met its emir or president, prime minister and senior ministers. These started with formal meetings, followed by frank off-the-record discussions covering not only the country's economic situation but also politics and diplomacy.

When I arrived to take up my post, I discovered that, for the first time, the chamber had committed itself to funding and organising a large trade exhibition at Olympia in London, in 1993. The country concerned – Saudi Arabia – was the most important. The export documentation for Saudi Arabia formed around 60 per cent of our income so this had to be good or there would be serious problems. It was a good example of why Abdul Karim needed help. The man whose responsibility it was to plan the exhibition was leaving. He told me how relieved he was that he was now out of it. I quickly understood why on opening the file to discover it contained a single A4 sheet of paper with the figure £50,000 written on it.

I had never organised a trade exhibition before but I knew that £50,000 was a risible sum. Organisation is actually simple but I have noticed over the years that few people are good at it. I simply applied the basics of organisation, found out from Olympia what they required and, with their help, identified all the components needed. The new total was £350,000.

The exhibition was a success and, in 1994, that led to the chamber being asked to organise the first Gulf Co-operation Council trade exhibition anywhere in Europe. The budget was no problem this time as each Gulf chamber paid for its floor space, while our chamber did the hiring of the stands and the publicity.

I approached Margaret Thatcher, by then Baroness Thatcher, to officially open it, as she was extremely popular with the Gulf governments. Although we were miles apart politically and had had a rough exchange during her final speech in the Commons, when I denounced her policies and she my socialism, she happily accepted. Her speech was excellent but the Saudi minister's speech welcoming her was badly delivered. The Arab ambassadors, some from states where women were excluded from the workforce and much else besides, applauded her enthusiastically and jostled each other to have a word with her. As she left the exhibition, she said to me, referring to the Saudi speech, 'Jim, you really must get these people to learn how to speak in public.' She was seemingly unaware that Arab ministers appointed in the Gulf states were all technocrats who never needed to justify themselves in debate and so had no need to develop skills in public speaking.

The chairman of the chamber was a retired ambassador, Sir Richard Beaumont. Dick was old-style English public school and Oxbridge. He had been a member of the British delegation at the United Nations Security Council, where he had a hand in drafting the famous Resolution 242 in the aftermath of the Six-Day War, also known as the Third Arab–Israeli War. He had been head of the Foreign Office Middle East Section and ambassador to Morocco, Iraq, from where he had been expelled by Saddam Hussein, and Egypt.

He taught me a great deal about how the Foreign Office worked internally and about the histories and personalities of the various dynasties that controlled the Arab countries. He told me that, during WWII, as a young foreign office official, he went into the desert on a motor bike with bags of gold to meet someone who, in exchange, supplied the Vichy French order of battle, before the British and Free French launched their attack to take control of Syria and Lebanon. Money talked then and still does in the Arab world.

Dick had a very close personal relationship with the key Arab member of the board, Sheikh Abdulaziz al-Sager from Kuwait. He was a member of one of Kuwait's important families which had, in a struggle with the ruling al-Sabahs, created a state where the ruler became more like a constitutional monarch with a freely elected National Assembly (– albeit male only – able to criticise the emir's government and bring it down if necessary. Sheikh Abdulaziz was the Speaker and became a strong and fearless counterbalance to the power of the ruling family.

His reputation as a democrat and believer in the people's rights and his record in fighting for them went well beyond the borders of Kuwait. Had the Arab world been blessed with more like him, it would be in a far better condition than it is today.

As chairman, Dick had to be diplomatic but, in private, he said that during a working lifetime in the region he had never seen the Arab world so bereft of outstanding leaders as it was now – one of the reasons why Sheikh al-Sager stood out. Self-interest, tribal interest and monarchical interest, in addition to playing the religious card when it suited, were the guiding factors he saw as blunting the potential power of the Arab peoples and their ability to be a successful part of the modern world.

When Dick retired in 1995, Abdul Karim asked me to find a replacement. This had to be someone with diplomatic, political or business experience at the highest level, to reflect the importance of the chamber in the Arab world. Fortuitously, Jim Prior, Lord Prior, who had been a Cabinet minister in both the Heath and Thatcher governments and was chairman of the General Electric Company (GEC), the largest manufacturing company in Europe, was about to retire from that position. I had known Jim when I was in the House of Commons. He was a one-nation Tory and a farmer who could be tough but civilised in debate. We had got on well despite political differences. I paid him a visit at the GEC office in Mayfair. It is worth noting that it wasn't plush. GEC Chief Executive, Arnold Weinstock, ran a tight ship with no absurd grandiose expenditure or expenses. The City disapproved of him for not being adventurist enough. When he and Jim Prior retired, GEC had a portfolio of profit-making companies and £3 billion cash in the bank. It didn't take long for his successors to engage in 'adventures' resulting in a share price collapse from £12.50 to 6p and the company finally disappearing. Capitalists don't always make capitalism work well.

The upshot of that first meeting was that Jim and I ended up working together for seven years, travelling around the Arab world. Both avid readers, we swapped books and talked openly about political ideologies and the successes and failures of UK governments, and politics in general. We developed a close friendship and remained in touch in the years after we left the chamber. Both our wives were afflicted with Parkinson's and both died around the same time. I was due to visit Jim in his house in Suffolk in 2016 when he took suddenly ill and died. I lost a valued friend.

Our work at the chamber meant Jim and I had an inside track to information and free discussion with those we met in the Arab states. One trip to Libya was of special interest. We were taken on a visit to

Roman ruins by a Libyan scientist who opened up, in private, about the madness of Gaddafi's grandiose project to pump a great underground sea of fresh water, found in the south, up to the north. He explained why this was damaging to agriculture in the south and pointed out that setting up desalination plants in the north would be a more sensible option. But, he said, it was dangerous to talk scientific sense when the Great Leader did not want to hear it.

On our travels, we developed good relations with and open access to every UK ambassador. They were happy to talk frankly in private with their assessments of the countries they served. I recall one asking us rhetorically why Islamic jihadists did not attack Dubai which, with foreign women in bikinis on its beaches and easy access to alcohol, epitomised everything fundamentalists denounced about the West. There are literally hundreds of thousand British and American expats working there. It seemed an obvious target for the jihadists so why was it seemingly exempt and safe? Every diplomat and intelligence officer knew the answer – Dubai is where major drug transactions and money laundering can be safely done by various non-state actors and it is in the interest of the jihadists and others to keep it free from attack. But so important were and are relations with the UAE, of which Dubai is a crucial part, no Western government would or will engage in any negative comment in public, choosing instead to praise the admirable development there which, of course, is true but not the whole story.

But the truth is there to be seen from non-governmental Western sources. In July 2020, the US Carnegie Endowment noted in a report 'a steady stream of illicit proceeds borne from corruption and crime,' while Transparency International points to 'Corrupt and criminal actors from around the world operate through or from Dubai.' But hand it to Dubai's leader and his advisers: millions of dollars are spent on PR, of such a volume to drown out the truths they need to hide.

Arabs too practise what some would regard as hypocrisy but which I choose to call sensible caution in regard to how their states are run. In public, Arabs have nothing but praise for Arab leaders but that is not the same in private. Jim and I were given frank views and information about what people were really thinking. I was particularly friendly with a minister in a Gulf state and got the inside story of the practices, strains and tensions within the ruling groups from him. He also shared his private scorn for the failure of Gulf rulers to develop civil society because they were afraid of any real movement towards democratic accountability and the loss of power that would bring.

197

I had had an interest in the Arab world for many years before I was first employed by the chamber but I could not have gained the knowledge of their culture and politics to the level I did without being in the position given to me. That does not mean I am an expert. For people like me, who have experience and a wider knowledge of the Arab world than most others, it is wise to always bear in mind that if you do not speak and read the language, as an expert does, there will always be gaps in fully understanding how decisions are made. Some knowledge is not complete knowledge.

The politics in that part of the world makes ours look like a nursery school in comparison. I can recall a number of occasions when two Arabs greeted each other warmly in a way that any Westerner would regard as a demonstration of close friendship, when in fact they hated each other. What all the Arabs I met said contemptuously in private about Yasser Arafat and his corruption was never uttered in public. But even they had their limits of believing one thing and saying and doing another. After Arafat signed the Oslo Accord, he came to London to be presented at a huge reception in the Egyptian embassy. The chamber had to be present and be seen to be present but none of the Arabs would go. I was sent to shake his hand.

Over lunch one day, my friend Fakhri Shehab asked me if I felt we were on the same wavelength and had a perfect understanding of each other. I said jokingly that his English was actually better than mine. What a mistake. He said, 'Always remember that, while you write from left to right, Arabs write from right to left and that is how we think.'

My work with the chamber frequently took me to the Gulf states because these were the main Arab markets for British companies. With the exception of Saudi Arabia, the others all had very small populations, with Arabs outnumbered by workers from developing countries and Western European ex-pats. These states had formed the Gulf Cooperation Council (GCC) – or, more formally, the Cooperation Council for the Arab States of the Gulf – in the correct belief that, separately, they would count for little in the world arena but that, in a bloc whose members had massive amounts of oil and gas, they would count.

Although the visitor would see Western influence in the five-star hotels and magnificent shopping malls springing up in what had been desert, things were not Western politically. Rule by kings and sheiks had resulted in most government ministries being headed by technocrats who, although educated in Western universities, were devoid of political skills when compared with their counterparts elsewhere. It has taken time for Gulf governments to produce a cadre of foreign and trade policy specialists and, even now, monarchs still make the key decisions.

My job in the chamber was to be as helpful as possible to ministers who asked for advice in creating their own development policies. But my main area of work was aiding the Gulf chambers and the private sector to understand the world institutions which set the economic framework and rules of international business. There were big gaps in private sector knowledge.

All Arab governments were late to the international game of trade group building and were amateurs in the hands of professionals. An example of this can be seen in the GCC–EU free-trade discussions and in the attempt by Arab states to join the World Trade Organisation (WTO), where a legal capacity, sadly lacking, was vital in negotiations. In the former, there had been round after round of meetings over ten years, with the EU skilfully stalling. To help the leaders of the private sector get an understanding of how the EU worked, I wrote a number of documents on its history, structures, politics and trade policies. These were given to delegations I organised and sometimes led, to the Commission in Brussels and to the parliament in Strasbourg, where a Scot, the Labour MEP David Martin, was exceptionally helpful.

I had a difficult time with the first EU mission. Members of the Gulf chambers showed a truculent reluctance to go to Brussels and kept asking me to justify the expenses of doing so – something I could not do until they got there. But, once in Brussels, after meeting the UK ambassador to the EU as well as commissioners and other officials, the tune changed. They realised just how much they didn't know and the visit gave them the opportunity for frank, open briefings from the EU side. Other missions followed and were very successful, especially for the younger members of the delegations. I watched them develop a growing confidence in meeting and debating with Commission officials on trade issues.

I was responsible for our chamber organising the European side of the first ever EU–GCC Industrial Conference. Held in Oman, 300 Arab and 300 EU business leaders met for a week-long discussion during which the EU side learned a great deal about what was happening in the Gulf economies.

With the WTO, the chamber set out to provide educational material and seminars in the Gulf on how that organisation worked, and the issues facing decisions by the GCC states in seeking to join. Abdul Karim and I went to Geneva at the request of a Saudi minister to meet Pascal Lamy, then the director-general of the WTO, to find out why the

Saudis seemed to be coming up against a brick wall. It turned out that the stumbling block was the USA so Lamy arranged for us to meet the American delegation. It was led by a female lawyer with an exceptionally sharp mind. She explained that the Saudis came along time and again asking for changes in WTO rules and never seemed to grasp the idea that it was they who were applying to join the WTO, not the other way round. She asked if we would help to get that simple fact over to them. It was not a message easy to convey to the Saudis, who can be very touchy, and I was happy to leave it to the diplomatic skills of Abdul Karim.

Again, I gained much from the job. I got a much better understanding of how the EU operated at all levels, as well as about the importance of the WTO to world trade and economics, the benefits that flow from *freer* trade because, actually, there is not a great deal of free trade in the world and the problems and advantages that have arisen due to its rules-based system.

Development economists have levelled valid criticism at the tri-partite group – the World Bank, the International Monetary Fund (IMF) and the WTO – that forms the dominant structure of the world economy, pointing to its negative influences on poorer countries trying to find their place in the modern world of manufacturing and advanced technology and add value to agricultural products. As economic power shifts to Asia, policymakers there and elsewhere in the developing world have started to question the present institutional structure in which rules are set that regulate international trade and give the World Bank and the IMF great influence. These are western constructs. The World Bank, the IMF and the General Agreement on Tariffs and Trade (GATT) all came out of the Bretton Woods Conference in 1944, at which the USA's economic power and policy dominated. Change is inevitable but what change and at what pace will be a growing debate in the near future.

Although, as I write, Scotland is not an independent state, there is a Cabinet secretary for external affairs but little or no attention seems to have been paid to the role of these three powerful institutions and so Scotland has not joined in the debate about how they should be reformed or replaced with others that more accurately reflect the world that exists now.

It may seem foolish to suggest that a small nation, with only devolved power, could be a force for change. But a small nation, whatever its status, can contribute to the development debate because, when it comes to thinking about how changes can be made, ideas are not the sole province of large states. An idea carries no nationality and, if it has sufficient merit to gain wide acceptance, then it can make changes, no matter its source. The fact that we are not joining the debate, I take as a sign of the provincialism that I fear came along with devolution.

*

A good part of my work at the Arab–British Chamber of Commerce was looking after Arab interests. After the great privatisation of UK public assets, the Thatcher government was showered with praise both at home and abroad. British-based consultants thought they would take advantage of this free publicity by seeking to promote it and make money, elsewhere. Some targeted the Gulf states as all of them have huge public assets.

At a promotional meeting in Jeddah, I listened to a British consultant' spiel on how Saudi Arabia's government could, to its advantage, privatise water and electricity and so overcome one of the big problems they had of people not paying their bills. When faced with unpaid bills, companies often resorted to cutting off people's supplies. But cutting off water and air conditioning in Saudi where, on some exceptional days the temperature can reach around 50 degrees centigrade, was a mad idea. After the meeting, I asked the speaker if he was serious in believing he could sell the idea of privatising these utilities to a Gulf state? He was taken aback but then he had never been in Saudi Arabia before his lecture.

In Bahrain, I was part of a meeting in which a consultant was advocating the same idea. After he had set out the beneficial wonders of privatisation of water and had taken some questions, the chairman asked if I had any comments. I took pleasure in explaining that water can be a hot political issue and cited the fact that even Mrs Thatcher had not dared privatise it in Scotland. The reason for that I said was that we Scots tend to believe that water is a gift from God and no one should make a profit from it – not, of course, strictly true but an excellent point to make in debate in a Muslim country. There was no chance of the Bahrainis being won over after that. The speaker was very angry with me afterwards, claiming my job was to help him punt British business. I explained that, no, my job was to protect our Arab friends' interests first.

I did, of course, help British business. Throughout the Gulf, British people in senior positions in companies, both Arab owned and international, had formed British business groups. They worked closely with UK embassies to inform them of opportunities and assist British companies seeking to open new markets for their products or services. I was invited to their meetings and to chair the annual meeting. There was always a goody bag. One had a splendid T-shirt with the Union Jack on the front. I used to threaten Margo that I would wear it outside, in the supermarket. I was also a member of the Saudi British Joint Business Council and the similar body in Bahrain.

My travels in connection with the Arab–British Chamber were not confined to the Gulf states. I also made visits to others, some with special problems. Lebanon and Sudan were among those with 'special' problems in the sense that, in an Arab world teeming with problems, their problems were exceptional. Egypt and Syria (at that time) would be held to have 'normal' problems.

During the centuries of Ottoman rule, Lebanon had been an integral part of Syria but, when France took over Syria in 1919, they carved out Lebanon in 1922, giving favour to the minority pro-French Christians, leaving the Sunni and Shia Muslims, and the Druze simmering. France did not relinquish control of Lebanon until November 1943, during wartime when De Gaulle, leader of the Free French, was persuaded to do so. But the legacy of French colonial-constitutional engineering remained in place. With a Christian president, a Sunni prime minister and Shia presiding over the parliament forming the deadly combination of politics and religion, it was a ticking time bomb. To add to the toxic mix, Syria had never accepted losing Lebanon and then there were the thousands of Palestinian refugees and their armed militias.

Any mishandling of this delicate situation would lead to trouble and eventually Lebanon erupted into a civil war in 1975 that lasted until 1990. The count of the dead and injured is estimated at between 120,000 and 380,000. When a chamber delegation visited in 1994, the destruction we saw in the capital, Beirut, was like that of a German city after the RAF had bombed it in World War II. The Syrians took advantage and, at the war's end, began an effective military occupation that lasted for years.

We found the president in a despondent mood. Yes, the fighting had stopped but there was nothing that could be done about Syrian control. Lebanon was too divided to achieve any form of national unity and there were no external powers to call on for help. The prime minister, Rafic Hariri, was more optimistic about what he could achieve despite the Syrian occupation, which he thought would eventually cease under Arab and international pressure. He was proved correct in due course but has never been forgiven by the Syrian regime. In the meantime, he was concentrating on restoring the economy and mobilising the considerable capital owned by Lebanese in the large diaspora – a million people had emigrated – to undertake reconstruction and restore the country to its previous status as an oasis within a grim Arab world – a place where Arabs and others could mingle and enjoy a cultural life not available elsewhere in the region.

But the tensions between the Sunni, Shia and Christians could be felt in the air. Hariri was assassinated in 2005. Most believe the Syrian government was responsible. His son, Saad Hariri, became prime minister, only to be ousted in 2019 as factionalism again ripped its way through Lebanese politics. The irony is that the Lebanese are among the smartest people on earth. Wherever they go in the world they flourish but, at home, their differences seem unbridgeable. Perhaps, sick of the corruption, division and instability, a new generation, who have been demonstrating in 2020, will find the necessary unity across the religious lines.

*

The film *Khartoum* (UK, 1966) gives the impression of Sudan as a country solely of desert. That is false. It has enormous natural resources, an abundance of water and some of the richest soil found anywhere on earth. The only time I ever saw Jim Prior excited was in Sudan when he was in animated conversation with agriculturalists. 'You could plant a stick in this and it would grow,' he said to me. Properly run, Sudan could feed the whole of Africa. But its economic potential and the social development that could flow from it have been blocked by internal convulsions over religion and by military coups. As a result, the south of the country peeled off and became the separate state of South Sudan in 2011.

I made two visits to Sudan – one with the full board of the chamber in 1997 and again in 1998 with Jim Prior to attend a conference aimed at outside investors. It was a sad event. Government departments had produced well-researched papers outlining the vast resources of the country and the investment opportunities they offered. But the only attendees were business people from Sudan itself, none of whom had the kind of capital the conference was meant to attract. They had turned up simply because the government department organising the conference had to report a good attendance to the president. This kind of behaviour is a marked feature in some parts of the Arab world, where pleasing the man at the top, even if it means falsifying information, is what really matters.

Sudan had gone through a very bad period when, on taking power, the military regime sought to impose Islamic Sharia law on the whole country and engaged in widespread violations of human rights. Jim and I met the then president, Omar Hassan Ahmad al-Bashir. Now deposed by the military he led, he is on trial for his crimes – committed by that same military under his command. He was very confident of his grip on power but had a limited understanding of the principles of sound economic development, claiming, as these rulers do, that he was in power with the support of the entire population. We met him not long after Bill Clinton had sanctioned a cruise missile attack on the Al-Shifa pharmaceutical factory just outside Khartoum in August 1998. The US claimed that it manufactured lethal chemicals. The Sudanese said it was privately owned and produced medicines for human use and veterinary products for animals. It seemed, on the evidence of soil samples taken after the attack by respectable scientists from the West, that the Sudanese were correct.

During that visit we met an extraordinary man little known in the West but famous in the Islamic world – Hassan al-Turabi. After his death in 2016, Al Jazeera broadcast a series of programmes on his life. He was an Islamic scholar whose influence went well beyond Sudan but was also a Sudanese politician. His scholarship and political career show a man who could change his mind on doctrine and secular governance. He was an influence for bad and good in Sudan, as is reflected in his various trips to prison.

A key figure in pushing the regime of Omar Hassan Ahmad al-Bashir towards the introduction of Sharia law, he had, however, mellowed somewhat when we met him in his new role as speaker of the National Assembly. In that role, he was taking a lead in the 'national dialogue' that was meant to heal old wounds. He was charismatic, unlike the president, and was in a different class intellectually. He was well aware of the gulf between Western thought, built upon the precepts of the Enlightenment, and his view of Islam. He was extremely courteous and did not avoid discussion of difficult subjects. But he made it plain he saw Sharia law as God's law and thus superior to any system that human beings could produce. It was our only meeting with him but we came away with the impression that, for all his ability, like the president, economic development was not a subject he cared much about.

The Arab Spring, when it seemed citizens of a number of Arab states were rebelling against dictators and reaching for democracy, had no immediate effect in Sudan but, more recently, there has been something of a revolution, especially among the young. I would like to believe that the military–civilian government will eventually produce a purely civilian government with the military subordinate to it, but . . .

That 'but' is there because of what has happened elsewhere as the Arab Spring turned out to be a new winter of authoritarian control, particularly in Egypt and Syria, while Libya has disintegrated and Tunisia struggles as the Gulf rulers impose greater control. People who took action against the status quo thought they had won when the old rulers were toppled. They were, sadly, handicapped by a lack of experience in creating solid organisations capable of carrying through a democratic revolution and resisting the regimes' counter-attack when it came. The 'regime' nature of what they faced was not fully understood. The toppling of Mubarak and Omar Hassan, for example, did not remove the regimes which were formed of powerful vested interests that were still intact and untouched when the leader crashed. Principal among those forces is the military, not only the beneficiary of special privileges of pay and conditions but also as owners of profit-making parts of the economy. The Egyptian military, for example, is the country's dominant economic actor. It didn't take long for that caste to re-instate itself as rulers of Egypt when the demonstrators who ousted Mubarak mistakenly thought the generals were under an elected government's control.

But there is also a third factor that, hopefully, will have profound effects for the better in all Arab states in the years ahead. Young people make up a third of the population in the Arab region. More in touch than their parents with the rest of the world, they are better educated and have the capacity to think outside the boundaries set by their rulers. Repression will continue to be a tool used by those who rule today but next time there is an Arab Spring it will not so easily morph into an Arab Winter.

*

Scottish Enterprise (SE) is the Tory successor to Labour's Scottish Development Agency (SDA). Margaret Thatcher was opposed to this kind of public role in the economy but the Scottish Tories were not and this gave their ministers a problem – how to meet Mrs Thatcher's expectation that the SDA would be abolished while not getting rid of it? They devised Scottish Enterprise – 'enterprise' being a plus word for Mrs T. There was not much difference in reality between SE and SDA.

It may have been my connection with the Arab business world, which I laid out in my response to the public notice inviting applications, that enabled Michael Forsyth, the Tory Secretary of State, to overcome objections within Scottish Enterprise and appoint me to the board for three years in 1996. I was reappointed for another three years by Labour Secretary of State Donald Dewar in 1999.

I got the impression that Scottish Enterprise's first chairman, Professor Donald MacKay, thought I would be purely political with nothing to offer on the economic and business sides to the board. That was not the view taken by Crawford Beveridge, the chief executive. He told me privately that I was one of the few politicians who understood what SE was there for. I had the advantage over all other members that I had been on the Standing Committee of the House of Commons that had set it up and had the unique experience of seeing how it actually worked, rather than how it was meant to work in the eyes of the Commons committee. I had no problems with the second chairman, Ian Wood of the Wood Group. Until Brian Souter joined the board, I was the only nationalist, indeed the first SNP member, to serve.

That was the irony. I was well dug into the board's work but not once was I asked by the SNP leadership to contribute to their policy development on SE. I would have been happy to do so. When Brian Wilson became the Labour Scottish Office Minister responsible for the agency in 1997, he and I had a private talk about how it operated. The same private conversations took place when he became minister at the Department of Trade and Industry, and later at the Foreign Office, when I could provide him with insights into the Arab world. Brian and I have not had an easy political relationship, on many occasions vigorously disagreeing on the constitutional issue, but that did not prevent either of us from sitting down and discussing matters with a view to pursuing the public good.

During the passage of the Scottish Enterprise Bill in Parliament, I tabled an amendment that would have enabled the agency to be independent of the Scottish Office. I argued that it should be given a broad remit along with its budget and then allowed to get on with it – much like the Irish Development Agency could. My own vote and that of the Lib Dem MP, Ray Michie, were the only votes the amendment got. As we broke for lunch, Tory MP Allan Stewart told me he and his colleagues all agreed with me but they had been whipped to say no as ministers and civil servants were not prepared to create something they could not control.

The first set of papers I received as a board member had a double reference to some agenda items. On asking why, it was explained that those papers had gone to the Scottish Office first. SE was on a leash.

Crawford Beveridge brought weight, international business experience and a quiet but effective authority to a post which is not an easy one. When he decided to go back to international business, the job was advertised worldwide. A small group of the board made the selection and conducted interviews. I was not one of them. When the chairman announced at a board meeting that Robert Crawford was their choice, I said it was an excellent one. Robert had been the SNP research officer when Margo was deputy leader but I also knew him when he worked as a senior official at the Scottish Development Agency, through my job with the Arab–British Chamber. Robert was dynamic and imaginative and he had a big independent streak – not the characteristics that would endear him to the civil servants in the Scottish Office who wanted to keep SE on a tight leash.

After I left the board, I read critical reports about him in the business section of newspapers. The source was obvious. Some of the stuff was scurrilous invention and eventually he left and took his great talent elsewhere. I was correct in that amendment I had tabled. If a development agency is to be effective, it must have a policy agenda free from the electoral cycle that dominates the lives of politicians. It has to be given a remit by politicians, based on discussions with the agency itself, and then left to get on with its work, able to take the risks that are inevitable in making economic and business decisions, without being worried and manipulated by ministers anxious about a coming election date.

21

Middle Eastern Tragedies

The Gulf War and the Israel–Palestine Tragedy

The Soviet war in Afghanistan, 1979–1989, the first Gulf War, 1990–91, to evict Iraq from Kuwait and the second, in 2003, to depose Saddam Hussein may appear to be different events but they are links in a chain contributing to the turmoil in the Muslim world, especially its Arab parts, and in that turmoil's effect upon security in the Western states.

Both Sunni history and Shia history are ones of building great, magnificent civilisations, followed by long periods of decay and decline. The past 100 years have been a particularly bad period, with most Muslims subjected to Western domination, seemingly without any inner strength to resist. But underneath the Western panoply of control, there was movement, starting in Egypt in 1928 with the writings of Hassan al-Banna, who saw a return to the Koran and Hadith as the only way the Muslims could recover control over themselves. He gave birth to the Muslim Brotherhood but his ideas went beyond its organisational boundaries. You can kill a person, as was done with the assassination of al-Banna, but not an idea.

There was no upsurge after his views appeared but enough of a movement for the Brotherhood and people like them to be oppressed, brutally, by Arab regimes, ether allies of Western powers or under their direct control, who felt threatened. Nasser in Egypt executed members of the Muslim Brotherhood, as was the case elsewhere. The Brotherhood went underground but al-Banna's ideas did not. You could say it was a slow burn but eventually there was a resurgence of belief in the fundamental values of Islam throughout the Islamic world. This became manifest in the 1970s and was very obvious from the 1980s onwards.

In 1973, armed Muslims, many theology students, during the Hajj pilgrimage, occupied the Great Mosque at Mecca seeking to overthrow the corrupt pro-Western al-Saud regime and 'purify' Islam. It took two weeks, with the help of French commandos, to subdue them. Sixty-seven were later beheaded. That was a harbinger of things to come. Most people in the West didn't get the message. When the Gulf Arabs banned oil sales to the West during the Yom Kippur War of 1973, a senior British businessman, in a private meeting with a cross-party group of MPs, said it was time to 'send a gunboat up the Gulf' to restore our control of the oil and this was greeted with some shouts of 'Hear! Hear!'.

Upper- and middle-class women in Egypt, who previously had been very Western in their dress and the hairdos, started wearing the hijab. I caught this development in my own small way when working with the Arab–British Chamber. Colleagues told me that Abdul Karim al-Mudaris had been a lad about London's night clubs when he was Arab League ambassador to the UK, but, when I met him he was a strict Muslim. When organising the annual dinner that Europeans as well as Arabs would attend, I would have an argument with him each year over the serving of wine – a number of Arabs were happy when I won. I caught the new wind too when Abeer, one of his Egyptian daughters, an English-educated, sophisticated upper-middle class woman, came one August for her holidays wearing the hijab. Her husband, Zaki, explained this was now standard among her friends.

But there were other much more potent signs within the Arab world itself. President Sadat of Egypt found it prudent to be seen praying in the Mosque and even Saddam Hussein was photographed at prayers. A great new mosque was built in Morocco, not a rich population, by public subscription.

This resurgence within Islam, a repudiation of past subservience to foreign non-Islamic powers, was there to touch, feel and hear. It was at this time the grey men in the Kremlin, with all the sensitivity of a dead tree, decided to invade Afghanistan. That war became Islam against the infidel, with Arabs in particular like Osama bin Laden, flocking to join the muja-hideen. The boost to the al-Banna idea was spectacular. The defeat of the Soviets was proof positive of its authenticity and being the correct guide to Muslim people everywhere and again especially in the Arab world from where Islam had sprung and within which were the holy cities. It is still a young religion. This is something that is hardly ever mentioned in the West but it is important in understanding Islam in the present day. In the Islamic calendar, this is the year 1441. We have not only witnessed a resurgence of belief but also the religious energy powering a belief that is more than five hundred years younger than Christianity.

This resurgence of Islam presented the Arab ruling groups with a potential problem of backlash from their populations in the first Gulf

War, when Western military boots came on to the ground of the land of the Prophet, in preparation for the expulsion of Saddam Hussein's Iraq from Kuwait. There were, however, no immediate adverse consequences, something helped by the Saudi king obtaining approval for this Western presence from religious scholars.

The Saudi regime was aided in its avoidance of the religious problem when George H. W. Bush skilfully brought Arab states into his coalition of military forces, thus avoiding what would otherwise appear to be a solely Western action. This Arab involvement was the reason he did not sanction an invasion of Iraq once Kuwait was free. The problem arose afterwards, with the United States now having military bases in Saudi Arabia, the holy land for Osama bin Laden and those many thousands who thought like him. Ridding Saudi of the USA military was his first demand. All the time they were there, anger simmered and the call to live only by the Koran and Hadith became more powerful, driving the call to drive the infidels out and revenge the perceived insult to Islam. The twin towers and 9/11 were the result.

Then along came George W. Bush, with his talk of a 'crusade', and his partner Tony Blair with their invasion and take-over of Iraq. I don't know if we should forgive them but they certainly did not know what they were doing, which was to poke a great big military stick into a theological wasps' nest – the Sunni–Shia divide, which was and is at its most intense within Iraq, where the Sunni minority has ruled and oppressed a very large Shia majority which has long and deep links with Shia Iran. Destroy Saddam Hussein's regime and release the Shia from the Sunni grip and, as they exercise the power of their numbers, sectarian violence becomes Iraq's fate.

As the Bush-Blair war drums were beating and as our anxieties at the Arab–British Chamber were rising about the consequences of an invasion, we did more on the political side of our life, in the UK, than was usual. Our Arab colleagues in the Gulf knew that an invasion and destruction of the Saddam regime would produce what they feared most – with Iraqi power removed, the geopolitical balance would alter and Iran would emerge as the regional power. Precisely what happened.

What could we do? Perhaps very little but Jim Prior, as chairman, convened a series of private meetings with former ambassadors and academics, all with detailed knowledge of the Arab states. The purpose of the meetings was to try to open up channels to Downing Street about the consequences of what the two Western warriors had in mind. Two things stand out in my memory from those meetings. Firstly, when one former ambassador said the USA and UK were about to 'enter a quicksand', he was corrected by David Gore-Booth, another former ambassador, who said, 'No, we are about to land in treacle.' And, secondly, an academic warned that beating Saddam's military forces was one thing but letting loose the various forces inside Iraq and elsewhere was quite another. He managed to have a meeting in Downing Street but told us afterwards that Blair was deaf to the reality.

Arising from the meetings, a number of former ambassadors wrote to Blair seeking to persuade him not to go to war but he dismissed them as 'Arabists'. One would think that views from Arabists, that is people who know the region intimately, would carry weigh, but it seems the opposite was the case.

After the invasion, with the US and UK forces tied down with insurgency, Jim Prior arranged a meeting with Sir Jeremy Greenstock, who had been the UK ambassador to the UN at the time when negotiations were conducted over a possible second UN resolution, the one Blair sought but did not get. Jim, Abdul Karim and I met Sir Jeremy over a private lunch.

It was October 2003, and Sir Jeremy was about to take up a position as the UK's Special Representative in Iraq working with Paul Bremer, the US-appointed administrator of the Coalition Provisional Authority ruling Iraq. A man with no experience of the Arab world, Bremer blundered from day one of landing in that country, in May 2003. He barred the Ba'ath Party members from any governmental involvement depriving the country of an administration and making it ungovernable. He dismissed the whole of the Iraqi armed forces overnight leaving them with no income but still fully armed. It is doubtful if, in the entire history of imperialism, there has been such a calamitous appointment.

Sir Jeremy was very open in his discussion with us, knowing we would not make anything he said public. We needed to know what the real position was as the UK Foreign Office saw it from within so that we could quietly pass on the information to the Arab ministers and business people with whom we had had continuous contact. He obviously thought the Bremer appointment by Bush a huge handicap. He said he would be taking an Iraqi-British civil servant with him as his private secretary – someone who could go out beyond the Green Zone in central Baghdad and find out what was really happening. He noted that Bremer had no such aide and nor did he think he needed one.

When asked about the UK government's influence on US-Iraq policy in general, he said it represented around 10 per cent. When asked about his likely influence as nominally the No. 2 in Iraq, he said 10 per cent of 10 per cent. He wound up our lunch by saying that this was

A Difference of Opinion

now October but, if by December we and the USA had not solved the domestic problems in Iraq, with proper utilities supplied to the people and stability and security on the streets, then we faced 'catastrophe'.

We three left that meeting despondent. Iraq was governed by an American ignoramus and we had little hope that Sir Jeremy, for all his undoubted ability, would be able to correct or stop Bremer's flow of mistakes. He was going to a no-win situation and the people of Iraq were facing hell, as proved to be the case.

Abdul Karim's Arab secretary, Bernadette Yacoub, was an Iraqi Christian. In touch with her family back home, their message was stark – that Christian community, one of the oldest in the world, was being attacked and decimated by Islamic zealots operating without restraint.

The Soviets in Afghanistan, the eviction of Saddam Hussein from Kuwait and the subsequent decade of punitive sanctions on Iraq, followed by the Bush-Blair incursion, set loose consequences that are still playing out today in the Middle East. The Arab world is no longer even nominally united but split. Iran, no matter what the Americans do, is a major regional player and Turkey is seeking to resume the influential role of the Ottomans. Israel too is a player and fluid in its choice of partners, whether they be openly identified or engaged with in secrecy. The prospects of these peoples living in peace and security are not good.

The Palestinian–Israeli Tragedy

I have had a lifetime's interest in the Israel–Palestine tragedy. Even when ten years old and reading the newspapers as I did, it was impossible not to know about the events there between Jew and Arab. The main news on the wireless was full of it. Large billboards advertised jobs in the Palestine Police. Britain still held the mandate for Palestine, given it by the League of Nations in 1919. I had well-formed views on the issue by the time I became an MP in 1970. In my first week, Maurice Miller, then a Glasgow MP, invited me to take an all-expenses-paid visit to Israel with a view to becoming a member of Labour Friends of Israel. I declined. I could, correctly, be described as pro-Palestinian and a severe critic of a succession of Israeli governments. But I do not wish to see the state of Israel eliminated, which is a fantasy held by some Arab groups and the Mullahs of Iran – a fantasy that makes them blind to reality. My bent in favour of the Palestinians is because I know the harm done to them by the creation of Israel and how badly they had been deceived and treated by the British. The collective punishments and destruction of homes that Palestinians suffer today at the hands of Israel with its

212

superior force are not new experiences for the Arabs. It was standard British practice in putting down the Arab revolt in 1936 when, incidentally, the major general in charge of the British Army there was Bernard Montgomery.

In trying to prevent the growing Jewish presence in Palestine, the Arabs attacked the Jews, committing appalling atrocities. The Jews engaged in a two-stage violence – first against the British, using terrorism to drive them out and second against the Arabs after declaring independence and during the fighting to defend it.

The Arabs in and outside Palestine cannot write objectively about their role from the 1930s onwards because it involves shameful episodes, including inner betrayal. Israel, by brilliant diplomacy and equally brilliant public relations in the West, has managed to airbrush Jewish pre-independence violence out of history. Convenient historic amnesia afflicting both sides enables them to clutch firmly to their own black-and-white version of history. There are more shades of grey and darkness in the historical relationship between the Jews and Arabs than some of today's participants and supporters are aware of. But, until historical truths are acknowledged and admitted by both sides, reaching a solution today remains entangled in the myths that keep both captive in a destructive relationship.

Today, when Israeli leaders condemn the Palestinians as terrorists, one can but smile. In pursuit of driving the British out, the Jewish terrorist groups, Irgun and Lehi – Lehi, *Lohamei Herut Israel*, 'Fighters for the Freedom of Israel', is also known pejoratively as 'the Stern Gang' – were assassinating British officials, soldiers and policemen and attacking government buildings. The assassinations began before the war ended – Lord Moyne, British Minister of State, Middle East, was murdered in Cairo on 6 November 1944 when Britain was still fighting Nazi Germany. The Stern Gang did the killing, claiming it as 'a step towards forcing the British Government to leave Palestine'. Even UN personnel were not safe. Count Folke Bernadotte, a Swedish diplomat, was made UN mediator in an attempt to end the 1948 fighting. Denounced as a British 'stooge', he was assassinated by the Stern Gang on 17 September 1948. Among those who planned his killing was Yitzhak Shamir. He and Menachem Begin of Irgun became Israeli prime ministers. In Israel, naturally, they are not seen as terrorists but as freedom fighters – pretty much the same as the Palestine Liberation Organization (PLO) in its terrorist days saw its people.

The first big post-war terrorist event in the world was the destruction, in 1946, of the King David Hotel in Jerusalem, the centre of the

British mandate administration. The bomb planted by Irgun murdered ninety-one people. In London, a young Jewish woman tricked her way past the man at the entrance to the Commonwealth Office, by saying she was desperate for the toilet, and planted a bomb that would have massacred hundreds. It didn't go off.

On the Arab side, there was violence too, as they sensed that their position was being undermined. They were poorly organised, untrained, badly led and suffered from treachery. In the years before WWII, the Zionists did not openly declare their intention of creating a Jewish state. The tactic was to buy land and expand the Jewish presence both in terms of territory and increase in numbers. The Arabs objected to the British authorities allowing this to happen. At a morning meeting, Arab 'leaders' – that is to say prominent families – would make their protest to the British and, in the afternoon, sell land to the Jewish Agency whose purpose was to facilitate Jewish immigration, purchase land for them to work on and represent Jewish interests to the British Mandate.

After the war, the recently formed United Nations proposed the solution of partition – two separate states. The Arabs rejected it. On 14 May 1948, the State of Israel was declared at midnight in part of Palestine. The new state was almost immediately recognised by both the United States and the Soviet Union and Israel was admitted to the UN in May 1949. The surrounding Arab states attacked to eliminate the new state. They were defeated. Israel expanded beyond the borders of the territory it had claimed in its May declaration and refused to let the Palestinians who had left their homes to return.

The Palestinians fled their homes because of acts of terror when war came. It is indisputable that a massacre of Palestinian civilians, including women and children, took place, at the hands of Israelis, at the Arab village of Deir Yassin. The Jewish Agency for Israel condemned the atrocity but terror was loose among the Palestinian population and many thousands fled. Terror and atrocity was not on one side alone. A convoy of Jewish civilians, academics, doctors and nurses was ambushed and the people slaughtered. The 1948 war was inevitable. Israel could only be created as a state by declaring sovereignty over land that Palestinians held as being theirs. Arab states were bound to intervene, seek to eliminate the new state and drive the Jews of Palestine into the sea.

The seeds of its inevitability were sown by the deadly ambiguity of the British government's 1917 Balfour Declaration, a three-paragraph document for the information of the Zionist Federation that was made public. It expressed the Cabinet's 'sympathy with Jewish Zionist aspirations' and went to state that:

> His Majesty's government view with favour the establishment in Palestine of a national home for the Jewish people, and will use their best endeavours to facilitate the achievement of this object, it being clearly understood that nothing shall be done which may prejudice the civil and religious rights of existing non-Jewish communities.

In forming this new British policy, Jewish leaders had been consulted but not Arabs. Moreover, Britain was at war with the Ottomans, the rulers of Palestine. It was easy for the imperial mind to give commitments on territory it did not presently hold.

Population figures show how important that declaration was once Britain did hold power over Palestine, after 1919. In 1890, 43,000 Jews lived in Palestine, compared to 57,000 Christians, many of them Arab, and 432,000 Arabs. By 1929, there were 84,000 Jews, 71,000 Christians and 589,000 Muslims and, by 1931, those figures were 175,000 Jews, 89,000 Christians, and 730,000 Muslims. In 1947, they stood at 630,000 Jews, 143,000 Christians, and 1,181,000 Muslims. Israel, today, has a population of 9.15 million, of which 6.6 million are Jewish and 1.8 million are Arabs. That steady increase in Jewish numbers from 1929 would eventually bring sufficient strength to declare a sovereign state, with the inevitable Arab reaction. Britain had never developed a policy for self-government in Palestine and that deadly ambiguity of the Balfour Declaration, promising a homeland for Jews without in any way disadvantaging the Palestinians, made it impossible to do so. Assailed by both sides in Palestine, receiving a public relations pasting outside, especially from the USA, with the deaths and the costs of occupation mounting, the British government threw in the towel and passed the problem to the United Nations.

Although the USA might now be ambivalent, Western powers have gone back to the UN principle of partition – a two-state solution but with a much smaller one for the Palestinians than was on offer in 1947. The two Oslo Accords, one signed in 1993 and the other in 1995, held out that possibility but it has been strangled by Israel's illegal settlement policy. An Israel–Palestinian federation is out of the question because Israel has declared, as policy, that it has to be known as a Jewish state. The Palestinians would probably reject it too. The wells of hatred on both sides have been too deeply dug for any form of a single entity to be considered.

A Difference of Opinion

Later in life, with a formal involvement with Arab organisations, I found my Arab friends railing against Western hypocrisy and double standards, citing the treatment of Iraq under sanctions in Saddam's time, while Israel could dismiss UN Security Council resolutions with open contempt, with no price to pay. That is because Israel is subject to Chapter VI of the resolutions which carries no requirement to comply, whereas Iraq fell under Chapter VII where sanctions are imposed if not obeyed. Whatever the legal niceties, the Arabs are, of course, right – most Western countries do apply double standards when Israel is involved. That state breaches international and humanitarian law with impunity and, were any other state to conduct itself as an occupying power like Israel does, it would be designated a pariah under worldwide sanctions.

That Israel is not in that category is due to a number of factors, the first of which is that it enjoys the protection of the USA. And then there is a combination of other reasons which include guilt felt by European Christian and post-Christian countries over centuries of persecution of Jewish people, clever diplomacy and a well-constructed and delivered narrative about Israel as the only democracy in a region of tyrants, Arab states' double-dealing by pretending, for public consumption, that Israel should not exist but being in concert with it in private and Palestinian leadership that is plain awful – Arafat was a disaster but he was not the only one.

Before the keyboards rattle and social media fills with demands that I apologise for my anti-Semitism in condemning Israel for its breaches of international law, let me state why I would not apologise. The International Holocaust Remembrance Alliance definition of anti-Semitism, with which I agree, has eleven contemporary examples of what can constitute anti-Semitism, the eighth of which states: 'Applying double standards to it [Israel] by requiring . . . a behaviour not expected or demanded of any other democratic nation.' I do expect all democratic nations to act differently in international law and human rights compared to authoritarian states. I don't believe Israel should be held to a higher standard than the United States, the UK, Canada, Australia or France, for example, but I do believe it should be held to the same standard and, when it fails, as when they fail, it should be as open as they are to criticism and, when necessary, condemnation. France in Algeria, the UK over the Hola death camp in Kenya, UK interrogation practices in Northern Ireland, USA carpet-bombing and use of agent orange in Vietnam, the US–UK illegal invasion of Iraq and the US rendition programme, a euphemism for torture by other hands, have all invited condemnation. Why should Israel's policy of collective punishment,

216

the destruction of a family's home or confiscation of Palestinian land for illegal settlements escape condemnation? If Israel goes ahead with annexation of much of the West Bank, how could that be acceptable because it is Israel?

Of course I recognise that Israel, unlike the states I mentioned, has faced and continues to face unique national security threats and its citizens have a genuine cause for fears about their personal security. Constantly living with this situation will pose difficulties in maintaining its adherence to international law but that is a reason for lapses not a blanket excuse for all its actions.

The state of Israel is supported by many Jews who are not Israeli citizens. Some, like the American Israel Public Affairs Committee (AIPAC) in the USA, will back the actions of the Israeli governments no matter what they do. But there are many others, such as J Street, also in the USA, and in other countries, including the UK, who are critical of Israel, the state, and its conduct in the occupied Palestinian territories. When, in 2019, the prime minister of Israel, Benjamin Netanyahu, announced his intention of annexing the West Bank, there was a massive demonstration in Tel Aviv by Israelis against it. Within Israel there are many Jews in the peace and civil rights movements who are the strongest critics of the settlements policies and who seek a genuine two-state solution. If I was, say, a British Jew looking at the long history of persecutions and massacres that culminated in the Holocaust, I would have a built-in bias towards Israel and I would not think I had any dual-loyalty problem by knowing that, if anti-Semitism ever again reached dangerous levels, anywhere, there was a place – Israel – to which Jewish families could go and be safe.

The peculiar thing about anti-Semitism is that it is not racist in the normal sense of the word. Racism is born of a belief that other peoples are lesser humans and so can be treated in an inhumane manner. But anti-Semitism comes from the opposite position – that Jewish people are alleged to be superior in societies and use power gained from that superiority to control the countries in which they live, and by extension the world. That is an even more dangerous myth than the usual racist trope, as history shows.

The histories I have read record how humans have moved around the world over the ages, conquering land and killing peoples; sometimes the numbers of dead have been mind boggling. It is usually numbers that history records. But it was not just the number that, only once in my life, forced me to lay down a book and stop reading. It was the people. That happened in 1960 when reading *The Rise and Fall of the Third*

Reich, by William L. Shirer (Simon & Schuster, New York, 1960). He reprinted an affidavit from a German civilian eyewitness, submitted to the Nuremberg Tribunal, of the execution of 5,000 Jews, by Ukrainian militia and German Einsatzgruppen commandos, outside the town of Dubno in Ukraine. When the Chief British Prosecutor presented it in evidence, he made no speech. He just read it. First to a stunned silence, then to the sound of tears as even the hard men in the court started to cry. I am not ashamed to say it had the same effect on me in 1960 and still has today. I will not reproduce the whole of that long heart-rending affidavit from Nuremberg but I believe it should be compulsory reading for every young person before they leave school. It would be an unpleasant experience but would show what allowing anti-Semitism to flourish can bring in its evil wake. It began by recording that men, women, and children were forced to completely undress and went on:

> Without screaming or weeping these people undressed, stood around in family groups, kissed each other, said farewell and waited for a sign from another S.S. man who stood near the pit, also with a whip in his hand. During the fifteen minutes that I stood near the pit I heard no complaint or plea for mercy . . .
>
> An old woman with snow white hair was holding a one-year-old child in her arms and singing to it and tickling it. The child was cooing with delight. The parents were looking on with tears in their eyes. The father was holding the hand of a boy about 10 years old and speaking to him softly; the boy was fighting his tears. The father pointed to the sky, stroked his head and seemed to explain something to him. At that moment the S.S. man at the pit shouted something to his comrade. The latter counted off about twenty persons and instructed them to go behind the earth mound . . . I well remember a girl, slim and with black hair, who, as she passed close to me, pointed to herself and said 'twenty-three years old'. I walked around the mound and found myself confronted by a tremendous grave . . . I looked for the man who did the shooting. He was an S.S. man who sat at the edge of the narrow end of the pit, his feet dangling in the pit. He had a tommy-gun on his knee and was smoking a cigarette.

In the Israeli–Palestinian conflict, the long trail of blood has never dried. There are no signs that those in leadership positions can find another language to speak to each other in except violence. Neither side has produced the kind of statesmen needed to bring it to an end. Yitzhak Rabin might have. He has no successor of the same calibre on the Israeli side and the Palestinians are ill served by what passes for their leadership today.

Where is the Israeli leader who can insist that the Israeli people acknowledge that serious harm was done to Palestinians whose land was taken by force and that the 1948 Palestinian exodus – the *Nakba* – was indeed their catastrophe? This needs to happen so that a solution with some justice can be found. The present methods of occupation are not only a humiliation of the Arabs but also a stain on Israel's reputation on human rights. On the Palestinian side there is no leader willing to stand up and tell the truth – that Israel is a state recognised as such by the international community, that it will remain tenacious in safeguarding its Jewish character, that, as a nuclear power, it is not going to be eliminated and that there will be no right of return for the Palestinian refugees to the land they lost.

Both are, of course, tall orders. If Israel was to admit illegal confiscation of Palestinian land and harm to another people, as essential to its creation, then it would put a question mark against its founding narrative of having a moral right to be where it is, through divine gift. An Arab leader telling the Palestinian refugees a blunt but awful truth – that their dream of return is just that, not a reality – would not last long. And so the tragedy continues, violence met by violence, met by violence. Israelis are not secure, the Palestinians are impoverished and the world community impotent.

The Palestinians are now faced with a new chapter of their story – betrayal on the altar of state interests by Arab gulf rulers as they bring into the open and formalise what were previously back-channel links to Israel. The UAE is establishing full diplomatic relations with Israel. Bahrain, now effectively controlled by Saudi Arabia, has done the same. Oman has not gone as far but did host the first official visit by the Israeli prime minister in October 2018. Qatar continues with the back-channel and doesn't bother to hide it. It is an open secret that it is only a matter of time until Saudi Arabia, the big catch for Israel, joins the UAE and Bahrain.

These Gulf rulers have acted, formally and informally, to engage with Israel because they all – the Gulf states and Israel – face the same adversary – Iran. The benefits will be that the USA will unlock the supply of modern weapons hitherto denied them for not recognising Israel, access to Israel's own formidable weapons industry and a second nuclear-powered 'friend' – Israel – to provide an arms'-length deterrent to the Iranians. This Gulf–Israel rapprochement has been widely welcomed in Western capitals as a big step forward in achieving a final peace between Israel and the Arabs. I am not so sure. These were rulers' decisions and it is hard to believe they carry the support of the Arab street. It is a disaster for the Palestinians as Israel was not required to pay a price for its foreign policy success. Netanyahu did not cancel his policy of annexing most of the Palestinian West Bank – he only postponed it, leaving annexation for a future moment of opportunity when the Gulf states are too entangled with military and investment deals to be able to protest effectively. A few days after Bahrain's formal recognition, Israel announced there would be another development of 5,000 houses on Palestinian land. Only the EU and the UK protested.

Blair and War Crime

> Laws are spider webs through which the big flies pass and the little ones get caught.
>
> Honoré de Balzac

After the US–UK invasion of Iraq in 2003, there was a lot of talk about Tony Blair being guilty of a war crime but nothing concrete emerged until the SNP, led by Alex Salmond, and Plaid Cymru commissioned research and used it to seek a House of Commons impeachment of the prime minister, in November 2004. There was no chance of success in that arena but a criminal case from February and March 2003 had been making its way, court by court, to the House of Lords where a decision on the criminal appeal could open or close the door on an indictment of Blair for a war crime. That was not the issue before the judges but the legal principle upon which they had to decide had consequences one way or the other.

Briefly, around twenty people had broken into an air base in both February and March, damaged property, were arrested, charged and taken to trial and found guilty. Their appeals were based on a claim that they were justified in their actions because the British government was committing the war crime of aggression and they, therefore, had a valid defence in English law in trying to prevent that crime being committed. The legal issue to be determined was whether the war crime of aggression was or was not incorporated in English and Welsh domestic law.

I was not alone in following the case as many realised that, if a court found in favour of the appellants, then Blair could be in trouble. The importance of what was at stake came before a five-judge bench in the House of Lords, who heard legal arguments over four days, before giving a long, detailed decision on 29 November 2006 (UKHL 16). The judges acknowledged that aggression was a war crime in public international law but that it had not been transposed into the domestic law of England and Wales. Blair was off the hook.

But that judgment only applied south of the border. I thought it worth a try in Scottish jurisdiction. However, as there was no case in the Scottish courts, unlike in England, that provided a legal peg upon which the war crime issue could be argued, a case would have to be made out on its own merits. I set about trying to produce one.

It took six months, during which I wrote to and received replies from noted international lawyers. None laughed off the idea – all of them were helpful and encouraging. I trawled the internet and other sources of information, examined international law, the scope and limitations of the International Criminal Court and debates in the House of Commons. My two years of training in international law at Edinburgh University proved to be most helpful. I discovered emails between senior officials working for Blair and Condoleezza Rice, President Bush's National Security Adviser, confirming that Blair had committed himself to regime change in Iraq in the full knowledge that this was aggression – a war crime in international law ever since the Nuremberg Tribunal.

Nearing the end of my efforts, there came the fortuitous election result of May 2007 and the installation of the first SNP government at Holyrood. Surely this would be an opportunity to bring Blair to justice? After all, the SNP had been among the most vociferous in condemning the Iraq invasion as being 'not in our name'. Was not its opposition against the Gulf War a factor in its election victory over Labour? Did not the new First Minister, Alex Salmond, seek to impeach Blair? And was not the Lord Advocate a member of that government?

I produced and submitted a substantial document to the Lord Advocate on 8 June 2007, asking that Blair be indicted for the war crimes of aggression for the purposes of regime change. Margo MacDonald chaired a meeting with the press in the Scottish parliament, where I sought to explain international law and how Blair had breached it to a Scottish press corps more used to reporting on issues like the NHS, education and transport.

There is protective legislation providing that no one should be tried for a crime which did not constitute a criminal offence under national or international law at the time it was committed but Blair was not protected by it because, since Nuremberg, aggression was a criminal offence in international law and war for regime change was also a crime. Blair was well aware of these facts when conspiring with Bush to wage aggressive war against Iraq for regime change.

I spent six months researching various British and US sources, and found a significant amount of government material in the public domain, from books, articles and leaked emails, especially from within the USA. Here are some extracts from my submission to the Lord Advocate. They make Blair's culpability clear. In Col. 722 of Hansard, 18 March 2003, Blair told the House of Commons, 'I have never put the justification for action as regime change.' Documents from a year before that show he lied. Cabinet office paper, 8 March 2002, Paragraph 11: 'In considering the options for regime change below, we need to first consider what sort of Iraq we want.' and in Paragraph 26: 'Option 3 comes closest to guaranteeing regime change. At this stage we need to wait and see which option or combination of options may be favoured by the US government.'

A memo from the prime minister's foreign policy advisor, David Manning, to the prime minister, 14 March 2002, with Downing Street Chief of Staff, Jonathon Powell, copied in, read: 'I had dinner with Condi on Tuesday; and talks and lunch with her and an NSC team on Wednesday (to which Christopher Meyer [British Ambassador to the United States] also came). These were good exchanges, and particularly frank when we were one-to-one at dinner. I attach the records in case you want to glance. Iraq: We spent a long time at dinner on Iraq. It is clear that Bush is grateful for your support and has registered that you are getting flak. I said that you would not budge in your support for regime change but you had to manage the press, a Parliament and a public opinion that was very different from anything in the States. And you would not budge either in your insistence that, if we pursued regime change, it must be very carefully done and produce the right result. Failure was not an option.'

Cabinet office paper, 21 July 2002: 'When the Prime Minister discussed Iraq with President Bush at Crawford in April, he said that the UK would support military action to bring about regime change.'

From British Ambassador to the United States Sir Christopher Meyer, 18 March 2002 by e-mail to Sir David Manning in Downing Street: '1. Paul Wolfowitz, the Deputy Secretary of Defense, came to Sunday lunch on 17 March. 2. On Iraq I opened by sticking very closely to the script that you used with Condi Rice last week. We backed regime change, but the plan had to be clear and failure was not an option . . .'

Then there was Blair's claim that he had no alternative to abandoning pursuit of a second UN resolution because the French President Jacques Chirac had said he would veto it permanently. Chirac's alleged threat to veto came during an interview but it showed that, far from laying down a permanent veto, he had only referred to the situation while the weapons inspectors were still investigating. The following passages show the difference between Blair's deception of the House of Commons and the reality of the French position. Blair, speaking of his war resolution in the House of Commons, Col. 765 Hansard, 18 March 2003, seeking to justify action without a second UN resolution, highlighted France's position thus: 'For that country to say that it will veto such a resolution *in all circumstances* is what I would call unreasonable.' (emphasis added)

Extracts in English from a transcript of Chirac's interview made available by the French on 10 March 2003 showed that it was not the absolute veto Blair claimed it to be:

> Chirac: 'We have said 'We want to disarm Iraq' (UN), we unanimously chose the path of disarming him. Today, nothing tells us that this path is a dead end and, consequently, it must be pursued since war is always a final resort, always an acknowledgement of failure, always the worst solution, because it brings death and misery. And we don't consider we are at that point. *That's why we are refusing to embark on a path automatically leading to war so long as the inspectors haven't told us 'We can't do any more.' And they are telling us the opposite* (emphasis added).

Chirac was then challenged on Iraq not complying with the inspectors a hundred per cent:

> 'No, the inspectors say that cooperation has improved and that they are today in a position to pursue their work. And this is what is of paramount importance. It's not for you or me to say whether the inspections are effective, whether Iraq is sufficiently cooperative. In fact, she isn't, I can tell you that straightaway . . .'
>
> 'Not sufficiently. But it isn't for you or for me to decide that, that's for the inspectors to whom the UN has entrusted the responsibility of disarming Iraq to say. The inspectors have told us, "We can continue and, at the end of a period which we think should be of a few months" – I am saying a few

months because that's what they have said – "we shall have completed our work and Iraq will be disarmed". Or they will come and tell the Security Council "We are sorry but Iraq isn't cooperating, the progress isn't sufficient, we aren't in a position to achieve our goal, we won't be able to guarantee Iraq's disarmament." *In that case it will be for the Security Council and it alone to decide the right thing to do. But in that case, of course, regrettably, the war would become inevitable. It isn't today.*' (emphasis added)

I was astonished that not one MP in the House of Commons had read Chirac's interview, spotted the difference between what Blair claimed Chirac had said and what he had actually said and challenged him with the truth.

After having considered the material I sent, the Crown Office explained that it would not be taking action against Blair. Firstly because the power of the High Court to create a new crime was no longer used and, secondly, because, although the English case was not binding it would be persuasive and it was highly unlikely that a Scottish Court would take a different point of view as Scots law too had not incorporated aggression as a war crime. In acknowledging this decision, I pointed out that, once again, Goering's gibe at Nuremberg that the only justice handed out in war crimes is victors' justice had been proved true again.

The consequences of the invasion of Iraq were immense in geopolitical terms, in the stimulus they gave to radicalisation in the Islamic world and in the production of new threats to civilian security in Europe and America. But more important was the deaths, those maimed, those tortured, and the scale of destruction. British military dead number 179. US military deaths in 2003 were 486, rising to 849 in 2007. No one knows the real number of Iraqi dead. The estimates range from 130,000 (admitted to be too low as it only reflects deaths reported by the media) to 600,000 in an academic study.

With no chance of a British prosecution of a man who shared responsibility for all this, a number of us looked elsewhere. First was the International Criminal Court. It began its work in July 2002 and its statute does list aggression as a war crime. But that proved a dead end because, when including it in the statute, the state signatories did not agree on its definition, leaving it to become an indictable war crime only much later and after years of haggling. Not until July 2018 did they reach an agreed definition but there was one important caveat

– this newly defined law was not retrospective. Blair was safe from that court.

The only route would be to find a state which classes aggression and regime change as crimes in domestic law and whose criminal justice system would be prepared to prosecute Blair. I worked with a Quaker group in York to try to find such a country in Europe but we were unsuccessful. Maybe one day Blair might land by accident in Iraq, where jurisdiction will not be a problem.

22

The Road to the
Independence Referendum

I ended my full-time job with the Arab–British Chamber in late 2002. I was not fully retired due to my *Sun* column continuing – although I was finally sacked in 2005 – and the monthly column I wrote for Mandy Rhodes, editor of *Holyrood* magazine. Apart from these, my only political role, outside the Blair document, was to support Margo MacDonald in her Scottish parliament election campaigns in 1999, 2003, 2007 and 2011. I returned to playing golf regularly and, above all, I had a growing number of grandchildren to keep me busy.

Margo and I had bought a small two-bedroomed villa in Portugal in 1990 with the aid of a bank loan. Later, with another bank loan, we extended it to four bedrooms. The villa was to play a key role in our lives thereafter, especially after Margo was diagnosed with Parkinson's in 2001. She would do her Parkinson's exercises for 45 minutes in the pool each morning and the same in the afternoon. She learned Portuguese and we made a very close friend in Joaquina Alexandre Cavaco, the woman who looked after the villa for us and who also plied Margo with all the local gossip.

Those days in our Villa Maria were the happiest ones of our married life. It was home. We were relaxed, had great fun with the grandchildren and knew the local restaurateurs well. Margo could still keep in touch with her office and her pals in the media. Her mobile phone bill was very large but it was never charged to the parliament and she did not claim many of the expenses she was entitled to. I write this not to suggest she was morally superior to other MSPs. The need to keep receipts for telephones, mobiles etc. and the filling in of forms were things she found irritating when she wanted to get on with important matters. There was no chance of her staff doing her expenses forms as her receipts were all in various and many plastic bags. Throughout our married life, I had to take care of the family administration. I remember coming home once from Saudi Arabia on leave to find her crying because she said she had no money. She was in full-time well-paid broadcasting work so I couldn't understand why. I found all her pay cheques in unopened envelopes in a plastic bag.

I was quite happy to be the political spouse. As a former Royal Navy rating I could take on all the housework no problem. I easily coped with doing the washing, ironing and cooking and generally making sure Margo was kept in the best shape possible. I could drive her around, sit at the back of her meetings and then, once home, do a reverse of Govan and tell her where I thought she could do better.

In the run-up to the 2014 independence referendum, as it became obvious that Margo's Parkinson's had reached a stage when she could not campaign in person, she insisted that I should come out of retirement and do so. I could not refuse that order. She had a long period in hospital with infection and, a week after she was discharged, we received a visit at home from a doctor from the Western General Hospital who told us she had only three months at most to live. Next day, came a visit from her GP Dr Keith Donaldson whose care of her was exceptional, to confirm the information. That was then followed by a visit from her consultant at the Edinburgh Royal Infirmary, Dr Tom Mackay, who also had her under his care. He told me privately that three months was the maximum. We had coped with all sorts of problems and difficulties in our lives but this was different. For Margo, it was bad enough not to be able to campaign but what was worse was that she would not live long enough to vote for something she had devoted her life to.

She insisted that the cause was too important for me to back out, even temporarily. So I mixed going to evening meetings with spending as much time caring for her as I could during the day. It was difficult. When I was out she was well looked after by her young carer, Claire Carriere, who she treated like a daughter. It was typical of Margo to encourage Claire to be more ambitious and urge her to become a nurse – something Claire had always wanted to do. Claire told me later that Margo's advice and encouragement had changed her life. She is now a fully trained, university-graduate nurse.

The cause for Margo was all. Her willpower was something extraordinary to witness. Ill as she was and dying, she got herself dressed and made up and then did a long interview for the BBC in our home, with Jackie Bird, about her views on independence, including on Alex Salmond. It was a monumental physical and mental effort. In the end, she did not have three months – just three weeks – and she died on 4 April 2014, aged 70. I was devastated. We were two halves of one whole. We did not always agree and often argued fiercely but we sparked off each other and needed each other to function. I have never been the same since.

Before starting to campaign, I had written a book, *In Place of Fear II: A Socialist Programme for an Independent Scotland* (Vagabond Voices, Glasgow, 2014). The title was borrowed from Nye Bevan's book, *In Place of Fear*, first published in 1952, that was such an inspiration to my generation of socialists. It sold well and seems to have been widely read.

Researching the material and discussions with Margo provided a role for her in the campaign and I was grateful to have the help of Peter Warren in digging out material and making suggestions. I also debated my ideas with a number of close friends who were going to join me in the campaign.

The book sought to address several matters in the ideological sphere. The Left needed to be bumped out of the mindset that had seen it present socialism as no more than romantic anti-capitalism. Capitalism is capable of generating and releasing great technical and productive forces on a scale that has, in many countries, transformed the health and living standards of billions of people, making it, to date, the most successful economic system produced by humankind. There are two different classes of capital we have to address – large capital and local capital. The latter, being rooted in the community, poses no threat to it. But the former, far from being an unalloyed benefit to billions of human beings, exploits them and brings a great deal of misery. I quoted Hugh MacDiarmid's description:

> Above all, I curse and try to combat
> The leper pearl of Capitalist culture
> Which only tarnishes what it cannot lend
> Its own superb lustre.

I took the opportunity to answer the Right-wing canard that the private sector creates wealth, whereas the public sector spends it by pointing out that carefully directed spending by the state, in the public sector, also creates wealth.

There was one idea my friends advised me to abandon due to their concern that it would be regarded as ridiculous and so devalue all else in the book. I asked Harry Burns, then Scotland's Chief Medical Officer, about the idea to get his reaction. He was an enthusiastic supporter. I put it in the book and I am glad I did. I called it *The Robert Burns.*

Among the issues I thought long and hard about was how an independent Scotland could get aid to people in poor countries. I did not mean countries 'poor' in terms of natural resources but 'poor' in terms of their citizens living in states where the elite use tribalism, the coercive forces of the police and the military and a corrupt judiciary to plunder wealth at will. I had seen enough of the 'aid industry' to know that much of what is poured in with good intentions from rich countries ends up in secret bank accounts.

I was aware that the Royal Navy could not man or operate both large aircraft carriers being built because it did not have enough sailors in the service to man them or the number of escort ships required to support them. So I hit on the idea of an independent Scottish government acquiring one of them during the division of assets and naming it *The Robert Burns*. It would have a dual role. Its primary one would be to act as a hospital ship visiting areas in Africa and Asia to provide medical care for the poorest people and training for local health workers. Its secondary role would be to take on a humanitarian role in areas devastated by natural disasters. This, in my view, would mean that every pound of aid would be spent where it was meant to be spent. I fully costed it.

My friends were proved wrong. At every meeting, the audiences supported it with strong applause. I was reminded of Winnie Ewing's slogan way back in 1967 – 'Stop the World, Scotland wants to get on.' The audiences' response showed this was the kind of generous, practical contribution our nation wanted to make to those in need, when we joined that world. Even today, six years later, people stop and tell me the idea still resonates in their minds.

We are not independent and there is no aircraft carrier. But why is a hospital ship not a key part of the Scottish government's international aid programme? At present, from a restricted budget, that aid is aimed at one country only – Malawi. Given that the UK aid programme is now very large – 0.7 per cent of GDP (around £15 billion) – would it not be a good idea for the Scottish government to ask for 9 per cent of it, our national contribution, combine it with its own aid budget and build a hospital ship on the Clyde that would serve the needs of a number of countries whose people lack medical care?

Before its publication in November 2013, Alex Salmond claimed the White Paper 'Scotland's Future' would be as eloquent as the Declaration of Arbroath. It was anything but. His introductory preface was stale and the following pages of text turgid. Not a document to inspire, it essentially set out to explain that independence would be change-no-change.

The obvious weakness, stunningly clear, was the proposal for a currency union between Scotland and UK. That, I described in a *Daily Record* article was 'nonsense on stilts'. I was roundly attacked for that in the Twittersphere, with people insisting that we all had a duty to line up behind it. But that I would not do. No one in the SNP leadership or in Alex's Fiscal Commission, which had produced the idea, had spotted the blunder – to create a currency union between two countries requires them both to agree and, if one says no, it cannot happen. George Osborne, the UK chancellor, had, right at the start of the campaign, been gifted a veto over a key part of Alex's policy. He used it, leaving the yes side with no credible answer to the question of what currency we would use in an independent Scotland. This was crystal clear when Alistair Darling beat Alex in the first TV debate. Some think that was a seminal moment.

I sought to get that flaw sorted by meeting Crawford Beveridge, chairman of the Fiscal Commission. I told him, no matter how technically correct his group may think a currency union was, it was a political disaster as it gave the Westminster chancellor the whip hand, which he had used. To be fair to Crawford, he listened, seemed to grasp the political point and said he would go back to Alex. The first minister would not budge.

It was the same error with the corporation tax rate being reduced below the UK level. When I debated with Neil Findlay MSP in front of a large group of Unison members at Crosshouse Hospital near Kilmarnock, he homed in on it, attacking Alex Salmond as wanting a pro-boss economic policy with no regard for the workers and urged them to vote no.

Outside the tiny circle in the Scottish ministerial group and the Fiscal Commission, there had been no consultation with Yes groups, with many not connected to the SNP or SNP backbenchers either. They might be grateful for Alex getting the referendum but were not prepared to campaign and promote policies they did not want, and many did not want the Scotland depicted in the White Paper. Right from the start there was a lack of unity producing a discordant note as public meetings got under way. Only SNP MSPs stuck to the White Paper. At meeting after meeting someone on the platform would start a speech with 'This is not about Alex Salmond and the White Paper'. That was a sign of weakness.

I spoke at a fair number of meetings with Colin Fox, leader of the Scottish Socialist Party, and it proved a pleasure to see how, when engaged with a wider variety of people than would normally be the case for those who had sprung from the old Militant tendency, he developed a new breadth to his politics. An interesting point I picked up was the discontent, indeed the dislike, working-class people had for elected politicians in general, whom they regarded as an out of touch elite. When this was raised at meetings, I didn't play to the gallery. Yes, I replied, there is now an elite of professional politicians but this is the fault of the working class for standing back and refusing to take up leadership positions themselves. The point I made to Tony Benn, way back, that the working class would not come to parliament if it was for only one term was no excuse because there is no one-term rule. The Scottish working class is betraying itself by leaving the legislative arena to others, whose priorities are not theirs. Our political class spends more time on and is more genuinely enraged by the debate on gender and biology than how to eliminate our large housing lists by instigating a construction programme equal to the task.

The Margo Mobile was conceived and built because I was determined that, although Margo was no longer with us in body, she was going to be there in spirit during the campaign. Our small campaign group created a travelling speaking platform like the Snappy Bus used in Govan but this time 'something classy to reflect the lady herself' as one of the donors said to me. Gil Paterson took on the job of vehicle purchase and modification. He did a superb job. It was unmistakeably the *Margo* Mobile. The team was: Iain Lawson as campaign manager; Gil in charge of the vehicle; Peter Kearney responsible for publicity; Calum Miller dealing with social media; and Heather Williams organising the timetable of campaign venues and booking hotels. We needed a professional driver and a back-up and Frank O'Raw and Jonathan Gillies filled those roles. They became part of what was a happy band. We had campaign meetings to set out what we were going to do, how we were going to get the message across and where we would go and allocated research responsibilities as new issues emerged. Heather liaised with local Yes groups and directed us to support them.

Our target was the Labour vote, which we knew was the vital component in the make-up of the electorate. We toured the country speaking around twelve to fifteen times a day and I was touched by the number of people who came up to us and said how pleased they were that Margo was so clearly identified with the campaign. As well as the speeches from the vehicle, I took part in ninety public meetings. At one public meeting in Partick, I shared a platform with a young woman, then nineteen years old, called Mhairi Black. Her ability to hold an audience and convey complex issues in understandable language and her grasp of social and economic facts were things I had never witnessed before in one so young. I invited her to join the team as I thought she would benefit from the experience. Her learning curve was remarkable. Iain Lawson and I both reached a quick conclusion that we had discovered political gold in Mhairi.

After the Partick meeting, I went for an interview at STV. I told Stephen Townsend, the programme producer, that I had just met a young woman called Mhairi Black and that her name was one he should remember. I don't think he took much notice. Another young woman who impressed me was Cat Boyd from the Radical Independence Campaign and she is also now making her mark on Scottish politics and the trade union movement.

Along with many others, we made significant inroads into the Labour vote, until Gordon Brown's intervention in the last stage of the campaign. I watched news reports of his speeches, which drew heavily on the history and achievements of British Labour, and my instincts told me that this was having an effect. The polls bore this out – before Brown, the Labour vote for independence was travelling towards the 40 per cent mark but, after his involvement, it dropped back to just over 30 per cent.

Nearing the end of the campaign came one of my serious misjudgements. I had become incensed watching the likes of the chief executive of BP and others Prime Minister Cameron had recruited for Project Fear warning the people of the consequences of independence on the basis of their concern for our financial wellbeing when, in fact, it was their ability to keep trading with us on their terms that they were really concerned about. These business tycoons had never previously given a damn about the people of Scotland and had shown no concern about the levels of poverty that were a blight upon our society. Now, there they were pretending to be concerned about our future if we voted Yes.

Towards the closing stages, on 12 September, I issued a statement warning them of a day of reckoning. It not only brought *The Daily Mail* and other unionist papers down on my head but it also got me a 1 a.m. telephone call from Alex Salmond in which he sought assurances that I would not repeat it. Most Yes activists thought it was a mistake and so I confess to the error. It gave the unionist media a stick with which to beat us and I take full responsibility for that. I reproduce the statement in full below. While I accept that it was a mistake in the context of the final stage, I think the defensive way it was repudiated by many in the Yes camp was an indication of how unprepared the movement was to tackle businesses that were in cahoots with a Tory prime minister, playing their part in instilling fear into people and thus subverting our democratic process. All those who told us of their deep concern for the Scots have, since September 2014, been conspicuously absent from comment or in providing suggestions on how we might tackle the continuing levels of poverty, poor productivity and low pay.

With the price of oil at around $64 a barrel, BP is still drawing vast amounts of oil from the Clair Field, and many countries continue to be involved in the North Sea oil industry. Yet the Scottish nation does not own even a cupful of the black stuff. So, when I reread the statement now, I think that, by showing what could and should be done with the sovereign power we threw away, it has validity.

No campaign fearmongers have had an effect on me – instead of retiring on 19 September, I am staying in. This referendum is about power, and when we get a Yes majority, we will use that power for a day of reckoning with BP and the banks.

The heads of those companies are rich men in cahoots with a rich English Tory Prime Minister to keep Scotland poor, poorer through lies and distortions. The power they have now to subvert our democracy will come to an end with Yes.

BP in an independent Scotland will need to learn the meaning of nationalisation, in part or in whole, as it has in other countries who have not been as soft as we have been forced to be. If it wants into the 'monster fields' in the areas west of Shetland, it will have to learn to bend the knee to a greater power – us, the sovereign people of Scotland. We will be the masters of the oil fields, not BP or any other of the majors. If Bob Dudley thinks this is mere rhetoric, just let him wait. It is sovereign power that counts. We will have it; he will not.

As for the Bankers. Your casino days, rescued by socialisation of your liabilities while you waltz off with the profits, will be over. You will be split between retail and investment, and if your greed takes the latter down, there will be no rescue. You believe in the market, in the future you will live with its discipline. Fail will mean failure.

As for Standard Life, it will be required by new employment laws to give two years warning of any redundancies, and reveal to the trade unions its financial reasons for relocation to any country outside Scotland, and the cost involved. It has never crossed the minds of our compliant Unionist media, especially the BBC, to ask the chief executive what his costs are on his proposed moves.

As for John Lewis, the question is whether the senior management consulted the 'partners' or took instructions from Cameron? Another question our supine BBC did not ask. There is now talk of boycott, and if it happens, it will be a management own goal.

What kind of people do these companies think we are? They will find out.

Why did Yes lose? The Scottish government's White Paper did not inspire. It promised constitutional change but no change in how the economy would work to promote prosperity and tackle poverty. The idea of a currency union was destroyed from day one. There was not one central campaign, one central theme, but several, with many speakers disowning the White Paper in favour of their own view of how an independent Scotland would work. Pensioners were ignored and became the target for the No side to raise serious doubts in their minds as to whether their pensions would be safe in an independent Scotland. My own statement also helped defeat us. The root cause of the defeat lies in recent history – that is, the SNP never building up the independence vote over the years from 1992 to 2014 and the decision of Alex Salmond to keep all discussion about the White Paper before publication within his small group of acolytes.

When the White Paper was published, Margo was ill so I went to pick her copy up. I was standing beside an SNP MSP and asked him what the difference was between us. He said he was an MSP and I was not. 'No,' I told him, 'when you pick up that White Paper, although you have had no input to it as an MSP, you will be bound by every dot and comma whether you agree with it or not. Whereas, if I disagree with it, I will be free to say so.'

On polling day, I thought we had won but the result proved otherwise with 55 per cent voting No and 45 per cent voting Yes. But there was a political dividend to the campaign. Many, many more people were now better educated politically than they ever had been. In the working-class areas, in the deprived areas, there had been huge meetings which were more like teach-ins, with policies and issues explored in depth. We found people thirsty for knowledge. I remember one meeting in an Edinburgh housing scheme when, at the end, a woman stood up and said she did not have a question, just a statement on behalf of herself and her neighbours. 'We have learned a lot in a few weeks,' she said, 'and never again will they pull the wool over our eyes.' I wrote it down as it seemed to sum up an important aspect of the campaign's success.

I was aged seventy-seven when I campaigned in 2014. The effort involved and the impact of Margo's death left me utterly exhausted at its end. But I could still think and write. After a reasonable period following the result, I expected the SNP and the Yes central leadership to produce an examination of why we lost. Any group which loses a contest, whether it be in politics, sport or any other adversarial activity, usually seeks to find out why. It never happened.

As far as I am aware, the only detailed examination of the campaign from the committed Yes side and why we lost to Project Fear is in the book I wrote in September 2015 – *In Place of Failure* (Vagabond Voices, Glasgow, 2015). In it, I examined each of the twelve main components of the unionist Project Fear where the Yes response was inadequate and proposed how, next time, we could answer decisively. I took the opportunity to flag up a few economic matters that are overlooked or inadequately examined, such as the value – or not – to our people of the whisky industry. The independent economics consultancy firm Biggar Economics, in a study published in 2012, and Professor John Kay, in 'Economic Policy Options for an Independent Scotland', presented a very different insight to the one we get from the Scotch Whisky Association. This is a superb public relations organisation and has either deliberately or inadvertently – take your pick – avoided any consistent examination of how the whisky industry operates, what value it brings to the economy compared to the value it could bring and where its substantial profits end up. As Professor Kay noted, 'I think the benefits to Scotland from the whisky industry are really quite disappointing. The largest producers are not based in Scotland. Their profits go mostly to people who are not resident in Scotland. They don't pay much tax in Scotland, and we don't think they pay much tax in the UK.'

There are around 10,000 jobs in the whisky industry in Scotland. However, given that 83 per cent of it is in foreign hands, it is not owned by Scots. That has meant, as Biggar calculated, £3.03 billion of profit went out of the country. Our politicians don't help to get the people focused on the industry, any more than the Scotch Whisky Association does. When Diageo announced plans to close the Johnnie Walker plant in Kilmarnock in 2009, a huge rally against the closure was attended by the leaders of the main parties. The local Labour MP and former Secretary of State for Scotland, Des Browne, had a message for Diageo, which went down well with the crowd but was arrant nonsense: 'You seem to have forgotten that you don't own Johnnie Walker. The people of Kilmarnock do.' Diageo *did* own it and, in March 2012, the Kilmarnock plant *did* close. Whisky is a source of wealth, and the wealth flows out of the country, and will do so as long as Diageo, or some other private group, owns it lock, stock and barrel.

I am not suggesting the nationalisation of the whisky industry. It would be easy to gather knowledge of its operations inside Scotland and how its distilleries work but whisky is a commodity sold in many countries through marketing and sales systems and contracts with agents. Because we know so little about how these systems and people operate, it would not be easy to take the industry into public ownership. What I am suggesting is taking a public stake in its shareholding, with seats on the board of every large whisky-producing company like Diageo, both of which would provide what is missing now – public influence on its strategic decision making and substantial public income from the profits coming from the product. The Scottish government's publicly owned investment bank would be the ideal instrument to carry out such a policy.

The drop in the price of oil shortly after 2014 and the price crash when Covid-19 forced a shutdown of much of the world economy mean that no one any longer mentions oil as an important present or future economic factor in the Scottish economy. Unionist politicians and columnists never tire of saying what a fool Alex Salmond was to predicate his White Paper on oil at $100 a barrel and what a catastrophe it would have been if Scotland had become independent. The unionists have wiped the floor with the SNP, which now seems terrified to mention the word. The oil industry is relegated to the back business pages of our newspapers, and rarely gets a mention, other than the drop in price, on our television screens. How easily a nation can be robbed of its wealth.

The unionist anti-oil story is consistent both in the purpose and in the telling. Oil found in Scottish waters has to be discounted as an important source of long-term wealth to enable the myth to continue that Scotland has been and forever will be a subsidised part of the United Kingdom. This requires that the truth be hidden and, when it cannot be hidden, the public message is that it will not last forever, production is declining and it is, therefore, foolish to build any kind of economic model that has oil as an important component and, if you have to talk about oil, talk about the tax revenues not the black stuff itself. In recent years, there is the added political value to unionists that, being a fossil fuel, oil is condemned as a CO_2 danger to humankind and should be kept underground. Thus the Scottish nation is held spellbound in a combination of ignorance, lies and a sense of guilt, while other nations take away its wealth.

In 1974, as the importance of the oil discoveries in the North Sea became evident, Gavin McCrone, head of the government's Scottish Economic Planning Unit, delivered a paper to the UK government showing that 'the advent of North Sea oil has completely overturned the traditional economic arguments used against Scottish nationalism. An independent Scotland could now expect to have massive surpluses both on its budget and on its balance of payments and with the proper husbanding of resources this situation could last for a very long time'. When the McCrone Report reached the new Labour government, Willie Ross, as Secretary of State, suppressed it.

What could not be suppressed, of course, was what was happening in the North Sea, and so began the 'It won't last forever' mantra, allied to stories – and 'stories' is a good word – that it not lasting forever were true. Nor was much emphasis ever allowed to focus on the fact that the North Sea was an oil *and gas* asset.

*

On 20 August 2014, in a review for the UK government on how to maximise the remainder of British oil reserves, Sir Ian Wood, who had built an international company on oil servicing and was, therefore, an 'expert', told the nation that there were only about 15 billion to 16.5 billion barrels of recoverable oil left in the North Sea, meaning that no more than 35 years of oil and gas production remain. He warned, 'The loss of significant offshore oil and gas tax revenues as the North Sea runs down will have a big impact on our economy, jobs and the balance of payments, with significant increases in household energy bills – and a very adverse impact on the legacy for future generations in an independent Scotland. It means our young voters must be fully aware that *by the time they are middle aged, Scotland will have little offshore oil and gas production* and this will seriously hit our economy, jobs and public services [emphasis added].' A dismal picture but untrue. I hope the reader noted that, again, the emphasis was on only oil tax revenues, not the black stuff? It was reported in *The Herald*'s business section on 11 July 2017 that the Wood Group had secured the contract for services to 'the giant Culzean gas field in the North Sea . . . one of the biggest discoveries for 20 years'.

As for Scotland having little offshore oil and gas, I doubt if many Scots, having been told to forget about oil, will have heard of Lancaster, Catcher, Kraken, Mariner, all recently described as 'giant' fields in the North Sea. Then there is Clair Ridge, another, even bigger giant, not in the North Sea, but west of Shetland, into which $4.5 billion is being invested.

Of course, one day, oil and gas production will dwindle to inconsequential levels but not in the short time Sir Ian Wood forecast. Clair Ridge alone is reckoned to be at least a forty-year field, if not more. But oil wealth today can, in a real sense, be stretched in value far beyond the day when the last barrel is extracted. That happens when a country uses it for two purposes. One is to see it as a capital resource, for investment in the home economy, and as a 'bank' for the future in the form of a sovereign wealth fund, as Kuwait, Abu Dhabi, Saudi Arabia and Norway have done.

I cannot emphasis enough that we should concentrate on the oil more than on the tax revenues. Oil prices fluctuate and, when at their lowest levels, generate little or no tax revenue. But, even when the price falls, the oil itself is still sold at a profit – that is why it is imperative to get the Scottish nation an 'ownership' share of it. I am not, as with the whisky industry, proposing to nationalise the whole of the North Sea or Clair Ridge. But I do argue that an independent Scotland should take a percentage of the ownership of each field and, therefore, a percentage of the profits. If the price of a barrel goes away up, then an extra bonus would be the tax revenue. There is nothing new in that. Other nations across the world have done exactly the same – in the Arab states, they have gone from virtually no ownership to full ownership, in stages. That is not a policy I am suggesting. The North Sea fields and the fields in the Scottish Atlantic Margin, west of Shetland, require considerable investment capital, which Scotland would not be able to mobilise and, therefore, a partnership with oil companies who can access the capital required seems sensible.

If Scots don't wake up – and that includes rejecting the ludicrous 'climate emergency' policy of the Scottish government, whose logic is to keep the oil underground – then we shall, as I said many years ago, have the unique distinction in the developed world of being the only nation to discover oil and get poorer.

Four final points on oil. It has many uses in our industrial society – not only as a fuel. It will continue to be in high demand as a primary energy source as Asia, Africa, Latin America and Central America continue to develop. Its price will always fluctuate but, even in the depression created by the Covid-19 pandemic, it remained around $40 a barrel. Most important of all, for a small country of five million like Scotland, oil is a far greater capital resource than it is for a country like England with its population of almost 56 million.

23

Margo MacDonald

Born Margo Aitken in Bellshill Maternity Hospital, Lanarkshire, in 1943, her father was a local GP. She had two younger siblings, Anne and David. The father walked out on the family and paid no maintenance so they ended up living in a caravan, supported as best she could by their mother, Jean. There was no money but Jean, a nurse, had aspirations for her children and each succeeded in education and later life. Margo could have gone to university but went instead to Dunfermline College of Physical Education which, despite its name, was in Aberdeen. At school, she was competitive both in education and sports. She was dux medallist in her primary school. After qualifying at 'Dunf', as it was called, she became a gym teacher in Hamilton.

In 1965, she married Peter MacDonald, who owned and ran a pub in Blantyre and they lived above it. She was married to Peter when she won the Govan by-election in 1973. When she married me in 1981, there was no name change. The only time she was called Mrs Sillars was when attending an Arab function with me in London or, occasionally, when someone wrote her an insulting letter. Just exactly where the insult lay, we could never understand.

She was not aware of her political gifts until she joined the SNP in 1966 but the party recognised them. Before the Winnie Ewing victory in Hamilton in 1967, the SNP was of no account in Scottish politics so no one outside the party knew of her. My first contact with her was over the telephone in my STUC office in 1969. She was the SNP candidate in Paisley. I had never heard of her. Margo had wangled a meeting with the Paisley Trades Council. Jimmy Jack, STUC general secretary, also lived in Blantyre and had got wind of Margo's ploy. As I was responsible for the trades councils, he told me to instruct Paisley that they were not to meet and give her a platform. I duly did so in writing. Then came the phone call from this person calling herself Margo MacDonald, asking me by what right I had barred the trades council from meeting her. I told her that, as she was not part of the trade union movement, it was not necessary for me to gave her an explanation. It was simple. The trades council would not be meeting her, period. I recall that she was not complimentary. I forgot all about her.

Then came Govan in 1973. She arrived on the national scene from nowhere, with an almighty political bang. She was undoubtedly a nationalist but she spoke a different language to most of them. She was in tune with working-class people and her concept of nationalism matched theirs – pride in being Scots with its tradition of egalitarianism, concern for the underdog and revulsion at the poverty blighting so many lives And she was able to generate in their minds a belief that they were capable of changing the world they lived in. She could also go beyond the working class and touch something within Scotland's middle class and ignite their interest in her views on independence. She was the kind of a political leader that was rare in Scotland. She was, for me and my Labour colleagues, a danger.

I doubt if I spoke more than two words to her when she came to the House of Commons as the centre of attention to the press inside and outside. I did notice how nervous she was in delivering her short maiden speech – a good one but it did not set the heather on fire. A subsequent speech she made was marred by getting the numbers on oil wrong by quite a big margin. I used her gaffe in my own speeches against the SNP in the February election.

As I have said elsewhere, I was delighted when she lost Govan in February 1974, believing, as any MP would, that deprived of the title and the platform of the House of Commons, she would disappear and be no longer a threat to Labour. I didn't know her then. What I didn't realise was that her best platform was not the chamber of the House of Commons but the public meeting where she could develop her ideas and engage in discussion with people. Margo was very much a people person.

It didn't matter that Margo was no longer an MP. She had arrived and nothing could bury her. Far from becoming no threat to Labour, she was a bigger threat, pulling in huge audiences to public meetings all over Scotland. And there she was, on television, another natural medium for her, a debater of the first rank. She was also able to write. Of course, everybody can write using the alphabet but not everybody, including politicians, has an ability and style that can weave words in a way that captures the reader. She had it.

Margo was also a thinker. It was from her pen that came the first ever mention of the 'social union' that exists and will exist, no matter the final constitutional arrangement, between Scotland and England. I remember a Labour colleague in the Commons saying to me after he read it that it was a strong phrase coming from a Scot-Nat.

My next meeting with Margo was along with Teddy Taylor, Tory MP from Glasgow, in 1975. She phoned to suggest that, as we three were in favour of leaving the EEC, we should campaign together, and show that there was a wide body of opinion for getting out. I recall we did a couple of meetings outside factories, but they were not successful. That was because Teddy started off saying he detested nationalists, and deplored socialists, but necessity brought him here with us.

Margo is seen by most as a politician but she was proudest of being a journalist and she made her mark in that profession after her marriage to Peter broke up. Her articles appeared in a wide variety of newspapers in Scotland and England. As a radio and television broadcaster, she was a success. She had a genuine interest in people which enabled her to be one of the best phone-in hosts. She was an international figure, invited to the United States by broadcasting companies and to a Puerto Rico conference along with Rosalynn Carter, the US First Lady. As a broadcaster, Margo was held in such high esteem that she interviewed several international figures including President Lech Walesa of Poland and François Mitterrand of France. Margo spoke French and Mitterrand spoke English but she told me, if she was having difficulty finding the right French word, he would not help her out with advice in English.

During her journalist years, in 1992, she interviewed Jean-Marie Le Pen, President of the French National Front, for television, as many others from all parts of the Western world had done. In her column for the *Edinburgh Evening News* in 2002, with Le Pen only 3.28 per cent behind Jacques Chirac in the first round and in the run-off in the French presidential election, many were asking how could this happen. When Margo dipped into that long-ago interview to analyse why he had won those votes, John Swinney didn't like it. Let Tom Peterkin, a leading journalist at the time, explain, in his article of 27 April 2002:

Margo MacDonald has been rebuked by John Swinney, SNP leader, after she described M. Le Pen as 'charming' and 'intellectually tough'. Mrs MacDonald said, 'His logic was difficult to fault' when she asked him about people who had emigrated, legally and illegally, to France from Africa. M Le Pen told her that skin colour and country of origin meant nothing to him, but he objected to immigrants failing to embrace the culture of their adopted country.

Margo MacDonald

The Peterkin article went on, quoting Swinney:

> I told Margo MacDonald, both in writing and in a meeting, my profound disagreement with her about the article she wrote. I want to make it equally clear that the SNP holds the policies of Jean-Marie Le Pen in total contempt. His politics have no place in our democratic debate.

The journalist noted that the letter had been leaked to the press, 'leading to the suggestion that some SNP members are behind a campaign to discredit Mrs MacDonald as the party begins to select candidates for the 2003 Scottish elections'. He reported Margo's statement that, in her article, she had tried to explain how such a '"repugnant politician as Le Pen" had attracted wide support'. She said, 'Mr Swinney has himself told me that he does not consider me to be either racist or fascist, and I think most people who have worked with me will agree with that assessment.' Of course, there was an intention of forcing Margo out of the parliament because she was not toeing the party line and demonstrating too much independence. It was not well hidden and John Swinney's confected outrage was one sign of it.

In June of 2002, she was before a disciplinary tribunal, accused of having missed a vote without permission and briefing a Sunday newspaper against party policy. The latter was a joke, considering the briefing being done against her by the leadership. But a written warning was given. The coup de grâce came when she was relegated from first to fifth position on the Lothian list, a position guaranteed to get her out. The public and media reaction to Margo's rejection was universal condemnation of the SNP. *The Daily Record* leader summed up the general mood by advising her to 'Gaun yersel, hen'. I was sure she would win when standing as an independent. The SNP launched personal attacks on her, many claiming that she would fail, with activists from Edinburgh South writing to the *Edinburgh Evening News* saying her vote in 1999 owed nothing to her personally and that at best she would gather only a handful of votes. In the 2003 election the SNP South Edinburgh vote slumped to 4,396.

Politics is, as they say, a rough trade but what makes democracies work as a peaceful and civilised method of managing differences of opinion is the self-restraint that top-quality politicians exercise – their ability to know where to draw a line in attacking opponents. The people have this quality in abundance, as they have proved time and again with their strong disapproval of personal attacks and character assassination or the release of personal information designed to wound without justification.

In the case of Margo, the SNP leadership failed the test of self-restraint, which cast them in a poor light. Margo had been diagnosed with Parkinson's but was under excellent medical care and perfectly able to continue as an MSP. But now she was outside the SNP tent, the leadership thought it would be a good idea to sink her candidacy by telling the media that she had Parkinson's.

When Margo was diagnosed, we decided that she should say nothing in public about her condition as she was fully functional. We also thought it would be better to take our time and tell our grandchildren when they were a bit older and more able to understand why Grandma's hand was shaking a bit and why she could be slow in doing some things. We were denied that important privacy by the SNP's tactic. Our eldest grandson, Stephen Martin, still a child, learned about his granny's condition at primary school from one of his friends whose parents had read it in the newspapers. He went home very upset thinking his granny was going to die. The leak backfired badly on the SNP. Margo won as an independent. In later years, she was very forgiving of those who had leaked the story.

She was brave politically. As an MSP she took on two difficult subjects – prostitution and assisted dying. The first was highly controversial and the second was an ethical minefield. Edinburgh had operated a 'safe zone' for prostitutes. The police knew where they were and the women knew they could call on them if attacked. The zone was, understandably, not popular with many of the public and was threatened with closure. Margo not only talked to the women in Edinburgh but also to prostitutes from Sweden and Holland. She got to know the women in Edinburgh, understood the circumstances that led them to this 'trade' and how it worked, including the role of pimps. She did not moralise. Safe zones made the women safe and so she defended their existence. She came under attack from fellow MSPs and a group in Glasgow was determined to end prostitution. When she pointed out that prostitution was not going to be legislated away, her critics exclaimed that slavery had been banned and so could this 'trade' in human beings. A rather premature claim, it turned out, sadly, to be. Margo took her case to women's groups, including church groups, outside the parliament and found a great deal of support for what she was trying to do.

She knew her attempts to get an assisted dying Bill through parliament would not succeed. There were MSPs who privately told her that they agreed but saw it as political suicide if they did so publicly.

The reason she pressed on came from her personal experience of close friends dying the most awful deaths and the need to put it squarely on the public agenda, as a first step in a long battle. The strongest opposition came from the Catholic Church yet, among the people she could call friends was Cardinal Keith O'Brien. When he fell from grace and lots of his fellow Christians were adding to his woes, she made a public statement: 'He was my friend, he is my friend and he will remain my friend.'

Was Margo faultless? Of course not. She was like everyone in political life – she made mistakes. It could be said that, in valuing her independent mind and right to speak it, often standing square against the leadership view, she disqualified herself from holding the offices which would have allowed her to do what she could only otherwise urge others to do. There are those who would regard that as a bad mistake. But a Margo MacDonald, who put her career ahead of expressing her opinion, would not have been Margo MacDonald. What she was known and appreciated for and what made her influential was that people knew what she said was what she thought – even when they disagreed with her.

Margo did have flaws. Her mind and system of thought did not combine naturally with economics. She was a poor administrator and Stephen Maxwell once remarked that, if she had paid more attention to detail in her senior positions within the party, she would have been more effective. There was obviously a book within her but she lacked the self-discipline to sit down and get her head into the nitty-gritty to produce one.

But the big flaw – due, I believe, to the experience of her father walking out – was the need to be liked. Beneath that tough exterior there was someone who could be hurt. Alex Neil once said that, if Margo got ninety-nine votes out of a hundred, it was the one against that mattered. That was a Margo not on public display but some sensed it and knew they could aim for a weak spot. I could never convince her to be like me, with not a care what anyone says.

She was classless. One day, on my way to the local supermarket, I was stopped by a Morningside lady and she asked, 'Are you Mr Sillars?' When I said I was, she continued, 'I do like your wife but I don't like you.' She struck up a relationship with Camilla, Duchess of Cornwall, which began with Margo being impressed by Camilla's make-up after seeing her on TV one night. The next day, she got Peter Warren, her office manager, to phone Kensington Palace to find out what mascara Camilla had used and he got the information for her.

That was Margo. She spoke as an equal to everyone. She could be deadly serious, flippant, sympathetic and critical. She was fun to be with. She never tailored her talks to a particular audience but gave them her views unvarnished. I was immensely proud of Margo. She could easily have taken a back seat and rested on her national reputation but she was a campaigner and, of course, brought a very independent mind to the Holyrood parliament. It is not surprising that people tell me she is missed.

On writing the announcement of her death, aged 70, on 4 April 2014, helped in what was a shattered state by our friend Peter Kearney, I described Scotland as having been 'robbed of one of its greatest talents, and that the brightest light in the Scottish political firmament has gone out'. At her insistence, we held a private family funeral. But I didn't want Margo MacDonald to go out unnoticed. So, with great help of the parliament organising staff, a memorial was held for her, on 25 April, in the Assembly Hall on The Mound, where she had first taken her seat in the new Scottish parliament. It was to be a celebration of her life.

I particularly wanted our grandchildren to know what an exceptional person their grandmother was. To them she was Grandma, Granny Margo, Granny, and only that. Our eldest granddaughter, Roseanne Reid, on the day the newspapers gave massive coverage to Margo's death, said she had no idea how famous her grandma was. I took with me a life-sized cut-out of Margo, used in her first Scottish parliament election, which I kept in the garage, on to the stage so that, in a sense, she too could be there.

To a packed hall, Alex Neil and Elaine C. Smith paid their tributes, The Proclaimers sang the Hibs anthem 'Sunshine on Leith' and I made the most difficult speech of my life. Bob Scott, from the Humanist Society, who conducted the memorial, had a copy in case I didn't manage it. But I did.

I will not reproduce the whole speech, just passages that I believe both capture the essence of Margo and the love and admiration not only I had for her but others too. I began:

> On the 19th of April 1943, a star was born, that we came to know as Margo MacDonald. Noticed by only a few in her formative years, that star burst forth into Scottish life, in all its splendour, when she won the Govan by-election in 1973.
>
> Thereafter, she captivated friends, opponents, and the people of Scotland through her intellectual power, radiance, beauty, warmth, humour, humanity, and colossal talent, for the

next 41 years. Charismatic is an inadequate word for Margo. She was dusted with magic.

Our friend Jim Walker, from his base in Hong Kong, devoted the first seven paragraphs of his weekly economic analysis, sent to clients worldwide, to this memory of his first meeting with her in 1986, when he was a young academic. 'She was instantly engaging, enveloping, enlivening, and enthralling ... She treated me with the affection for which she became famous ... She oozed integrity, humanity, and beauty of spirit that lifts your soul to heaven. Margo MacDonald left everyone she met better for the experience.'

In her last days, the one thing that pleased her most was a private visit from Alex Salmond. Her relationship with him, like mine, had deteriorated but her getting back on to the old footing for one last time meant a very great deal to both of us.

The last non-family member to see Margo alive was Fiona Ross who was not a Yes voter but a bosom pal. Margo's life's work was a passionate pursuit of Scottish independence but she refused to relinquish her friendship with Fiona and others who fundamentally opposed her on the issue. After Fiona left, Margo talked to me about her anxieties with the divisions that would arise during the independence campaign and I reflected her views in the closing part of my speech:

So in my final remarks I bring a final message from Margo for all engaged in the campaign. There will be harsh statements on both sides. The debate will be fierce. There will be verbal wounds inflicted. But, if we conduct ourselves in the run-up to the 18th September the Margo MacDonald way, the divisions will be much easier to heal. The Margo MacDonald way is to recognise that you are dealing with opponents not enemies, not with ogres but with fellow human beings, with whom you can disagree but do so without malice – and where the exercise of mutual respect is a civilised corrective to uncivilised abuse, an abuse which, if unchecked by both sides, can so easily mutate into an irreversible corrosive influence on the conduct of public life.

24

Europe and Brexit

Although not heavily engaged in the Scottish political scene because of the priority given to my job with the Arab–British Chamber of Commerce, I continued to contribute views on Scottish and UK politics. During that time, I produced pamphlets reviewing the policy of independence in Europe, which showed a mark shift in my position since the 1980s. That first pamphlet published in October 1999 said this:

A United States of Europe?

In addition to earlier comments on the undesirability of creating a United States of Europe, it is worth noting that today's issue of the single currency is not about the economics of the European Union. It is a major stepping stone to a federal superstate. The adoption of the single currency removes one of the core aspects of national sovereignty, control over the currency and reserves, and transfers it to Brussels . . .

A federal EU will require, in addition to monetary and fiscal policy, the other core sovereign competencies, defence, foreign affairs and law and order to be similarly transferred to Brussels. That would not amount to Scottish independence in Europe. It would keep us as a vassal state of an all-powerful centre.

I did not like the EU direction of travel, towards a United States of Europe, whose creation was bound to suck out the sovereign power of member states. I had many discussions with people in the EU Commission in Brussels and was struck by the 'world power complex' they had developed. I recall being told that their aim was to create what would be a new super state equal to the United States and the Soviet Union. I thought that another superpower was not what the world required. Nor did I want Scotland to regain its sovereignty only to have it transferred to a new central organisation in Brussels. Those years of practical engagement with the Commission, allied to thinking, brought me to a change of policy on the EU, by seeing more advantage in membership of European Free Trade Association (EFTA) and the European Economic Area (EEA). This shift from EU to EFTA meant continuation of ties to the EU but with greater scope for the exercise of national sovereignty.

*

In 2015, to my complete surprise, David Cameron, caving in to the threat UKIP posed to the Tory Party, decided to hold a referendum on leaving or remaining in the EU. I thought he would have toughed it out. Cameron's move was ill starred from the beginning. He negotiated 'changes' to the UK–EU relationship which were so trivial they never figured in the referendum campaign itself. Instead, the UK government gave us Project Fear again with George Osborne forecasting an economic nightmare – not only if the UK left the EU but also if people just voted Leave.

I intended to vote Leave and do nothing more until two former Labour MPs, Nigel Griffiths – with whom Margo and I had been friendly for years – and Tom Harris, decided to take part in the Leave campaign. With all the Scottish political parties lined up in favour of Remain and the SNP government projecting its own version of Project Fear, I didn't expect anything but a Remain majority. However, as the question was whether the UK was to leave or remain, every vote we gathered would count in the grand total. That proved true. The 1,018,322 Leave votes in Scotland proved a substantial help in taking Leave over the winning line, where the overall UK majority was 1,269,501 – a fact overlooked in subsequent debates.

I approached the issue *with* two minds but not *in* two minds – one as a Scot seeking the best way to independence and the other as a citizen of the UK. They were not incompatible, however strange that may seem. The first was an imperative but let me first explain the reasons I voted Leave in the context of UK–EU relations. I do not like to be ruled by people who cannot be dismissed, as is the case with the EU Commission, the President of the European Council, the Council of Ministers and the top body, the European Council, which is drawn from the presidents and prime ministers of the member states. And I do not like government by secrecy. During the 2016 referendum campaign, I asked people at meetings to name me two EU Commissioners

249

except Jean-Claude Juncker, the Commission President, who is always in the news. They could not and that included the UK Commissioner – a democratic deficit if ever there was one.

Although the EU is one of the world's largest economic blocs and protects its agricultural products with high tariffs, it has inherent weaknesses both constitutionally – some outlined above – and economically. Its founders and successors in the Commission and in Berlin and Paris want to create a new superstate but it lacks the homogeneity essential for that purpose. The 28 member states have different histories, different political systems arising from those histories, different points of geopolitical references, significant cultural differences and, above all, a lack of intimate knowledge about each other that is crucial to the success of such a polity.

Let's take that issue of intimate knowledge of each other. What do we really know about what makes people tick and what are the conditions and issues that matter to them in the cities, towns and villages of, say, Poland, Hungary, Italy, Germany and Lithuania, to mention but a few states? What does a Slovakian know about the Midlands of England or Shetland and what do we know about Slovakia or Slovenia and their people? In the polity that is the UK and no doubt within the separate polities that make up the member states of the EU, there is a bond between each constituent part. Even if Scotland and the UK separate politically, we will remain in a social union forged over centuries of shared history, intermingled families and the emergence of a shared political culture.

Nothing marks the lack of essential homogeneity of the EU more than the fact that no pan-EU political parties engage in the European parliamentary elections. These are fought within each state along national party lines. In their respective 2014 EU manifestos, both the Tories and Labour boasted about what their MEPs had done for Britain and each had a distinctively nationalist line. It is only when new MEPs gather in Brussels that they start to cobble together eight political groups in order to make the institution work. I am certain that most electors in most member states and the media could not name them.

This situation means there can be no European parliament from which a pan-EU government can be drawn. That in turn means continuation of the same unelected power structures. The sole right to initiate legislation lies with the unelected European Commission. It also supervises member states' policies to ensure they adhere to EU law and can refer them to the European Court of Justice for alleged breaches. Few outside a tiny circle of government official will know about COREPER

– the Committee of Permanent Representatives, from the French *Comité des représentants permanents* – with its key role in EU decision making. It is the committee of all member states' ambassadors to the EU. Under Article 240(1) of the Treaty of the Functioning of the EU, all agenda items for Council of Ministers' meetings, except agriculture, must go to them first. That is where the bargaining takes place. The Council of Ministers, when it meets, need not accept their recommendations but it usually does. COREPER, of course, is unelected and meets in secret. The Council has elected members – government ministers from each state – but they are elected to each states' parliament and not by a pan-European electorate. They too meet in secret. The whole thing is a fabricated form of democracy – an EU constitutional construction that is inherently weak because it lacks electoral legitimacy.

Then there is the economic weakness. The EU is an indisputably large market of over 500 million people, many in states that are highly developed in terms of commerce, industry, technology and sources of financial expertise and investment. It trades in world markets as one and is often described as a trade superpower. So where can its weaknesses lie? It is not in its declining share of world trade, as some critics claim. The EU economy has grown but the economies in other parts of the world have grown faster. The entry in to world markets of countries such as Vietnam, Indonesia, the Philippines, Brazil, India and China was bound to affect the EU's comparative performance – as has been the case with the USA. The weakness lies in a policy of single-market rules that impose the rigidity of one-size-must-fit-all, which removes flexibility and smothers innovation. That the same rules should apply across a swathe of countries – large, small, some with geographic proximity to big internal EU markets and others for whom distance is a commercial handicap – is nonsense.

Then there is the issue of how the treaties address the matter of the respective power of capital and labour. At the Labour Party special conference on the EEC in 1971, I denounced the Rome Treaty, the foundation of the EEC, as encapsulating the ethic of capitalism. In the Viking and Laval judgments of the European Court of Justice, in which capital versus labour was the basic issue, the ECJ came down in favour of the right of capital over any rights workers may have. Let me be clear, I am not saying the court was in error. It ruled correctly in its interpretation of the treaties that form the legal basis of the EU – capital is superior in law to labour.

Viking was a Finnish company operating a ferry service to Latvia. It sought to reflag from Finland to Latvia, to take advantage of cheaper labour. The Finnish workers sought to prevent the move through strike action. The ECJ confirmed the right to strike as a fundamental one but ruled that that was subordinate to the company's right to move its capital to where it wanted within the EU.

Laval was known as the 'posted workers' case. A Latvian company with a contract to rehabilitate a Swedish school brought over its own workers on cheaper rates than the agreed trade union level in that region of Sweden. Again the ECJ ruled in favour of the company. When extolling the virtues of the EU, one never hears about such cases from the lips of leaders in the SNP, yet it has a trade union group that is 15,000 strong.

But it was on the strategic ground of independence that I anchored my campaign. As in all previous elections, I set out my reasons in detail, this time in a pamphlet 'The Logical Case: Why ScotLeave.EU makes most sense', 11,000 of which were printed and distributed by the Leave campaign in Scotland.

One of the most important lessons to be drawn from the 2014 referendum was that, as long as the UK remained in the EU, the EU would line up with the British state, one of its biggest net contributors, in presenting independence as creating serious uncertainty about the ability of a Scottish state to access traditional markets. In 2004, the EU told a Scottish parliament committee that there would be no seamless continuation of membership for a Scottish state and repeated that message in 2014. On independence, we would be out. We could apply for membership but would have to join the queue and our application would require unanimity of all member states – code for a Spanish veto. In short, we were told to get stuffed. That EU position contributed to the 'uncertainty' that dogged the case for independence throughout the campaign. So, central to my pamphlet was knocking the EU out of the independence equation. Let me quote from it:

> If the UK remains in the EU, then nothing changes. The Yes movement will be told, as we were in 2014, that there is no guarantee of EU membership because all 28 countries would have to agree and Spain would threaten its veto again. The EU is not in favour of member states separating.

I spelled out why membership of EFTA and EEA circumvented the EU and how, with greater freedom that comes through the exercise of sovereignty, Scotland would be in the same position as Norway and in a better position than, for example, Denmark, a member of the EU. Again, it was a difference of opinion from that of the party leadership.

As part of its preparation for the independence referendum, the Scottish government published a document in late 2013, 'Scotland in the European Union'. Presented by Nicola Sturgeon as Deputy First Minister, it set out specifically to rubbish the idea of our nation joining EFTA and the EEA. It trotted out all the old canards about Norway having to toe the EU line without being involved in discussions on EU policy. It is hard to accept but impossible to avoid the impression that she had not actually read the European Economic Area treaty between the EFTA and EU and failed to understand the influence external international organisations have on EU and EEA law-making, making the document so false in its claims. Perhaps this superficial treatment of the EFTA states' position within the EEA and internationally is due to the tedium of actually ploughing through detail. I invite the reader to do a little of that work on the EEA treaty as it will demolish Nicola's claim that Norway is a supine supplicant marching only to an EU drum beat, rather than the sovereign power which it is.

The EEA treaty has 129 Articles and a number of protocols, setting out the respective rights and obligations of its signatories. The EFTA states have no vote at the final stage of EU decision making at the Council of Ministers or in the EU parliament but are by no means out of the loop when new laws are being developed, or without powers to protect national interests. Articles 99, 100 and 102 are relevant. They provide safeguards when EFTA states' national interests are at stake and guarantee their involvement in new EU law development from first to last stages before a final EU vote.

Nicola Sturgeon's claim that the EU says to Norway 'Here's the new laws, now obey' is an absurdity. That is spelled out in the EEA treaty as she would have discovered had she or her advisers had cared to read it. Article 99 states:

1. As soon as new legislation is being drawn up by the EC Commission in a field which is governed by this Agreement, the EC Commission shall informally seek advice from experts of the EFTA States in the same way as it seeks advice from experts of the EC Member States for the elaboration of its proposals.
2. When transmitting its proposal to the Council of the European Communities, the EC Commission shall transmit copies thereof to the EFTA States.

At the request of one of the Contracting Parties, a pre-liminary exchange of views takes place in the EEA Joint Committee.

3. During the phase preceding the decision of the Council of the European Communities, in a continuous information and consultation process, the Contracting Parties consult each other again in the EEA Joint Committee at the significant moments at the request of one of them.

4. The Contracting Parties shall cooperate in good faith during the information and consultation phase with a view to facilitating, at the end of the process, the decision-taking in the EEA Joint Committee."

And Article 100:

The EC Commission shall ensure experts of the EFTA States as wide a participation as possible according to the areas concerned, in the preparatory stage of draft measures to be submitted subsequently to the committees which assist the EC Commission in the exercise of its executive powers. In this regard, when drawing up draft measures the EC Commission shall refer to experts of the EFTA States on the same basis as it refers to experts of the EC Member States.

In the cases where the Council of the European Communities is seized in accordance with the procedure applicable to the type of committee involved, the EC Commission shall transmit to the Council of the European Communities the views of the experts of the EFTA States.

As the pamphlet noted, Norway is able to exercise sovereign power if the EU tries to go beyond the boundaries of the EEA Agreement. When the EU sought to extend its competence to energy in the North Sea making Norway's oil and gas subject to EU regulations, it did not happen because the 'Norwegian government has taken the view that the proposed regulation by the European Commission falls outside the geographic and substantive scope of the EEA agreement'.

Statistics from 2000 and 2013, quoted in the pamphlet, are noteworthy. Norway adopted only 4,724 EU laws in compliance with the EEA Agreement, whereas EU member states each implemented 52,183 directives and regulations from the Commission which arose out of the

EU treaties to which Norway is not a signatory. The EEA is not a customs union and the EFTA states have negotiated over thirty free trade agreements in their own right.

Such has been the hollowing out of the intellectual capacity of the party membership, none seems to realise that, for all the adulation of the EU – the many visits, kisses and hugs by the First Minister to the EU mandarins and the attempts to keep the UK in the EU, by subverting the 2016 referendum – there has been absolutely nothing in return. The position of the EU towards Scottish independence remains as it was in 2014. Spanish governments' – on the Right and Left – vicious reaction to the foolish, illegal referendum in Catalonia shows a state not at all confident in its territorial security. A secure state would have seen off such a bungled referendum with sarcastic humour. But the insecure Spain we saw revealed cannot afford entry to a separatist Scotland. For them, 'Scotland' means Catalonia. When the Spanish consul general in Scotland made a speech saying Spain would not veto Scottish entry, he was sacked.

Why, given that the SNP government has played the cards for the EU against the UK government since day one of the 2016 referendum, and given its declared ambition to remain in or re-enter the EU later, has the First Minister not formally asked for an independent Scotland to be guaranteed seamless membership as a new state? Something for nothing is not a sensible state policy.

The day after the EU referendum result, Nicola Sturgeon made much of the fact that Scotland returned 1,661,191 Remain votes to 1,018,322 for Leave, causing her to claim that Scotland was being dragged out of the EU against its will. This was a change in the material circumstance of Scotland's position in the UK and thus grounds for holding a second independence referendum. She misjudged the public mood, which was against an early second referendum. She seemed also to have forgotten that, in going down to England to campaign, she legitimised the question on the ballot paper, which was whether the UK remained or left the EU.

There then followed, as I have been pointing out to some of my colleagues who are MSPs and MPs, a series of hostages to fortune likely to haunt the SNP in the years ahead. First, by rejecting the result because they didn't like it, they invite the same conduct by unionists in any future ballot on independence. Second, by arguing that a second referendum needed to be held on the details of the final 'deal', they lay themselves wide open to the same tactic on an independence referendum. Third, by deliberate attempts to subvert the referendum decision, including resorting to the courts and joining in the Miller case in the Supreme Court, with the Lord Advocate arguing, wrongly, that the Sewell convention prevented the UK government acting on its Brexit legislation without Scottish parliamentary approval. Fourth, by leaping upon every anti-Brexit forecast by the Treasury, Bank of England, Institute for Fiscal Studies and English-based think tanks, the party will find it impossible to reject their damning forecasts of the consequences of independence next time, as all such bodies did last time.

Scotland voting for independence on a Thursday does not mean the country becomes independent on the Friday morning. It would remain in the UK until it exited with an Anglo-Scottish treaty – the 'deal' setting out the terms of separation and the post-independence relationship with our biggest export market with 60 per cent of goods and services compared to 18 per cent with the EU. Copying the SNP template, we can anticipate the unionists urging the UK government to make the terms as tough as possible, yelling constantly about a 'hard separatist exit', finding reasons to challenge the negotiations in court and so create the conditions to demand a second referendum on the 'treaty deal' – a Scottish people's vote, as they are likely to say.

When Ian Blackford, leader of the SNP Westminster Group, announced in the House of Commons that the party supported a second vote on leaving the EU, I sent him an email asking if he had gone off his head. Never was a hostage to fortune so easily given. The others followed with the same lack of thinking.

It should have been apparent that the Leave win meant we were now living in a new political and economic paradigm. Shortly after the result, I wrote an article and did a long radio interview at the BBC with Isobel Fraser in which I said it was now wise to wait until the Brexit deal was done and thoroughly examined before launching any new drive for a second independence referendum because those supporting independence would have to make a case in a new situation and set out a revised set of policy approaches.

I did not anticipate that the parliament elected in 2017 would set out to make the journey to Brexit so difficult. It was clearly a mistake for Theresa May to hold the election and, when her majority evaporated, the new parliament became openly Remain. Whether the UK would leave the EU was not decided until the December election of 2019.

The EU referendum widened the already large gap between the SNP leadership and me, leading some party members to invite me to resign. I did not do so although I found it hard not to, given the imbecility of a number of statements made by SNP ministers and MPs about the economic consequences of Brexit both before and after the vote. There was no scare they would not adopt, no catastrophe they would not forecast.

There has been no let-up in the SNP's forecasting of a Brexit disaster. In the *Scottish Left Review* in November 2019 Tommy Sheppard, SNP MP for Edinburgh East, declared: 'The promise of Brexit was a lie. It isn't possible to leave and things to get better.' But what if it does get better? Another hostage to fortune? Egg on lots of faces. There hasn't been one single caveat hedging those forecasts of the actual result we have still to see on Brexit. The SNP has put itself in one corner called 'disaster'.

Experience should warn politicians about so readily accepting and parroting medium- and long-term economic forecasts whose reliability is questionable to say the least. The Institute of Fiscal Studies and the Fraser of Allander Institute, not to mention the UK Treasury, the Office of Budget Responsibility (OBR) and the Bank of England, all have prestigious titles but the results that come out of their computer models are only as good as the input assumptions and their record is nothing to shout about. The Bank of England forecast exports to fall in 2017 by 0.5 per cent – they rose by 7.2 per cent. It forecast business investment would fall by 2 per cent whereas it rose by 2 per cent – a large margin of error. The Office of Budget Responsibility has an outstanding record of error in forecasting. On 13 June 2015, *The Scotsman* was so impressed by an OBR forecast claiming there would be 'a dramatic fall in North Sea oil revenues over the next 25 years' that it gave it pride of place in a leader column. In response, in a letter to the paper, I pointed out a number of factors unknown to forecasters that should make us sceptical. Here are just a few: 'Forecasting the direction of the price of any basic commodity over 25 years requires a total understanding of the global economy, and society, not now, but in the future. Here are, among others, some of the things forecasting needs to know for certain – the consequences on its growth of China shifting to another economic model, will the Eurozone continue to see the triumph of politics over economics . . . the effect [Indian Prime Minister Narendra] Modi's policies have for India . . . will Africa develop its full potential . . . when will recessions occur and how deep they will be.'

In 2015, the average price of Brent crude was $52 a barrel although it had been lower at around $40. In December 2019, it was $64 per barrel. Covid-19 sent it crashing in 2020. How high it will rise again is wholly dependent on the great unknown of how the world economy will recover from the crisis created by the Covid-19 pandemic. How high it will rise again are not careless words. All governments will be driven to seek higher growth as the escape route out of the economic damage done by Covid-19 and oil and gas demand will rise. It will be amusing to watch governments doing verbal and policy somersaults as they go for growth with oil and gas in the engines, while claiming to remain virtuously 'green'.

Long-term economic forecasting of how the world economy will perform is not a science. It is not even a good guess. The world economy is people – over seven billion in more than 160 countries, whose production and consumption patterns are heavily influenced by governmental decisions, some of which emerge to confound the experts. Take China with a GDP per capita of US$91 in 1961. The country's Cultural Revolution which had taken place between May 1966 and October 1976 had left its society in shreds and China was dismissed by economists in the 1970s as of no importance – its 'iron rice bowl' economy produced little that the rest of the world wanted. But, while they wrote, those economists were not privy to decisions being taken in the secret conclaves of the Communist Politburo and Central Committee. It was in the latter, in December 1978, that Deng Xiaoping won the fight to pursue a new two-phase policy. First was the emphasis on inner economic reform with the de-collectivisation of agriculture, allowing private businesses to set up and start making it possible for foreign investment to come in.

There were no immediate world-shaking results. In 1978, GDP per capita was US$229, reaching only US$370 in 1988. Then came phase two – the one that set China on course to becoming an economic superpower. GDP per capita rose from US$829 in 1998 to US$1,289 in 2003. In 2018 it was US$9,769. China's GDP per capita in 2019 is estimated at US$10,099. Who could have forecast that?

The truth is that no one could have known how the UK economy would perform post-Brexit – even if it had taken place in 'normal' times. Yet UK politicians opposed to Brexit felt able with absolute certainty to forecast doom, destruction and disaster. And this was despite not knowing the details of any final trade agreement or whether trade between the UK and the EU trade was to be subject to WTO rules – a trade system used for some 48 per cent of UK exports to non-EU countries and thus not an untried system for British exporters. The unknown can be guessed at and speculated about but it will always remain unknown. Now, of course, Brexit is happening in a Covid-19 world which is not a 'normal' one. My own view is that Brexit is fortuitous. Unlike the EU states that are really going to be in trouble, the UK has the flexibility from full sovereignty on policy that they are denied.

Brexit also raised a question about statecraft. My differences with Nicola Sturgeon are not personal but how, like Alex Salmond, she has exercised total control over the party and the parliamentary parties and so, with no debate, errors have arisen. The handling of the post-Brexit relationship with Westminster is a case in point, where statecraft has been missing.

Statecraft is founded upon an objective assessment of the power relationship between states or, in our case, between governments with different powers within the single entity of the UK. The factors that come into play are complicated and interdependent. Where do interests conjoin and where are they separate? If separate, are the divisions large or small? What short- and/or long-term aims does each have? And how seriously do one side's aims affect the other's? Is there room for cooperative compromise and, if so, to what extent? Between confrontation and capitulation, which is the best choice? What language and tone should be employed? And, last but what should be foremost, will the people benefit or be adversely affected by decisions taken by one or the other? These precepts are always important. How they are applied by those with less power – as is the case between devolved Scotland and sovereign UK – calls for a special level of diplomatic skill. I question Nicola Sturgeon's.

With the final Brexit taking place within the context of the Union, it will have a bearing on Scotland's economic life and create new competencies for the Scottish government. Former EU powers will be coming north and will widen the policy debates that inform our political life. Devolved Scots could not demand a role in the UK's official negotiating team nor expect to play any part in the discussions. However, it would have been possible for the Scottish government to establish a cooperative relationship with the UK government to enable it to contribute to and have some influence on the mandate for the UK negotiators – this would have offered a greater degree of influence than was likely to be had from participation in the joint ministerial meetings between Westminster and the devolved administrations.

But here's the rub. The UK government would have to be convinced that it was not inviting a Scottish–EU cuckoo into its fold. The SNP refused to accept the 2016 referendum result and, with their members regularly going to Brussels and actually consorting with a foreign power, Westminster feared their negotiating hand was constantly being revealed to the EU side. Matters were not helped by Nicola condemning what she termed a 'Tory hard Brexit'. There have been different reports about the arithmetic but around 152 former EU powers will be given to the Scottish government as part of Brexit. However, 24 will be held back, on a time-limited basis. These pertain to matters such as animal health, food labelling and chemical regulation that would need to apply UK-wide. It seemed sensible and being 'time-limited' means they are coming. Ian Blackford MP, SNP Westminster Group leader, denounced this temporary retention, in June 2018, as 'shafting Scotland and the people of Scotland'. The First Minister, at the same time, launched her claim that Westminster was 'taking back' powers from the Scottish parliament. It became a cry of anger in the nationalist movement. Yet not a single power, in any of the Scotland Acts, was being taken back from Holyrood – Brexit meant more. How could any rational person expect the UK government, faced with a deliberate misinformation campaign that painted them as setting out to 'shaft' Scotland, treat the Scottish government as a partner it could trust? So, in my view, the Scottish government placed itself without influence on the UK side of the negotiations.

Now, it may be that the First Minister and the SNP as a whole set themselves on a deliberate course of dispute and confrontation with Westminster over Brexit. The tactics and language chosen might have been calculated to widen the gap, as many Scots see it, between Scotland and England, raise and exploit a sense of grievance – being shafted – and, by doing so, increase the independence vote. Many nationalists would applaud that policy and it has been in the playbook used by nationalist movements over the years. But it begs the question of whether the strategy between 2016 and 2020 has been in the best interests of the people of Scotland. Brexit has taken Scotland out of the EU and the terms on which leaving is final are important to this nation. The leader of a party that seeks independence but is the First Minister of a devolved administration is not in the position she would wish to be. But that is the one she was in the day after the Brexit result. She had to decide what was most advantageous to Scotland's people – enter the UK Brexit tent or stand outside and shout political abuse to arouse grievance. She chose the latter. I view that as a serious error even although an opinion poll, published on 15 October 2020, placed support for independence at the unprecedented level of 58 per cent.

It remains to be seen whether that figure is solid or a consequence of the surreal world we were plunged into with the Covid-19 pandemic, with the employment of the different presentational skills of the first minister when compared to those of the blundering prime minister. It will not be in the pandemic world that the next independence referendum is held and it will not be on the same question, or issues, as in

2014. Of course, whether there is a referendum will depend upon the result of the May 2021 Scottish parliamentary election. Gaining an overall majority and therefore a clear mandate will be difficult because of the electoral system, in which the more constituency seats the SNP gains, the fewer the top up List ones it is allocated.

I view the Sturgeon strategy as an error because what will emerge, not just in any UK–EU agreement on paper but in practice, will shape Scottish policy on fishing, public-sector procurement, state aid, free-trade zones, exports and tariffs. That was so before the Covid-19 crisis and will be even more so as we try to put our economy back together and these matters will, in the event of independence winning the referendum, figure largely in any Scotland–UK treaty giving effect to that decision.

Let me take but two of them to illustrate.

Fishing

During the Brexit negotiations, the EU kept demanding the retention of the Common Fisheries Policy (CFP) which would give EU fishermen continued access to UK waters. Taking a hard-line stance, the UK government refused. Given the importance of fishing to parts of the Scottish economy and the opportunity that would emerge from getting out from under the CFP to rebuild the fleet and onshore business base, one would have thought the Scottish government would line up with Westminster in rejecting the EU claim, thus strengthening the hand of the UK which claims to be acting for the whole British fishing industry. But it seems not. It was widely reported in September 2020 that Scottish government ministers had met the EU negotiator Michel Barnier, telling him they were in favour of a compromise, thus undermining the UK government's position of asserting maritime supremacy – their key lever in the negotiations. No doubt there will be compromise but it is in the interests of the Scottish fishing industry to limit the compromise by expanding its rights to fishing areas which it has had to share under the CFP. That assertion of Scottish interests should have been transmitted to Brussels by Nicola Sturgeon to buttress the UK negotiators' position. The clear impression left is that the SNP is not only outside the Brexit tent shouting in but they are also shouting in for EU interests before those of Scotland.

Public Procurement

The EU single market rules prevented the Scottish government giving preference to Scottish companies when public contracts were above a certain level. EU policy also scuppered the SNP government's desire to demand that anyone bidding for a public contract had to pay the living wage. Out of the EU, there will still be procurement policy as the UK government will seek, within the UK single market, to eliminate unfair competition on large contracts. Is there to be a line drawn between size of contract that must be advertised UK-wide and those that enable the Scottish government – or the Welsh, the Northern Irish and English regions – to favour local companies, our small- and medium-sized enterprises (SME) sector? The answer is important. Will public procurement become more flexible and give the SME sector a greater chance of winning contracts, thus benefitting local and regional economies and creating jobs? So too are the rules to come on free-trade zones, and the ability of the Scottish government to give state aid to companies it believes it is in the national interest to help.

But was getting Scotland's national interest into the heart of these and many other matters involved in the final Brexit deal well served by the SNP government's stance? On the face of it, Nicola Sturgeon's view of statecraft is that she can advance towards independence best by being at constant loggerheads with Westminster, revealing it as an inherently anti-Scottish institution. That fires up the party but does it serve the nation's interests? I think not. I am not sure that it serves the independence movement well either.

My friend Ian Blackford, as part of the grievance message, has told the House of Commons repeatedly that the people of Scotland are sovereign and, when our wishes on Brexit are not being followed, it is an outrageous insult to us all. Politics and intellectual rigour do not combine easily but there are times when it does harm to ignore the former. When did Scotland's people have sovereignty and give it away? Not with the Act of Union 1707. The 'people' had no say then. But we had sovereignty on 18 September 2014, between the hours of 7 a.m. and 10 p.m. What the ballot paper asked the nation to decide was whether to keep it or hand it back to be absorbed into the sovereignty of the British state. Scotland's people did the latter. Until that decision is reversed, the interests of Scotland's people on jobs, wages, education and our relations with other countries call for statecraft to be practised on their behalf within the context of the whole of the UK.

If another referendum is held and a final victory won, there needs to be a total shift in how the Scotland–England relationship is seen and presented by both the SNP and Yes movements generally. I say England because, with its population of around 56 million people, it is dominant.

That is not an anti-English swipe – simply a statement of reality. We Scots used to bristle whenever 'England' was used in the media instead of Britain. It was never a slip of the tongue or pen. It reflected reality. In past Cabinet papers, speeches and political memoirs, you will find 'England' is the state referred to, not the United Kingdom. Take the example of Churchill's *History of the Second World War*. In the first volume, *The Gathering Storm*, published in 1948, he records that, on 27 September 1938 while 'the Fuehrer was at grips with his generals, Mr. Chamberlain himself was preparing to broadcast to the English nation'. Throughout his six volumes, he repeatedly uses 'England' when Britain or the United Kingdom would be more accurate. However annoying for the Scots, it was unlikely to have been otherwise given that the union of 1707 was a triumph for English foreign policy. If the situation had been reversed and Scotland had been the dominant power with the larger population, we Scots would have acted as the English state has done. Politicians, broadcasters and others down south are more careful now but careful language does not hide the fact that England's state interests will always come first.

Many of the statements made by SNP ministers and MPs at Westminster, together with those who write columns and letters in *The National* newspaper and the messages that stream out on social media, scream that Scotland is being ignored, insulted and not respected. The fact is no one sits in ministerial offices in London thinking of how to shaft Scotland. At the very worst, they simply don't give us much thought. That idea that deliberate 'Scotland shafting' is going on has a grip on the Yes and SNP minds and it has led to the policy of advancing the case for independence through manufactured grudge and grievance. The 'they are taking back powers' rage is an example. Grudge and grievance complaints against Westminster, combined with vitriolic attacks upon unionists via social media, make for a stupid policy. If Yes is to win next time, it will be on the basis of persuasion and that will require a better understanding as to why so many No voters held to the Union last time and still do. Unionists do not see Westminster as a malign anti-Scottish force and, in their rejection of any such claims, they become entrenched in their views and unreceptive to the idea of independence. Scottish unionists are not traitors to this nation and to suggest that they are or that they are not as Scottish as Yes voters is a mistake.

Perhaps my own journey from unionist to advocate for independence can point the way to how the Yes movement can address unionists and persuade them to vote Yes. When I took those first tentative steps away from belief in the Union back in 1972, I did not see the English as anti-Scottish but had a glimmering of the real nature of the UK, where realpolitik would always put England's state interests first. Over the years, that understanding grew and I began to develop the concept of a Scottish state interest and, with it, the positive not negative view that we could only develop our full potential if we disengaged from the Union and exercised independent sovereignty.

Oil was one of the learning points. From a UK (England) standpoint, facing a consistent and debilitating duality of a chronic balance of payments deficit and energy deficiency, it was essential to exploit the oil reserves in the North Sea as fast as possible to overcome those two serious defects – for a time. But what was good for the UK (England) interests was not so for Scotland. We needed a slower development to gain the knowledge required for our people of an industry that was new, and a slower rate of exploitation because a small country like ours did not need the torrent of production that UK policy dictated. What we needed was the Norway model, where a great deal of the wealth was kept under the sea as a significant economic reserve to be produced once Norway had established a domestic extraction industry and knowledge of the oil international market. But that was not possible with Scotland part of the UK. I remember attending a meeting for Scottish MPs, at the invitation of BP, when its chief executive denounced any policy of low production as being the kind of thing 'the blue-eyed Arabs of Norway' were imposing.

It is not anti-English to say that Scotland has always had a problem with England and its size and power. The Union of 1707 did not change that situation but compounded it. From William I – William the Lion – in 1165 right through to Bruce's wars of independence and beyond, Scotland has been in England's sphere of influence. We share the fate of other small nations which find themselves in close proximity to a much larger powerful neighbour. That is the hand dealt to us by geography. It is permanent – one of life's realities. Our national strategy should take account of it and we should be doing what can to diminish the influence England has. Being in England's sphere of influence is not necessarily a fatal trap.

I have come to the view that, because the Union negotiation was between two states, with Scotland in the weaker position, it has left a belief among Scots that it was an agreement to create a union of equals and, when such a belief has proved untrue in practice, it has created an undercurrent of anti-English feeling. Within the Union with England, we are not equal, never have been and never can be. A proper understanding of state interests should bring that reality into sharp relief and so perhaps help us get our relationship with England into a less negative perspective. State interests is not a concept familiar to thinking in Scotland. When speaking to audiences about Scottish state interests, I often draw a blank. But it is by explaining the importance of Scottish state interests that we can aid our people to see the positive reasons why we need independence. The essence of the case is that, whatever we may think of ourselves as a nation within the Union, we can in reality only be an economic province of the UK and that prohibits us from being what we could be with sovereignty – different and finding different paths to being successful and prosperous.

Even with independence, we cannot escape geography. We shall remain in England's sphere of influence and, being a member of NATO with Scotland as a neighbour in the strategic position as a main guardian of the Atlantic sea lanes, England has a reason to want to hold on to us. And this is also one of the reasons the United States wishes England to hold on to us. That is something a Scottish state will need to take account of in its foreign policy but, in the economic and social spheres, we shall have thrown off the constraints that are inevitable in an incorporating union. We shall break free.

And it is that potential sovereign freedom upon which we can base a persuasive positive optimistic case for how we can transform Scotland from its present status of a low-growth economy, with low wages, large areas of deprivation and continued migration of the young, into an ambitious nation fired by self-belief. Being a small nation is a significant advantage. Small countries facing great changes in the world can be nimble, can change course and can identify and solve problems far faster than large ones. The difference between a small robust ship and a giant tanker seeking to change course is the perfect example of where size matters. At present we are tied to a rather large ship of state. We need to cut that rope.

If we Scots get a clearer understanding of the reality of Scottish–English relations, we shall see that independence is not the final round in a grudge match but a significant change for the better in how our two nations view each other and treat each other.

25

Issues of Our Age

Standing against the Climate Change Groupthink

> We do not believe any group of men adequate enough or wise enough to operate without scrutiny or without criticism.
>
> J. Robert Oppenheimer

If you believe the Green lobby, CO_2 is a dangerous pollutant gas that sits up in our atmosphere like a malignant blanket over the planet; that human activity is increasing its thickness; that it is the most significant greenhouse gas driving the temperature ever upwards to the point when our earth will become uninhabitable; that falling numbers of polar bears point to how life is threatened with extinction; that the Thwaites Glacier in west Antarctica is melting due entirely to global warming; and that governments must act on a climate emergency by abandoning fossil fuels and instead adopting vast schemes of clean renewable energy generation by wind turbines and solar panels, at whatever cost.

CO_2 is not a pollutant. It is an essential building block of life. Without it, there would not be even one green leaf, one stalk of corn, one tomato or anything else to be found on earth. The amount of CO_2 in the atmosphere is 0.0407%. The largest greenhouse gas (95% of it) is water vapour. The polar bear, alone, isolated, on a piece of ice was the iconic image of dangerous global warming. It was used by Green groups to raise funds. That piece of marketing has disappeared. It is no longer a fund raiser because, despite Sir David Attenborough, in 2007, claiming the polar bear could be facing extinction, a report by Dr Susan Crockford in 2018, recorded that the predicted 67 per cent decline in polar bear numbers did not occur and that their numbers have, in fact, risen with those in the Chukchi Sea continuing to thrive. It is now tigers and snow leopards that WWF are asking us to adopt, both endangered by hunting.

In January 2020, a press release from Antarctic researchers declared that Thwaites Glacier could melt this century, with the cause being cited as global warming. This was seized upon by the Greens and was given extensive coverage by the media, with the BBC among the most vocal. What the press release did not say and the BBC did not report is that under that ice sheet are a number of volcanoes and, as scientists noted back in 2014, 'the subglacial water system of Thwaites Glacier may be responding to . . . basal melting driven by the evolution of rift-associated volcanism'. Volcanic hotspots under the ice are too inconvenient to the groupthink's grip on the media to be reported.

To claim that the science is settled is far from the truth. Many eminent scientists are contesting the climate emergency and have challenged the repeated claim that CO_2 emissions are responsible for the earth warming or the climate changing and point out that warming, cooling and climate changes have occurred throughout the planet's history. Here are but a few examples. During the Roman Warm Period from c. 250 BC to AD 400, temperatures were two to six degrees Celsius higher than today. The period from AD 535–900 was one of extreme cold when the Black Sea froze in 800, 801 and 829 and ice formed in the River Nile. In the Northern Hemisphere, the Medieval Warm Period lasted from c. 900 to 1300 and was followed by the Little Ice Age 1280–1850. There were no human industrial age emissions of CO_2 during most of those times yet changes in climate still took place.

As for wind turbines and solar panels, they are not magic devices with no connection to the 'dirty industrial processes that the Greens would want to bring to an end. The website windwatch.org reports that: 'According to the Northwest Mining Association, a single 3-MW wind turbine needs 335 tons of steel, 4.7 tons of copper, 1,200 tons of concrete, 3 tons of aluminium, 2 tons of rare earth elements.' Add to that the transport costs and they are not as green as we are supposed to believe.

It is true that the wind and solar energy are free but the turbines and panels do not convert it into a free or even cheap supply of electricity for business or the home. Green taxes and subsidies introduced to promote their development are being paid for by higher energy costs for all. In 2019, £1.3 billion was the subsidy cost. To that 'constraint' payments are now added . Sometimes wind does not blow when needed and sometimes it blows when not needed and the turbines have to be switched off. The owners are paid for not producing electricity and, in 2020, these, so far, have come to £835 million. One of the ironies of the policy is that, while the poorest people pay more for electricity, their cash goes to fill the bank balances of already rich landowners on whose land they are built. As I record in my book *In Place of Failure*, Sir Alastair Gordon Cumming will reap £10.874 million over the lifetime of the turbines on his estates, the Earl of Moray £7.5 million, the Earl of Glasgow £5.252 million and the Earl of Seafield £3 million. And they are not alone on this green bandwagon.

During one of the early conversations I had with the publishers of this book, I was asked why, in a political autobiography, I should insist on recording the public stance I have taken on contesting the views of the Green lobby. An activist and fellow author in the Birlinn range of books wondered why a politician like me should dive into what is a scientific matter and thereby risk demonstrating my ignorance. The answer to the first is that it would be an act of cowardice not to record my dissent from the prevailing orthodoxy. I know politicians and academics who privately believe that the 'climate emergency' and 'climate catastrophe' warnings are either wrong or exaggerated but feel it prudent to say nothing, lest they be viciously attacked as 'climate change deniers'. The answer to the second is that I have no such inhibitions and, if I was seeking a seat in Parliament, I would still speak out on this subject because it is the poor who are suffering from the price being paid for 'Green' polices. It is no coincidence that fuel poverty with people freezing in their homes in winter has risen in recent years. Politicians pass the Green laws and parroting that they are 'following the science' is no excuse for the harm they inflict on the poor by the increases in heating and lighting costs they impose upon them. The science should be rigorously interrogated by politicians. It is not.

This lack of interrogation has meant misplaced resources and wrong priorities. There are several estimates of what it will cost for the UK to implement its policy of going carbon neutral by 2050. The lowest, from the UK's Committee on Climate Change is £30 billion a year for thirty years, although it has resisted Freedom of Information (FOI) requests showing how that calculation was made. The 2050 target and expenditure are priorities for the government and opposition. As governments have no money except what they raise in taxes and borrowing, with the borrowing having to be paid by taxes eventually, what does that commitment mean for future tax levels and how badly will the allocation of that £30 billion a year to green objectives relegate other priorities such as housing, the NHS, education and alleviating poverty? In pursuit of the impossible goal of controlling the great forces that determine life on earth, we will enter an expensive fairyland of failure.

When a person or a group claims expertise and certainty on complex matters, as is the case on many occasions and is certainly so on matters affecting the earth's climate, I have never automatically accepted their findings as gospel. This is because experts have often been proven wrong. I also have an aversion to scaremongering, which has been a feature of climate forecasts by Green lobby groups, now surpassed by Extinction Rebellion which claimed on 10 October 2019 that billions of people will die because of climate change, with Roger Hallam its co-founder, in the same report, scaring children with forecasts of their early deaths, stating that children will die in the next ten to twenty years. Extinction Rebellion's Zion Lights said, 'Alarmist language works.' It doesn't for me.

One has to hand it to the Green lobby and the other alarmists for one expertise that is unmistakably impressive – marketing. How could anyone be opposed to Greenpeace or not be a Friend of the Earth? How, when confronted with 'Extinction', could human beings and their politicians not be panicked into declaring a 'climate emergency'? But slick marketing and clever labels don't mean we should believe those punting them. I don't and I am not alone – just one of those willing to say so. I am not a scientist but nor are the many celebrities, royal family members, thousands of activists, Extinction Rebellion warriors, primary school children and the high priestess of the new cult, young Greta Thunberg. But I have read extensively on the subject and talked to scientists and engineers – the latter being experts on the use of the data that goes into model projections.

For Professor Ian Plimer, the history of temperature changes on this planet shows that among the major phenomena causing it are the shape of the continents, the shape of the sea floor, movements of the earth's crust, changes in our planet's orbit, changes in solar energy emitted by the sun, supernova eruptions and ocean currents. In his book, *Heaven and Earth: Global Warming, the Missing Science* (Connor Court Publishing, Australia, 2009), he comments, 'If we humans, in a fit of ego, think we can change these normal planetary processes, then we need stronger medicine.' He might have added another truth – our planet is dynamic, driven by great unpredictable forces of nature, and, thus, it is impossible for humans to control and calibrate its climate so that the temperature is just 1.5° Celsius above that of 1850. Scientists and others who point this out and do not fall into line with the Green groupthink are labelled 'climate change deniers'. That is not a scientific term. It is a political act – a smear intended to prevent others from listening to them. In my view, much of what is passed off to the public as science is propaganda, buttressed by scaremongering. In the 24-hour global news coverage, what have been normal natural events throughout the ages are punted as evidence of the growing catastrophes that will engulf humanity, all due, allegedly, to global warming because CO_2 is increasing in the atmosphere. The noise generated prevents a proper examination of why there are great floods and forest fires and if, in fact, they are due to significant changes in the world's climate, because of that 0.0407 per cent of CO_2 in the atmosphere.

In 2020, when we saw great forest fires devastating parts of California, 'climate change' tripped off the tongues of commentators and Green activists. Hurricanes descended upon Florida and, as the TV cameras record flattened houses, again 'climate change' and the associated bogeyman of increased CO_2 are cited as the cause. According to Stop Climate Chaos Scotland, as reported in *The Scotsman* on 31.10.20, 'Millions of people are already suffering from droughts, floods, fires and food shortages.' Not only is this alarmist claim repudiated by the Fifth Assessment Report of the Intergovernmental Panel on Climate Change (IPCC) but it also ignores changes in the population of the United States that make its citizens more liable to suffer the effects of what are normal bad weather and other events. The IPCC report, published in 2014, states there is little evidence on a global scale of any drought since the 1950s. In its worst-case scenario, sea levels will rise by 0.83 metres by 2100 – quite manageable as the Netherlands demonstrates with a good part of its land below sea level. A paper from Johns Hopkins University notes that as world population rose to 7 billion, enough calories were produced to feed us all but that hunger 'remains a global crisis, largely because those calories are not evenly distributed across population, and much of the world's food supply is never eaten'.

A major factor in the damage done to people and property in the United States by forest fires and hurricanes is due to population increase and the resultant vast expanse of house building, business creation, the infrastructure that goes into the spread of urbanisation, and more people building homes in forest areas. When Franklin D. Roosevelt was elected president in 1932, the US population was 124.8 million. In 1945 it was 139.4 million. In 2020 it was 333.4 million. California's population rose from 10.5 million in 1950 to 39.5 million in 2019. Florida's has grown from 2.4 million in 1945 to 21.4 million in 2019. Territorially, neither the USA nor its states have grown. This population increase has brought additional vulnerability to communities from severe weather.

Green activists quickly claimed that the fires in California and Australia were due to 'climate change'. The governor of California, Gavin Newsom added his voice to those cries, which allowed him to attack Trump, but he also recognised that other factors had contributed to his state's fires – these included the consequences of urban planning allowing new housing to be built within forests to cater for increased population and the problems property owners have with clearing brush, which is a 'fuel load' just waiting for ignition. Governor Newsom noted there were 'hundreds of millions of dead trees' in the state. To illustrate the problem, he said his father had paid a $35,000 bill to clear 'a small little patch of dead trees' on his property. Researchers have found 'no relationship' between forest fires and climate change. What mattered were population, proximity to development and forest management – a tinderbox of dead trees and thick undergrowth.

The great fires that spread across Australia in December 2019 were held out as proof of the global warming catastrophe we face. But, in the UK's *Daily Telegraph* on 4 January 2020, a Dr Laurie Le Claire from Sydney pointed to an inconvenient fact: 'A few years ago Australia's Greens successfully encouraged state governments to declare an abundance of national parks where no human activity was allowed. This led to a build-up of dense undergrowth, even across fire trails designed to ensure firefighters could access fires and safely contain them.'

Contrary to the groupthink view that we are supposed to take for granted, there is no consensus about CO_2 taking humans straight to a burning hell. There is a body of scientific opinion that holds that increases in CO_2 are due to two causes – one, that more CO_2 is released naturally as the earth has warmed. CO_2 in the atmosphere is a mere 0.001 per cent of the total held in the oceans. In short, CO_2 does not cause global warming but is a consequence of it. The second cause is human activity but that only contributes a fraction to the increase. This is not a view that is widely known as the media swallows and regurgitates press releases from the Green lobby and seems oblivious to any counter views.

When Greta Thunberg, showing a level of anxiety that came near to terror, excoriated governments at the UN on 23 September 2019, telling them to panic, the Secretary General issued a statement saying humanity faced a climate emergency. Five hundred scientists and engineers from across the world wrote to him saying there is no climate emergency. These are the opening points they made:

The little ice age ended as recently as 1850. Therefore it is *not a surprise that we are now experiencing a period of warming.*

271

(emphasis added) Only very few peer-reviewed papers even go on to say that recent warming is chiefly anthropogenic.

The world has warmed at less than half the originally-predicted rate, and at less than half the rate to be expected on the basis of net anthropogenic forcing and land radiative imbalance. *It tells us that we are far from understanding climate change.* (emphasis added)

They went on to state:

Climate models have many shortcomings and are not remotely plausible as policy tools. Moreover, they most likely exaggerate the effect of CO_2. In addition, they ignore the fact that enriching the atmosphere with CO_2 is beneficial. CO_2 is not a pollutant. It is essential to all life on earth. Photosynthesis is a blessing. More CO_2 is beneficial for nature, greening the earth – additional CO_2 in the air has promoted growth in global plant biomass. It is also good for agriculture, increasing yields of crops worldwide.

There is no statistical evidence that global warming is intensifying hurricanes, floods, droughts and such like natural disasters, or making them more frequent. However, CO_2-mitigation measures are as damaging as they are costly. For instance, wind turbines kills birds and insects, and palm-oil plantations destroy the biodiversity of the rain forests.

There is no climate emergency. Therefore, there is no cause for panic and alarm. We strongly oppose the harmful and unrealistic net-zero CO_2 policy proposed for 2050.

In July 2020, *Apocalypse Never: Why Environmental Alarmism Hurts Us All* (HarperCollins, London) by Michael Shellenberger was published. He was a leading environmentalist for thirty years and climate activist for twenty of them. He is an expert reviewer for the IPCC in the preparation of its reports – a climate guru not a denier. Here is what he says: 'I feel an obligation to apologise for how badly we environmentalists have misled the public.' No Extinction Rebellion fanatic has better credentials. In an article in *The Australian* on 2 July 2020, explaining the reasons for his book, he said:

But until last year, I mostly avoided speaking out against the climate scare. Partly that's because I was embarrassed. After all, I am as guilty of alarmism as any other environmentalist. For years, I referred to climate change as an 'existential' threat to human civilisation, and called it a 'crisis'. But mostly I was scared. I remained quiet about the climate disinformation campaign because I was afraid of losing friends and *funding*. The few times I summoned the courage to defend climate science from those who misrepresent it I suffered consequences. And so I mostly stood by and did next to nothing as my fellow environmentalists terrified the public.[emphasis added]

He went on to say that, among the things he would like us to note are:

Humans are not causing a 'sixth mass extinction'

The Amazon is not the lungs of the world

Climate change is not making natural disasters worse.

It is a great pity that there is not a comprehensive compendium of the all the doom-laden forecasts arising from the models and coming from the Green lobbyists' keyboards so that we could judge them against what has actually happened. But I can record the following examples. Firstly, Professor Wieslaw Maslowski, University of the Naval Postgraduate School, Monterey, California, and Professor Peter Wadhams of Cambridge University, as lead scientists in the Polar Ocean Physics Group, were reported in *The Times*, on 15 October 2009, predicting that the 'North Pole will be exposed in ten years. You will be able to sail a Japanese car carrier across the North Pole and out into the Atlantic.'

Then there is the forecast made in 1988 by the Maldives government that the Maldives would be underwater in 30 years' time. Professor Nils-Axel Morner of Stockholm University, who undertook extensive fieldwork in the Arabian Sea around Maldives, called it the biggest lie every told. He wrote four times to the Maldives president with the good news that his islands were not in danger of being overwhelmed by the sea. But it was not a message that was welcomed, given the funds that were likely to become available to prevent the alleged disaster. But, if Morner couldn't get through, the reality has. In 2020, the Maldives government committed to building a new 3,400-metre-long airport runway to accommodate the largest jets. The intention is to increase tourist numbers from 1.5 to 2.5 million by 2023. It also aims to achieve $3.5 billion of investment over the next five years and is building a six-lane bridge between islands. Its advert on CNN boasts that, in one development, the villas are built right on the water's edge. Strange behaviour for a government whose whole island nation is said to be heading for a total submersion. Even stranger behaviour by the outside investors funding these developments.

The Tuvalu islands in the Pacific are another example of scare and stunts being different from reality. On 13 June 2019, *Time* magazine used a photograph of Antonio Guterres, the UN Secretary General, standing up to his thighs in seawater, in Tuvalu, as illustrative of an article warning that 'rising seas threaten to submerge' the island. As Bjorn Lomborg has pointed out in *False Alarm: How Climate Change Panic Costs Us Trillions, Hurts the Poor, and Fails to Fix the Planet* (Basic Books, New York, 2020), the sea level had risen but the interaction of waves, coral and sand had created a net land gain. In a scientific report in an edition of *Nature* magazine, published on 9 February 2018, it was noted that the Tuvalu islands will continue to 'persist as sites for habitation over the next century'. It was all there but the evidence was ignored.

One thing I do agree with Greta Thunberg about is that many governments have contradictory positions between what they spout and what they do. Bowing to the Green lobby but not acting as it demands is the cause of failure at the past jamborees in Paris, Copenhagen and Madrid. It is one thing to declare a climate emergency, as part of the political fashion of the day, but quite another to apply the remedies if there really is such a threat to humanity.

Our own Scottish First Minister declared a climate emergency in April 2019, and then joyfully opened a major extension at Edinburgh Airport. She is, of course, not alone. A real climate emergency would command decisive action to cut back on the millions who travel the world by air as tourists. But, at the World Travel Market in London in 2019, 77 ministers boasted to interviewers about their expansion plans. In the UK, Edinburgh, Glasgow, Manchester and Bristol Airports all have ambitious expansion plans, not to mention Heathrow's third runway. In India, the 2019 election manifesto of the winning Bharatiya Janata Party (BJP) states its aim is to build an additional 100 airports. In September 2019, the Chinese president opened the new giant Beijing Daxing International Airport. Air passenger traffic in China will reach 1.6 billion, through doubling the number of commercial airports to 450 by 2025.

Back in the UK, the British Tourist Authority recorded 38 million international tourists in 2016 and had predicted that number to increase by a quarter by 2025. Things were on track in 2019 when there were forty-one million foreign visitors but the contrast in Covid-19-hit 2020 when the figure was under ten million is stark. However, I have not heard the Scottish government declare we are abandoning our tourist promotion plans or that we should no longer host the Edinburgh International Festival. The blows delivered to the airline industry, hospitality and tourism, by the Covid-19 effect on the world economy have not wiped out those plans, just caused a hiatus. They will all be pursued with renewed vigour because they will have to be to assist the growth essential to world recovery.

When it comes to CO_2 policies, we really do enter the wonderland of Alice. Even if the developed Western countries meet their carbon reduction targets and cripple their economies in doing so, China and India and others may increase CO_2 in the atmosphere by 50 per cent. That is the conclusion drawn from examination of the 'Intended Nationally Determined Contributions' information which forms part of the Paris Agreement follow-up. China and India will do so by building more than 800 new coal-fired power stations and Japan by building thirty-six coal-fired power stations in the next ten years. And, as ministers from African countries declared in late 2019, they are going to deliver the electricity millions of their people who do not have any just now by using their coal resources. Ghana does not intend to keep its newly found huge oil resources underground forever – they are seen as a means of improving the country's standard of living.

The latest scare forecast being bandied about is that we only have twelve years to drastically curb CO_2 emissions or the end is nigh. If that were true and not bunkum, then, given the actions to pump out more CO_2 by many countries, we humans have had it. But I doubt if anyone in any government anywhere believes the game is up. Nor should people believe it.

It is not only politicians who find themselves enmeshed in the coils of reality versus virtue signalling. Even young Greta is caught in them. She has 3.7 million followers on social media and there is then an ever-widening circle of re-tweeting to many millions more. As my friend Peter Kearney has pointed out, this large network is not energy free. If Greta shut down her social media and flew by air, she would cut her carbon footprint substantially.

But perhaps the most glaring evidence of how the need to give Green signalling creates fairyland policies came in the statements by all three major UK parties in the 2019 election when they pledged to plant more trees. The Tories promised 30 million trees a year, the Liberals sixty million and Labour billions by 2024. As one sane person, with knowledge of forests, wrote in the *Daily Telegraph* letters page on 18 November 2019, the lowest, the 30 million, would require planting just short of 82,192 trees a day or 3,424 an hour. Another writer pointed out that no one in any party had calculated the acreage needed or the capacity to grow the saplings.

The present hysteria hyped up daily by the alarmists is nothing new. In my sixty years of public life, I have witnessed two similar scares. In 1972 the Club of Rome published *The Limits to Growth* which sold millions of copies all over the world. Its experts constructed a computer model of the world designed to predict the future for humans of five interrelated variables – population, food production, industrial production, non-renewable resources and pollution. The model had, of course, as all do, an assumption – that 'continued growth leads to infinite quantities that just do not fit into a finite world'. The model's conclusion on the effects of exponential economic growth and population increase was that humans are faced with a 'catastrophe' if both continue without changes in policy. It forecast that, if we continued on the path of seeking growth, the world would run out of resources and so governments must change the economic model developed after 1945, with people changing their habits lest they destroy the future for their children. I remember discussing it with John Smith. We were young MPs at the time and we both came to the conclusion that it was nonsense – as proved to be the case.

Continued economic growth has provided higher standards of living, better health care and greater longevity in the developed countries. In China, exponential economic growth has lifted 500 million people out of abject poverty and increased life expectancy to 75 years. In India, it has improved life expectancy beyond what anyone imagined could be the case when the country became independent – from 33 years in 1950 to 69.5 today. *The Limits to Growth* is a classic case of experts and their models being wrong, very wrong.

Another great scare appeared in 1996 over Bovine Spongiform Encephalopathy (BSE), mad cow disease, which had been found in dairy herds whose cows had been fed a protein supplement made from the remains of other animals. Scientists said it had crossed over from the animals to the human species through us eating meat products. In humans, it was named Variant Creutzfeldt-Jakob Disease (vCJD) although frequently it was simply called CJD by newspapers. The newspapers reported that Professor Neil Ferguson and his team at Imperial College London, using a mathematic model, forecast up to 50,000 deaths from CJD. Yes, the same Ferguson whose Covid-19 model of up to 500,000 deaths drove the UK prime minister to impose the lockdown in March 2020. His model was denounced as flawed the next day by other scientists and, when applied to Sweden, forecast 60,000 deaths. But there was no interrogation of his 'science' and into lockdown we all went.

The new BSE fear took wings. In the *Newsnight* programme of 20 March 1996, Jeremy Paxman interviewed Dr John Pattison, a scientist who predicted that 500,000 deaths might arise in the UK. A few days later, the *Observer* newspaper embraced this new Armageddon. Quoting the same *Newsnight* scientist, it foretold a death rate of 500,000 a year by 2016 and claimed that we would need euthanasia clinics, the NHS would collapse as it faced 'the strain of caring for more than two million CJD victims' and the rest of the world would be forced to place the whole UK in quarantine. The scare hit such a level that 4.4 million cows were destroyed although only a few showed any signs they were unhealthy. British beef was banned in the EU and many other countries followed suit with some only lifting it in 2016 and thousands of local butcher shops went bankrupt. The death toll in the UK over the years has been 177. The late author and *Sunday Telegraph* columnist Christopher Booker pointed out in his investigation, years later:

> Yet in May 1997, only fourteen months after predicting that the number of deaths from vCJD could eventually rise to 500,000, Dr Pattison confessed that his epidemic was not going to take place after all. The scientist who more than anyone else had engineered the BSE scare admitted that a continuing decline in the incidence of vCJD deaths now indicated that the final figure might 'end up at around 200'. (Christopher Booker and Richard North, *Scared to Death: From BSE to Global Warming: Why Scares are Costing Us the Earth*, Continuum, London, 2007)

My great regret is that I shall not be here in 2050 to see humanity still enjoying, in safety, this earth on which we live. But I hope that, perhaps in some second-hand bookshop, someone will pick up this book and find on this page the words 'I told you so'. Here are three pieces of advice in the meantime. When you are told repeatedly that you should always follow 'the science', remember that science is not dogmatic and, when it is pushing out the boundaries of knowledge, it is also standing on the brink of ignorance. Models are just that – models – and not reality especially when forecasting years ahead. Do not always conflate environment with climate – they are interrelated in many ways, of course, but not in others. It is not climate but over fishing that is destroying fish stocks. It is not climate but human misbehaviour with disposing of plastics that is polluting rivers and the sea. It is the desire of some humans to kill animals that is bringing some species near to extinction.

To Russia with Concern

> No government or social system is so evil that its people must be considered as lacking in virtue.
>
> President John F. Kennedy

The last political act I engaged in was to set up, in 2017, the 'Edinburgh–Russia Conversations' – along with Joe Farrell, Colin Fox, Tom Walker, Chic Brodie, Alex Neil, Jim Eadie, and Peter Kearney. Why? At the political level, UK–Russian relations are at their worst in the post-Soviet period. There is hardly one positive article on Russia in the Western media. It is often described as a Mafia (*Vory*) state, where corrupt organisations and oligarchs' interests are guarded by President Putin's authoritarian regime. NATO, at the political and military level, warns of its potential aggression towards the Baltic states and Poland and beefs up its military presence in both.

But is Putin Russia? Does his authoritarian method of governing leave no space for people to breathe in any oxygen of freedom? Can public opinion express itself or is the pattern of life total conformity? Why is Putin re-elected and how can he manipulate the constitution to keep himself in power? How has Russian society come to its present political condition? There are academics who know the answers to these questions but their knowledge rarely comes into the public domain and only those politicians and columnists who read the reports of the Select Committee on Foreign Affairs become acquainted with them.

If, as Western powers have done, you define Russia as an adversary, why did it become so after the collapse of the USSR? Is it worth talking to an adversary or should we maintain the flow of severe criticism of every Russian government action? Our group is interested in finding answers to those questions because we believe that engaging in dialogue is a sound policy – understanding where the other side is coming from and getting them to understand our views can reduce friction to the benefit of peoples.

Our model was borrowed from one that was created by the late Professor John Erickson of Edinburgh University. He set up the 'Edinburgh Conversations' when tensions in the Cold War froze contacts at the highest levels. Paradoxically, that is when contacts are most important and he was able to bring together, in Edinburgh, in total privacy, senior politicians and officials from the USA, UK and Russia who could engage in frank discussions.

In the scale of things, our small group is extremely modest and we are not in an arena where we can influence UK–Russian relations. But, by engaging with Russians, seeking a better understanding of the people and trying to find answers to the questions listed above, we can disseminate knowledge and understanding of Russia and its people, to others in Scotland – just as I am doing with this chapter. Is it not better to understand another people, rather than accept negative stereotypes?

It is a small contribution but we think it's worth it. So do Russians. Our aim has been to link with think tanks and institutions in Russia, of which there are many, and have frank discussions with academics and international policy experts. We have met a number of times in Moscow and St Petersburg and hosted one meeting in Edinburgh. There was value for both sides.

At the time this book was published, the Russian state today was only a little over 20 years old. Nonsense? No – the USSR finally collapsed in 1991 and, in the nine years that followed, Russians were not living in a well-functioning democracy under President Yeltsin, the most notable feature of whose rule was the theft of state assets. The former ambassador to Russia Sir Tony Brenton, in January 2020, noted that Putin 'remains popular among ordinary Russians who view him as the man who brought order after the chaos of the Yeltsin years and who won back Crimea'.

Before the USSR collapsed Russians lived for centuries under the Tsars, then had 70 years under Communist dictatorship. Except in the Baltic states, there has never been a tradition of democracy in the Russian Tsarist-Communist empire, so there was nothing to draw upon. A quick conversion to a Western-style democracy, which itself took hundreds of years to develop and mature, was never going to happen. No people can throw off a legacy like that with ease. That applies not only to Russia. With the exception of the Baltic states, all others that have emerged in the post-Soviet era have wrestled with quasi-dictatorships and corruption – Belarus being a recent example.

According to her citation, Svetlana Alexievich won the 2015 Nobel Prize in literature for 'her polyphonic writings, a monument to suffering and courage in our time'. No mouthpiece for Putin's government, her book *Secondhand Time: The Last of the Soviets* (English translation by Bela Shayevich, New York, Random House, 2016) provides evidence, from interviews with ordinary Russians, of how difficult it has been to move from being a Soviet citizen told what to think, to a Russian citizen no longer under control but with no experience of autonomy. The shambles and shock of the Yeltsin post-Soviet decade, which allowed Putin to emerge as Russia's saviour, can be explained by these admissions from two of the many Russians she records: 'No one had taught us how to be free' and, in the bewilderment of being enveloped in wild market forces, 'The discovery of money hit us like an atom bomb.'

It is in the international sphere that Russia has invited condemnation and sanctions for its aggression in seizing Crimea and funding and supplying the rebels in Ukraine's Donbass region. The Kremlin's lies in denying its share of responsibility for the mid-air destruction over Ukraine of the Malaysian flight MH17, a civilian plane travelling from Amsterdam to Kuala Lumpur on 17 July 2004, add to the general view in the West that we are dealing with a state that disrupts for the sake of disruption.

But when you are dealing with a state like Russia, you have to look deeper than the surface image. There are three factors that need to be grasped. Firstly, the Putin ultra-nationalist policy of restoring Russia to its Soviet era status is an impossibility with an economy no greater than that of Spain and so it has taken on the role of a spoiler with its cyber attacks. Secondly, there is the hangover legacy of the Russian–Soviet empire with its spheres of influence – the 'near abroad' as the Kremlin sees it. And the continuing influence on Russia's people and their strategic view of defence are rooted in Russia's searing experience of the Great Patriotic War against Germany. To understand is not the same as excusing. But it can explain.

The slow dissolution of the British Empire, with Indian independence in 1947 and Africa bursting free in the 1960s, gave the imperial British mind time to come to terms with its changed position. In contrast, the Russian Soviet Empire dissolved into chaos between the attempted coup against Gorbachev in August 1991 and 25 December of that year. In political time, it was gone in a puff of wind. Russian citizens went, in one short puff of that wind, from having a super-state to a shambles state in a matter of four months. This allowed the ultra-nationalists to claim that their USSR was undone by the West and President George H. W. Bush's boast, 'We won the Cold War', reinforced that belief.

By the time the final assessment was made by the Stalin regime of the material destruction inflicted on the Soviet Union by the German invasion, the former allies were in the Cold War land and, with the Soviets' policy of secrecy, little or nothing was known of its findings. The damage was staggering with the total destruction being 1,710 towns, 70,000 villages, 32,000 factories, 84,000 schools, 1,500 high schools, 6,000 hospitals, 13,000 km of rail bridges, 17 million cattle and that is only part of it. But it is not that material destruction which is at the root of Russian people's view of their national interest and so informs the Kremlin's foreign policy. It is the human casualties – 8.7 million combat dead and 19 million civilian dead. Of the young men born in 1923, 80 per cent are among that combat dead.

In the UK our war combat dead number is 470,000 and the civilian dead is 47,000. The Blitz and Dunkirk are lodged in the national mind. That war still has resonance and continues to influence our foreign and defence policies. Can anyone be surprised that the scale of the Soviet dead lies heavily on the Russian mind and is a contemporary influence on the country's foreign and defence policies?

The reader may think I am a Russophile, anxious to throw a blanket of explanation over the foreign policy of the Kremlin. So, let me quote from two figures in the foreign policy establishment of the United States. Robert D. Kaplan in his *The Revenge of Geography* says: 'Insecurity is the quintessential Russian national emotion . . . For what drove the Soviet Union to carve out an empire in Eastern Europe at the end of World War II still holds today: a legacy of depredations against Russia by Lithuanians, Poles, Swedes, Frenchmen and Germans, leading to the need for a cordon sanitaire of compliant regimes in the space between historic Russia and Central Europe.' (*The Revenge of Geography: What the Map Tells Us about Coming Conflicts and the Battle Against Fate*: Random House International, New York, 2012) Kaplan has served on the US Defense Policy Board and is a visiting Professor at the Naval Academy, Annapolis.

In the *Financial Times* of 31 May 2015, Thomas Graham, former staff member of the US Security Council, says: 'The West acts as if it had a Vladimir Putin problem. In fact it has a Russian problem. The Russian president stands within a long tradition of Russian thinking. His departure would fix nothing. Any plausible successor would pursue a similar course, if perhaps with a little less machismo . . . European states seek security in balance; Russia seeks it in strategic depth. That view grows out of its location on the vast, nearly featureless great Eurasian plain, across which armies have moved with ease.'

With the Eastern European states free from the Russian-Soviet Empire, where does the Kremlin find that strategic depth? It is not there. A possible Ukraine-NATO tie-up would add to the Russian sense of insecurity, with NATO right on Russia's border. That possibility see-sawed from 2008–2014 as anti-Russian and pro-Russian governments came and went within Ukraine. Put Ukraine in NATO and Russia's Black Sea fleet, which operates in the sea where it has a national strategic interest, loses its Crimea bases. On the same principle of 'vital national strategic interest' that saw the United States' reaction in 1962 to Soviet missiles in Cuba, no Russian president could allow Crimea to be lost to the Black Sea fleet and become a de facto NATO base. That is the realpolitik in the Ukraine–Russia relationship.

So, this young Russian state, carrying enormous historical baggage of oppression and still locked by its geography into its age-old strategic vulnerability, is one in which its people are judged by us and others on a democratic scale, when they have no history or experience of democratic development to draw upon. It is a tall order in such a short time scale. I repeat the point made earlier. Russia is not Putin. The Russian people are like us – they go for coffee in cafes, meet friends in restaurants, attend football matches, buy tickets for the cinema, go for walks with their children, worry about their jobs, about housing and what is happening around them. At the end of Putin's regime, because he is mortal, it will be those people who decide the form and shape of the political society and we shall be happy to discuss it with them and keep trying to understand them and hopefully help them understand us.

Some Reflections on a Long Political Life

From the foregoing two passages on climate change and relations with Russia, although always identified as a Scottish politician, the life I have lived and my interests have always gone much wider than the boundaries of my own nation. But I am a Scot and, as Nye Bevan said, if you want to change the world, perhaps starting with your own front door is a good idea. So, in these final passages, I come back and try to explain, first, why I am as I am and, second, to offer some concluding words on how the people of Scotland might break free from the narrow confines of the limited power available in the devolution settlement and from a political class that rules but does not rule well.

Much of my political life has been one of dissent from the prevailing majority view. I may have missed government office because of it but I have no regrets. I came into politics on joining the Labour Party with no ambition other than to help knock on doors and give out leaflets and I have never been tempted to temper my views, irrespective of the consequences, except in that short 'party hack' period to which I have referred.

Those without ambition for office in politics are the most dangerous of all because they are not constrained as others are by calculations for advancement. I am one of them. Tam Dalyell, Margo MacDonald, Stephen Maxwell, Dennis Skinner, Frank Field and Dennis Canavan are others. Being free from personal ambition, as distinct from ambition to improve the lives of others, means being free to state matters as you see them, irrespective of the consequences at a personal level. Neither I nor they and others like us are saints, unsullied by compromise. Compromise is essential and unavoidable in a democratic polity but there are some who, on major issues, draw a line, will not compromise and do not succumb to the calculation of advancement. I think that is for the public good, as has been proved, for example, by the independent valuable contributions Tam Dalyell and Frank Field have made.

My comments on ambition are not a way of condemning those who do seek office and the power it gives them to make decisions that have a practical effect. If all eschewed office, we would have no government. I am aware of the contradiction in my own case – I know and urge people to understand that 'power' matters and has to be wielded if things are to be done, yet I was willing, when Harold Wilson offered me a first job on the ministerial ladder, to turn it down for a cause that mattered more than the red box. I have never regretted that aspect of my political nature. As contemporaries and friends advanced, I never harboured any jealousy or had a sense of frustration. Policy is what has always mattered to me and the advice I was given in 1960, by Jackie Cowan, a sub-officer in the Ayr fire brigade and my mentor when I joined the Labour Party, that politics is about sowing seeds of ideas has been my lodestar.

Like anyone who has had a leading role in politics for over sixty years, my record is strewn with errors and misjudgements but it has also been marked with being correct. I have never been prone to accept 'received wisdom' without looking deeply and carefully into what it proclaims. What has been consistent in my life is adherence – not always successfully – to the idea of the application of intellectual rigour and that principles matter.

A Difference of Opinion

Macduff: Stands Scotland where it did?
Ross: Alas, poor country! / Almost afraid to know itself.

Shakespeare, *Macbeth*, Act IV, scene iii

Although much of this book has been about the long gone past and the recent past, I would like to complete it with some thoughts on the future of Scotland's people with special reference, but not exclusively, to the working class from which I come. It has been relegated in terms of political power as the trade union movement has shrunk. Half of Attlee's Cabinet in 1945 were blue-collar workers. In the Westminster Parliament elected in 2017, only 4 per cent were. I doubt if it is any different in the Holyrood parliament.

A new political class has emerged to lead and set an agenda for the working class – frequently an agenda that is different from what their needs and priorities actually are. In one of the most deprived areas of Edinburgh, the people are represented in the Scottish parliament by someone middle class, who lives in the Borders and sent her children to private schools. Not only there but also elsewhere, there is no match between working-class need and its representation in the corridors of power where policies are made. Somewhere, sometime, a new leadership group has to emerge from within the Scottish working class. The key is in its members finding again that high degree of self-confidence that my generation had.

But my concern is not exclusively about the working class in Scotland. As many middle-class families learned in the bitter lessons of the 2008 crash, being a lawyer or accountant or a professional manager with a degree in business did not eliminate the fundamental requirement for a good living – the ability to sell one's labour in a labour market. Whatever social class Scots find themselves in, the ability or otherwise to sell our labour is a common factor.

It is that whole community of Scotland I sit here worried about. There is no such thing as a nation standing still. It either progresses through rising to meet new challenges or regresses. I am not sure if our political class is yet aware of the scale of the challenges we face. Neither am I sure that the party I have been a member of since 1980, the SNP, understands the reality of geography and the geopolitical and economic framework it creates.

In his contribution to the Queen's Speech debate on 19 December 2019, Ian Blackford MP, leader of the SNP Westminster Group, cited Charles Stewart Parnell's 'No man has the right to fix the boundary to the march of a nation', a quote calculated to make nationalist hearts beat faster by providing an ethical legitimacy to the policy of independence. Of course, it is bunk. World history and contemporary situations demonstrate that geography, state interests, spheres of influence and geopolitical factors do just that – place limits on many national ambitions. The Kurds in the Middle East and the Catalans in Europe are two current examples. Scotland's geography locks it into a permanent relationship with a larger neighbour and, in geopolitical terms, it falls into the sphere of influence of the USA. We are also on the other side of the world from where the great expanding markets and technological dynamism are emerging. Handled badly, all of those factors will limit what this nation can achieve. Handled well, they can be overcome and, in the overcoming, be the springboard to the economic success and strength from which social evils can be conquered.

It is in that wider world that the great challenge to Scotland lies – a world that does not owe us a living but one in which our people will have to earn a living if we want the good life and the decent society that comes from the experience of prosperity. This has to be grasped by the people. It is a fact we evade at our economic and social peril. Facing that fact and acting upon it and rejecting the meaningless rhetoric which may be music to the ear but is a useless guide to what is needed.

Scotland has a population of 5.4 million in a world of 7 billion, many millions of whom are very clever. University World News noted that, during the educational disaster years of Mao's Cultural Revolution, Chinese science and advanced engineering were hardly noticeable but that is different today. It records that 'China is now the second largest research and development performing country' after the United States. The same report emphasises 'the quality of higher education lies in science, technology, engineering and mathematics – STEM – as critical to providing the advanced work skills necessary to strengthen an innovation-based economic landscape' – not areas in which, today, Scotland is noted for its accomplishments.

Scots are living in an evolving new epoch. During the period while colonialism ruled, from the sixteenth century to well in to the twentieth century, Western powers dominated the world with their economic, scientific, military and political power. That era is over. We are now in a time when power has shifted and will continue to shift to the Asia–Pacific regions. It is in this new world order that Scotland has to live and to live successfully in that world requires us to have powers that exceed anything that can be offered through the present level of devolution.

Scotland's future prosperity lies in exploiting the natural resources we have, which are substantial, and through investing in our greatest resource, our people, because it is they and only they who can make our nation world class in the sciences, technology, research and education – all as internal drivers but also the means by which we carve out our place in the world economy. We can do it – we have a heritage in which innovation and invention put us in the forefront of development in past decades. Today we have a number of first-class universities that we must make undisputedly world class to give us the leading edge in the technologies that will determine whether a country succeeds or not. If we make that our ambition, we shall make Scotland an attractive location for some of the best talent from all regions of the world and from all races – talent we should seek out and welcome. A Scotland that is transformed economically, technologically and intellectually is possible – indeed, essential.

To accomplish that goal we need to lift our sights to a new level of understanding what we need to achieve as a nation. We need to face the reality that we are not in a good place, that there is a clamant need for new political leadership and we need to find it and employ it. And it must be one that has vision, imagination and, above all, the driving ambition to carve out an eminent and successful place in the new world that is replacing the fading hegemony of the old one we were once part of.

No one can stop us except ourselves. Progress or regress? That is the choice Scots face in a world in which there will be no hiding place for failure. It is said that in 1707 we came to the end of an auld sang. Time to write a new one.

Epilogue

After completing the first draft of this book in 2020, with publication delayed into 2021 due to the Covid-19 pandemic, I undertook what may prove to be my last lap in politics when I accepted the invitation from organiser James Gillies to actively support the Free to Disagree campaign against the SNP government Hate Crime Bill.

I have deliberately not included this in the main text of the book because I want to bring out a stand-alone statement that shows the immense value I place on our inheritance from those who have gone before us, namely the right to think as we wish and speak our mind as we wish. I cannot conceive how a society can live in freedom and flourish intellectually if there is a bridle on the mind and a zip on the mouth.

Reading the Bill was a jaw-dropping moment for me. Having worked in countries where the media was controlled by government and citizens inhibited in what they felt able to say, I was astonished that a Bill could be introduced in Scotland, the land of the Enlightenment, that puts us in that same class of country where 'you had better watch what you say or it's jail for you, and that applies to any conversations you may have in your own home'. The Bill had more than a touch of Stalinist control about it.

I viewed it as 'one of the most pernicious and dangerous pieces of legislation ever produced by any government in modern times in any part of the United Kingdom' and fought it through letters pages, articles and Zoom meetings. As the Bill neared its final stages in the Holyrood parliament, I set out my position on it in *The Times* (5 February 2021), from which I draw the following passages.

> Is the hammer of the law the best way to tackle human failing, or is the cleansing, disinfecting air of open discussion more likely to be successful? I opt for the latter because while the law can shut mouths, it cannot shut minds, and it does no good for false ideas and prejudice to fester underground.

Scotland is a peaceful society. A foreign visitor would believe it has always been thus. History says differently. Across parts of Ayrshire are to be found cairns erected in the memory of the Covenanters persecuted by my old friend Tam Dalyell's ancestor Bloody Black Tam, for their adherence to the Presbyterian religion. In more recent times rampant sectarianism, proud bigotry, in the garb of anti-Irish immigration and anti-Catholicism, was the norm over much of the country. In 1923 the Church of Scotland published its infamous pamphlet 'The menace of the Irish race to our Scottish Nationality'.

I live and shop in peace in Morningside Road, Edinburgh. In 1935 10,000 took part in an anti-Catholic rally and riot there. Buses were stoned, the police used a baton charge to clear Morningside Road, there was fighting on Bruntsfield links. In 1936 Protestant candidates won election to Edinburgh city council. In the shipyards and elsewhere there was discrimination to deny work to Catholics. The poisonous question: 'Which school did you go to?' was standard in the West of Scotland. As late as the 1950s, a young man asking a young girl to dance would, as they waltzed, seek to find out if she was Catholic or Protestant. A Protestant marrying a Catholic, and vice versa, split families.

We are a different better society today. Sectarianism still exists. The Orange Lodges still parade but no longer annually swagger down Princes Street in great ranks. Rangers and Celtic remain the twin-centre of tensions but the former does sign Catholics, a change forced on it by common sense and the laugher directed at it as Celtic, when having a choice, would sign the brilliant Protestant knowing Rangers would deny itself the brilliant Catholic.

When Pope John Paul II landed in Scotland in 1982 we had travelled a long way from the 1930s Dark Age: what concerned most Scots was not his Catholicism but whether he would kiss our ground and recognise us as a nation. You could almost hear the nation's purr of satisfaction when kiss it he did. 'Most' did not include Pastor Jack Glass, whose rabid anti-Catholicism led him to denounce the Pope as the anti-Christ. Pastor Jack was tolerated and dealt with by deadly humour. When he denounced Billy Connolly, the Big Yin said the pastor was his 'lucky mascot', as the more he ranted the bigger the audiences grew. When Tom Winning was made Cardinal, Pastor Jack was there in

Rome to denounce popery. Passing him, Tom took no offence, simply saying with a smile 'It's a nice day for it.'

If you think the Pastor was a nonentity in those days, go and read the major obituaries of him in the *Daily Telegraph* and the one written by Brian Wilson in *The Guardian*. A Pastor Jack on any subject today would send Humza Yousaf reaching for a Bill to silence him. In the past we dealt with him and others differently, by the use of free speech. Therein lies the clue to our progress. We are different and better today because we were a free speech society, tolerating but openly contesting the intolerant, and flushing out bigotry.

However, progress made does not mean perfection. Racism, principally direct at Asians, is a scar on the face of Scotland. Whereas the Irish-Catholic migrants had strength in numbers and a well organised church to help provide solidarity and a degree of protection, as did their deep involvement with the Labour Party, such numbers and a wide protective framework do not apply to our latest migrant community. Therefore the hammer of the law, with the approval of the majority, whatever its effect on free speech, has already been used as a means to signal that the rest of us care for them.

That set of anti-racist laws has not eliminated racism. Just as with the failed attempt on football-based sectarianism showed, it is not possible to legislate racism out of society. That malignant social virus will be eradicated only by open discussion of its inherent falsehood and the wickedness and inhumanity that can flow from it. It is the disinfectant of free speech that will finally rid us of it.

Index

Index

Index

Michie, Ray 206
Mikardo, Ian 85
Middleton, George 67
Militant (extreme Labour group) 153
Millan, Bruce 100, 153
Millar, J.P.M. 51
Miller, Calum 231
Miller, Maurice 212
Milne, Jimmy 67, 92
Mitchell, Professor James 154
Mitchell, Jim (Paisley councillor) 178
Mitterrand, François 242
Modi, Narendra 257
Moray, Earl of 268
More, Iain 145
Morgan, Alasdair 179
Morner, Professor Nils-Axel 273
Morning Star (formerly *Daily Worker*) 69
Mountbatten, Lord 23
Movement for Colonial Freedom xiii
Moyne, Lord 209, 213
Mubarak, Hosni 205
Mudaris, Abdul Karim al- 141, 151, 192–94, 196, 200, 209, 211
Mugabe, Robert xiii, 134
Mui Ying (amah) 37
Mullin, Roger 103
Murdoch, Rupert 169
Mure, Robert 74
Murray, Alex 58
Murrell, Peter 185
Muslim Brotherhood 208
Muslims, westernisation of 209

Naimi, Ali Al- 137
Nakba, The (Palestinian exodus) 219
Napier, Alex 51
Nasser, Gamel Abdul 24, 208
National Council of Labour Colleges 51

National Health Service (NHS) Medical Staffing Committee 5m 66
National Industrial Relations Court 83
National Party of Scotland 63
National People's Congress of China 43
National Union of Mineworkers (NUM) 8, 80, 84, 85, 95, 116, 125
National Union of Railwaymen (NUR) 19, 20
NATO (North Atlantic Treaty Organisation) 265, 282
Neil, Alex 61, 99, 100, 102, 111, 114, 116, 154, 156, 158, 245, 246
Netanyahu, Benjamin 217, 220
Newsom, Gavin 271
North of Scotland Hydro-Electric Board 58
Norway, relationship to EU 253, 254
Nuremberg Trials 218, 221, 224

O'Brien, Cardinal Keith 245
Observer, The 32
O'Donnell, Tony 31, 32, 35
O'Farrell, Anne (first wife of JS) 26, 27
O'Farrell, Mary (niece of JS) 76
O'Halloran, Charlie 53–55, 59, 126
oil industry
    historic value of 236–38; future potential 238, 239, 264; sovereign wealth fund from 238; price fluctuations 257
Olympia Centre, London 194
Oman Chamber of Commerce 194, 199
Opium Wars 11
O'Raw, Frank 231
Order repealing the Assembly Act 144